IMAGES
of America

SPRINGVILLE

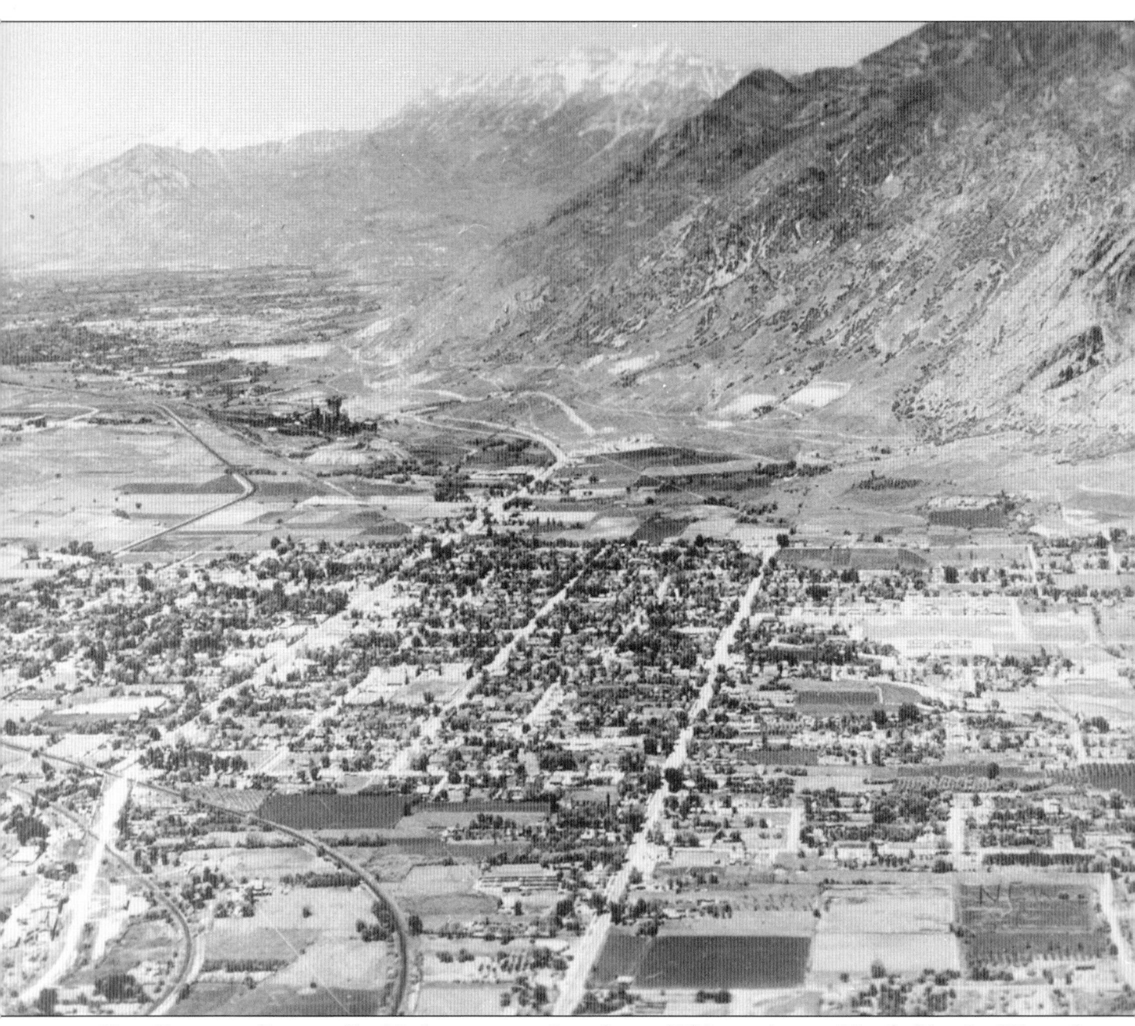

City Picture. Springville, Utah, is pictured in this c. 1950 aerial view. Nestled by the Wasatch Range in Utah Valley, Springville enjoys beautiful mountain surroundings. Utah Lake and the sparkling waters of Hobble Creek are nearby. This city is an exceptional spot to raise families, gardens, grains, and livestock. (Courtesy of M. Lee Taylor.)

On the Cover: H.T. Reynolds & Co. H.T. Reynolds & Co. built its second building at Second South and Main Streets in 1892. The third floor had a dance and entertainment center, the second floor was furniture and storage, and the main floor housed the general store. This brick and stone building was lauded as the largest department store in Utah County when it was completed. Historically, the company provided a coal and lumber yard, sheds for horses, and areas for delivery wagons in the back section of the property. Today, the building has been restored and is owned by Trivani International. (George Edward Anderson photograph, courtesy of the Springville Historical Society.)

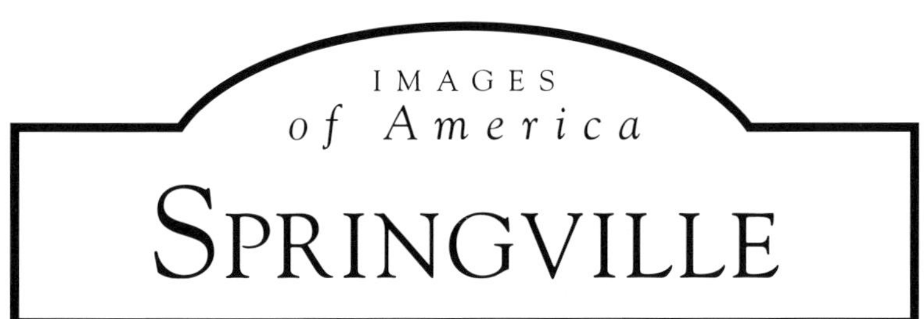

April Clawson

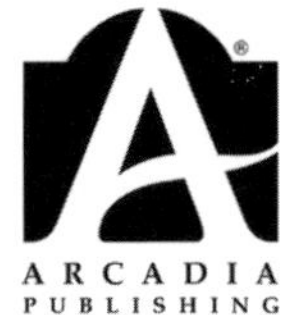

ISBN 978-1-4671-2489-8

Published by Arcadia Publishing
Charleston, South Carolina

Printed in the United States of America

Library of Congress Control Number: 2017935219

For all general information, please contact Arcadia Publishing:
Telephone 843-853-2070
Fax 843-853-0044
E-mail sales@arcadiapublishing.com
For customer service and orders:
Toll-Free 1-888-313-2665

Visit us on the Internet at www.arcadiapublishing.com

To the residents of Springville—may pioneerism flourish.

Contents

Acknowledgments

This book is a continuation of the previous Mapleton book. These two sister cities were founded within days of each other. In Mapleton, animals could graze and grains could be harvested. Springville had the most water resources and desirable land for homes and buildings. Each community deserves to have a separate history written about the incredible people who came, stayed, and planted the ground, making the cities what they are today.

The Daughters of Utah Pioneers Springville-Mapleton Camp (the DUP), has been a valuable resource for information and direction. Heartfelt thanks especially go to the Springville Historical Society committee members for the many hours of research they provided, and to the dedicated volunteers who answered my endless questions. The preservation of the city's many artifacts is due largely to these two entities and those past and present who continue to preserve them. They have been amazing individuals to work with, and if I could, I would add their names as authors of this book.

Thanks also go to my family for once again putting up with me during the endless hours of research and computer work.

I want to also thank my communication professors at Southern Utah University who let me use this book project as my master's thesis.

Once again, I acknowledge Alyssa Jones at Arcadia Publishing; her tenacity at finding me has been a blessing in my life. I have enjoyed writing these two books in the Images of America series, and I hope you will find this book interesting and informative.

INTRODUCTION

On September 18, 1850, the first settlers arrived in Springville, led by Capt. Aaron Johnson. The residents were very happy to have a place to live. During the past five years, these pioneers had endured many trials, hardships, and religious persecutions. This new land provided a place for establishing homes and farms and a way for them to live their religious beliefs without fear of violent opposition.

Hobble Creek was the first name the area was given in 1849. Oliver Boardman Huntington and Barney Ward were passing through and trading with the Utes. The men decided to put hobbles on their mares to keep their herd contained. The hobbles fell off, and the bell-horse waded into a nearby creek; Oliver followed their trail and eventually found all the horses. The creek and canyon still retain that name, but in 1853, when the city's charter was approved, the area was renamed Springville.

Early settlers hurried to build a fort to be ready for the winter months. Timber was cut down and hauled in, and desirable land was located for crops and grazing. They also needed protection and safety from the Utes, for a few of the previous encounters between the American Indians and the white settlers had not been peaceful.

After a couple of years, homes were built and a downtown area emerged, with a well dug and water shares appropriated among the residents. Soon after, a tax was issued to pay for and build the needed roads. In 1853, an election took place, and the first mayor, Gideon D. Wood, was sworn in. The settlers also built a meetinghouse that served the town in many capacities.

This book opens by highlighting Springville's past. There are still numerous residents who are descendants of the original settlers. Many individuals worked together to build this special place along the Wasatch Mountains.

Chapter two mentions the art museum and the local artistic culture. The city is a gathering place and destination for those who cultivate the arts. Historical points dotting the area make the city an interesting and fun place to tour.

Chapter three presents Springville's many cultural treasures. The weeklong events Art City Days and World Folkfest attract many visitors during the summer. The city has recently been named one of the best places to live in the state of Utah by the *Daily Herald* Reader's Choice Awards.

Most of these amazing preserved photographs are credited to the local artist George Edward Anderson (GEA). His wonderfully historic pictures are truly amazing to behold. Springville is an outstanding place. People stay due to its manageable growth, strong tax base, and the smart use of its land and resources. I hope you will enjoy this picturesque journey.

One

Hobble Creek to Springville City

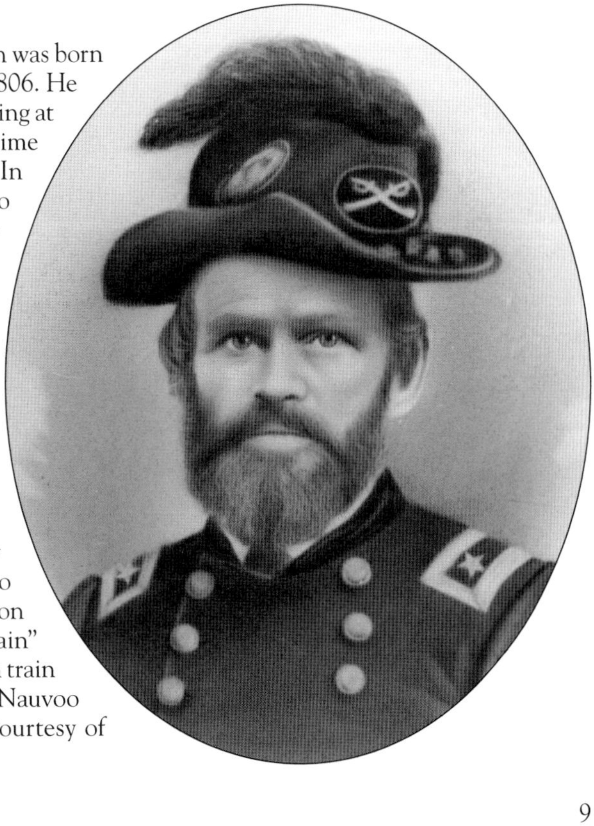

Capt. Aaron Johnson. Aaron Johnson was born in Haddam, Connecticut, on June 2, 1806. He was one of 13 children, and started working at the age of six around the farm. By the time he was 12, he was working like a man. In 1836, he and his wife were baptized into the Church of Jesus Christ of Latter-day Saints. Aaron arrived in Salt Lake City in the fall of 1850 and, under the direction of Brigham Young, was asked to start a colony in Springville, known then as Hobble Creek. Johnson is known as the founder of Springville and the town's first LDS bishop, and also became the first judge in Utah County. In 1857, he was elected brigadier general of the Peteetneet Military District. He served in many capacities and did all in his power to spread knowledge and useful information among the townspeople. The title "captain" was bestowed on him for leading a wagon train across the plains. He is pictured in his Nauvoo Legion brigadier general uniform. (Courtesy of the Springville Historical Society.)

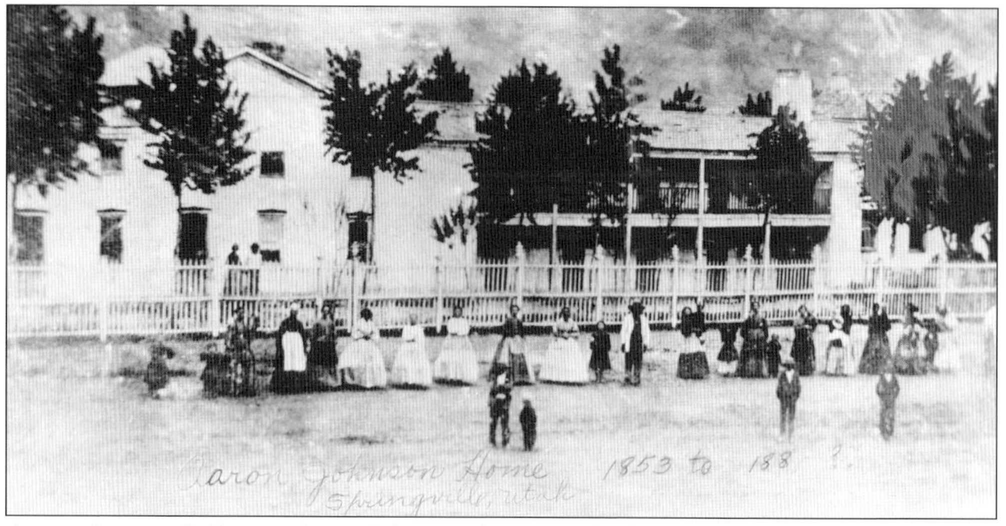

AARON JOHNSON'S FAMILY. Aaron Johnson's home was built on First North and Main Streets around 1852. It was a large adobe dwelling, two stories high, and at first had 12 rooms. Later it was remodeled to 27 rooms, and the home was now a block long. This dwelling was used as a school, for public gatherings, and as a meetinghouse, jail, post office, and dance hall. The people standing in front of the home are his 10 wives and children. He had lost two wives on the plains. (Courtesy of the Springville Historical Society.)

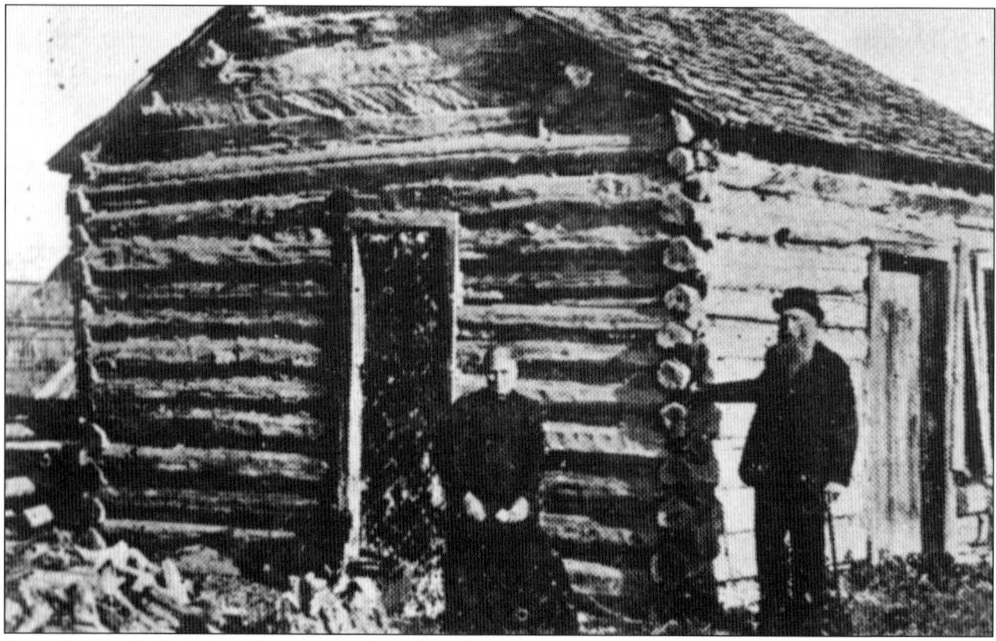

LOG CABIN. Polly Maria Perry Smith and William Smith are shown next to their log cabin. This was part of the original fort the settlers built and used during the first two years in Springville. It was moved from the fort to another location on April 27, 1852. The logs to build it were gathered along Hobble Creek and in the nearby canyons. It was known for a while as the finest home in Springville because it had wood floors. The Smiths raised 13 children there. Against all odds, remnants of the home still exist. Wood from this cabin was reused to build a shed attached to a home of one of William Smith's descendants. (Courtesy of the DUP.)

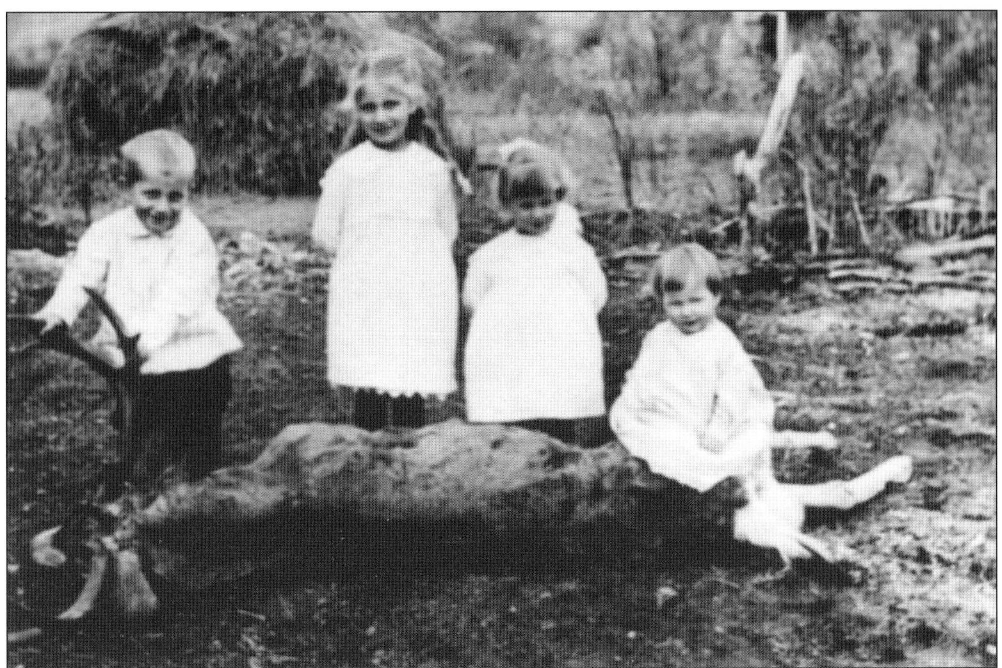

Deer. These unidentified children are posing with a dead deer. Fresh meat was a blessing. Residents were grateful for the abundance of wild game in the area. (Courtesy of the DUP.)

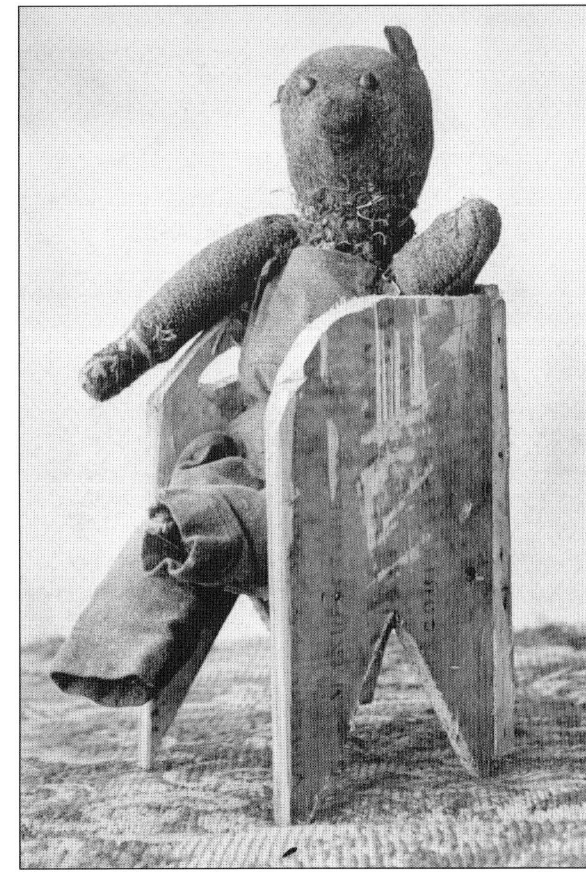

Teddy Bear. Even stuffed animals had a special place in children's hearts. In this picture, Helene Clark's teddy bear has his own chair, made just for him. (Courtesy of the DUP.)

Springville Jan-7th /78

To all whome it may concern, I hereby certify that I Moses Childs. eight or ten years sins. More or less, sold all my right. title, intrest, claim, and posion, of a certain field of farming land, and water claim to said land comonly known as the Buck Atchison field, situated about three Miles south east of Springville City Utah [illegible] (said land and water claim I bought of said Buck Atchison,) unto W.D. Huntington for the sum of ($50.00) fifty dollars to me in hand paid in witness where of I have set my hand and seal this 7th day of January one thousand eight hundred and seventy eight

witness

A Orlo Childs

Polly Childs

Moses Childs (L.S.)

1878 Deed. This 1878 deed between Moses Childs and W.D. Huntington was witnessed by A. Orlo Childs and Polly Childs. Before banks, signed papers and hand payments were considered normal transactions. The deed says in summary that Moses Childs is selling his land and water rights for $50, hand paid. (Courtesy of the Springville Historical Society.)

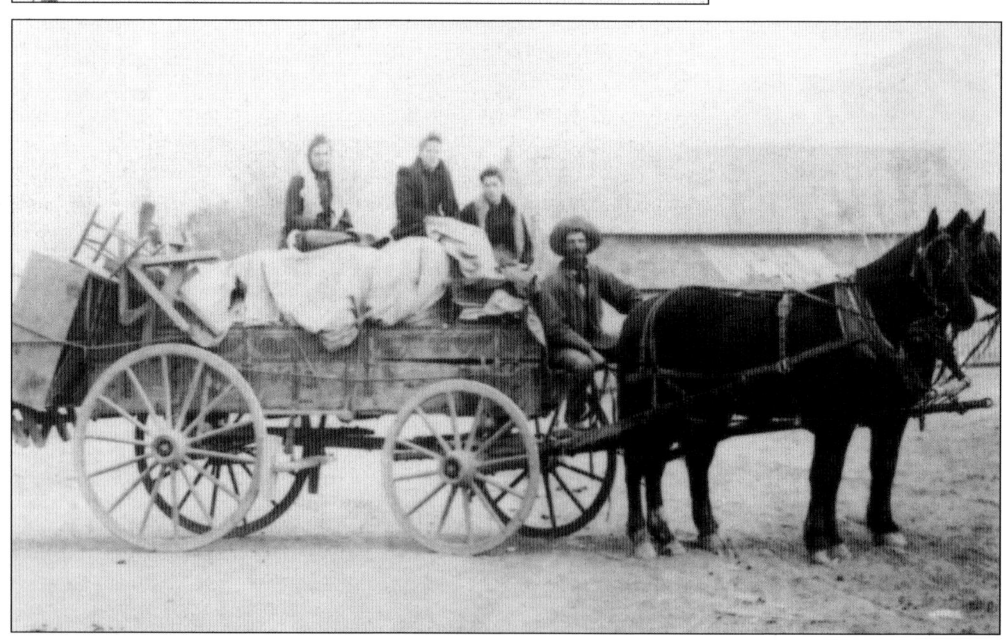

Moving Day. Eliza Roylance Harward and family are pictured on moving day. Everything owned by the family had to fit in and on the wagon. Eliza and her husband, Lenard, were blessed with 10 children, seven of whom lived to adulthood. Eliza died of a pulmonary embolism following a hernia surgery in 1916. The children were abandoned to the care of others, because Lenard had taken to drink. (Courtesy of the DUP.)

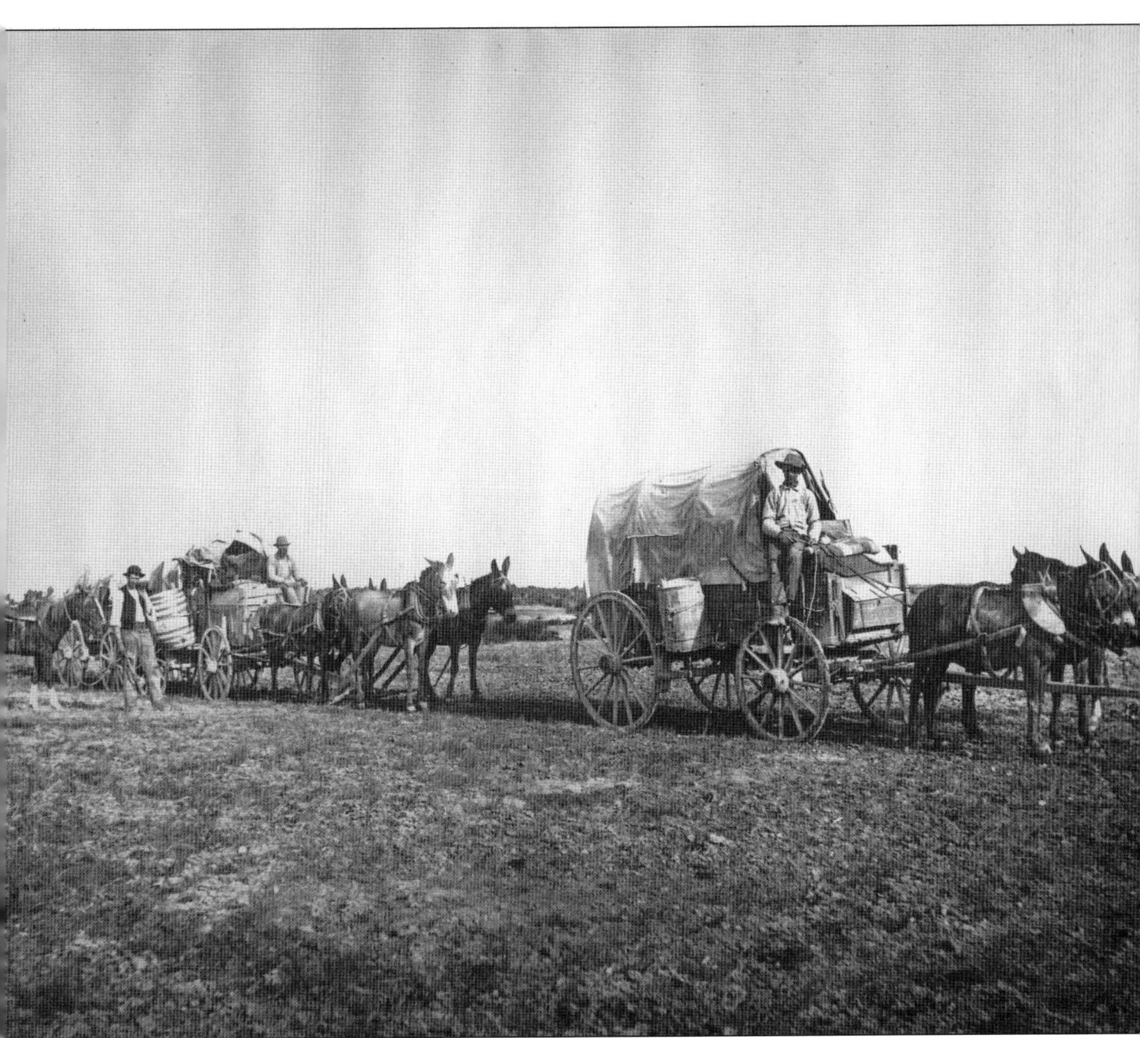

FREIGHT TRAIN. This picture depicts freight wagons moving goods and supplies. This was the way to safely transport people and goods: in a group with guns for protection. Eventually, as the West was settled more, horses and wagon trains were replaced by the railroad. (Courtesy of the DUP.)

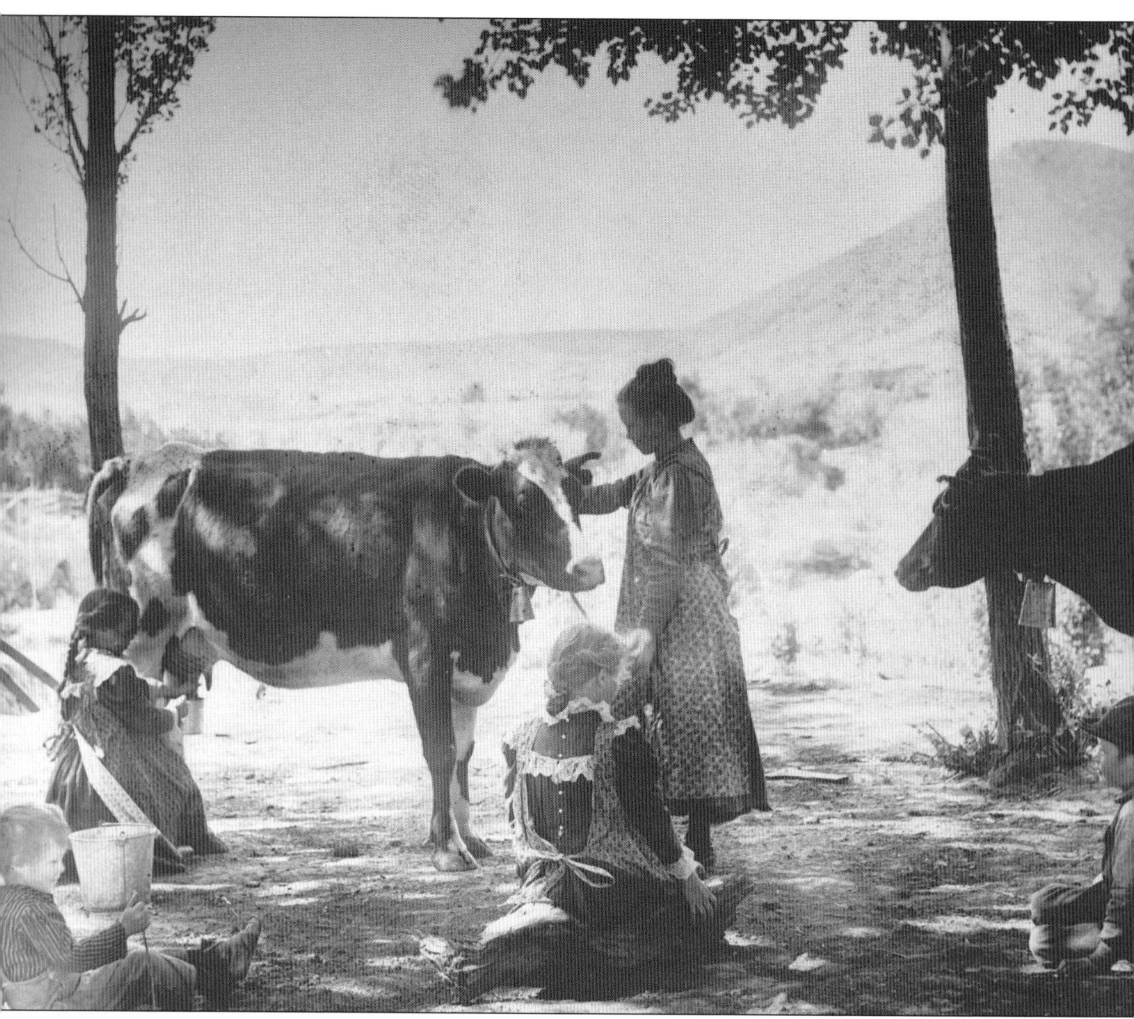

Drink of Milk. This photograph was taken around 1898. Christian Otteson's wife Sarah and some of their children are shown milking their cow. Animals were part of the family and received lots of attention. Otteson had one of the most desirable farms in Castle Valley, and was the first man to get pine logs for building a house from the Huntington Canyon area. (GEA photograph, courtesy of the DUP.)

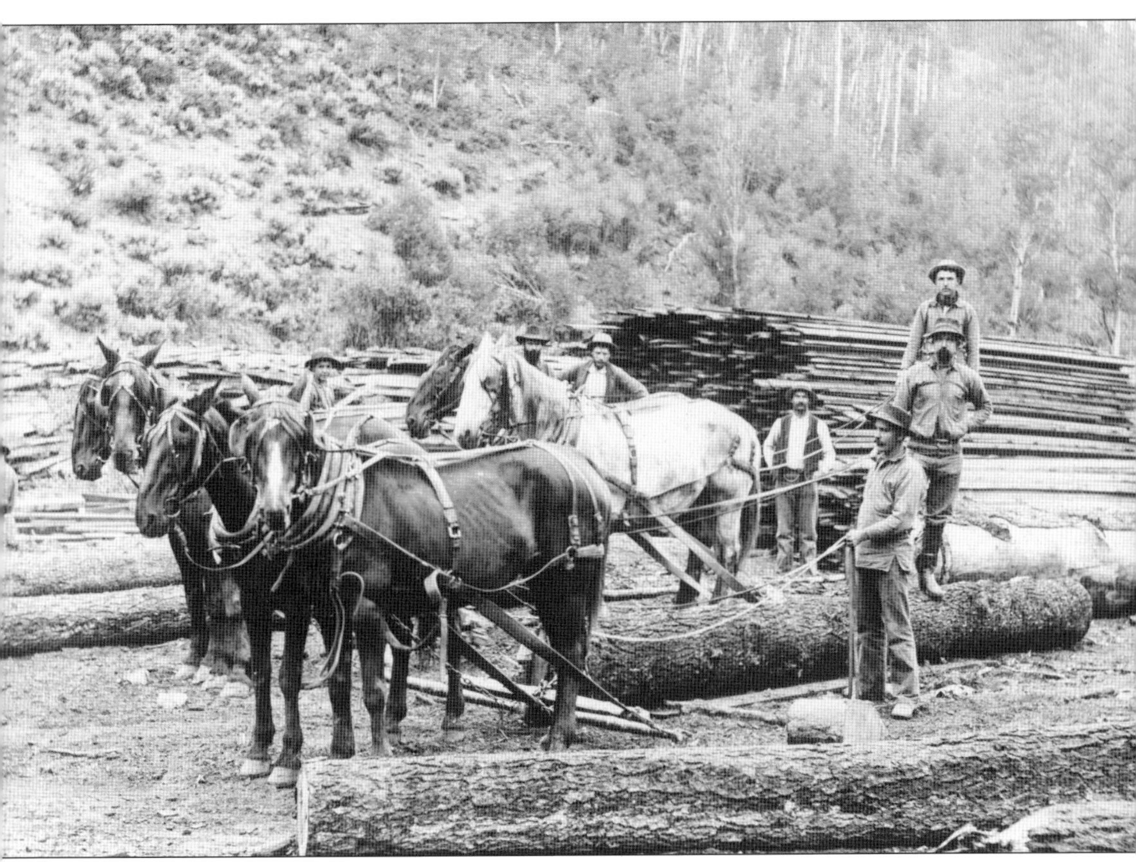

Hauling Wood. Thomas Burt's lumber and shingle mill was established on Thirty Oaks, located up the right fork of Hobble Creek Canyon. Burt Springs was named after the family in honor of their work. The small boy next to the horse's head is John Taylor Burt. The man behind the white horse is John Ford Burt, Thomas's son, who eventually ran the mill. (GEA photograph, courtesy of the Springville Historical Society.)

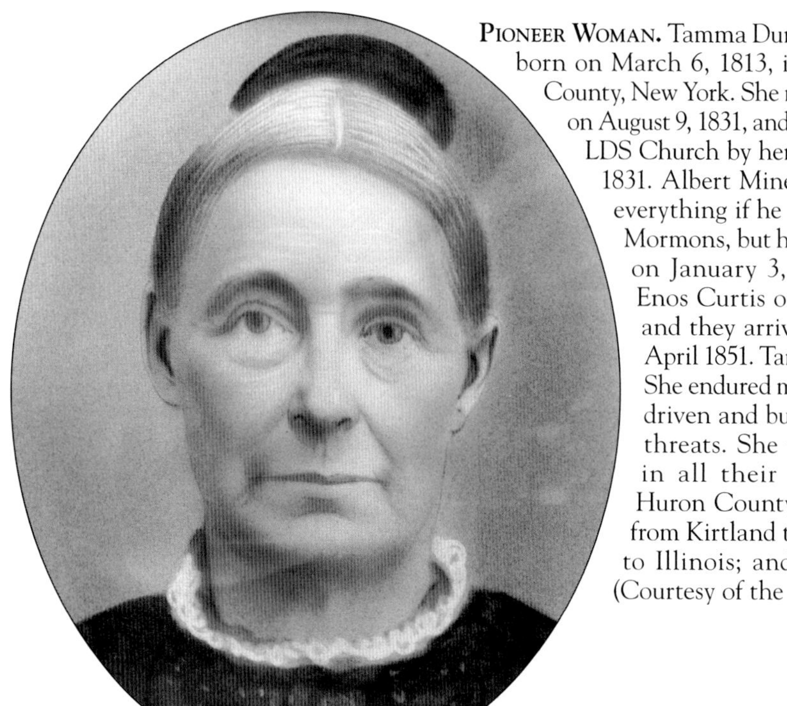

Pioneer Woman. Tamma Durfee Miner Curtis was born on March 6, 1813, in Lennox, Madison County, New York. She married Albert Miner on August 9, 1831, and was baptized into the LDS Church by her father in December 1831. Albert Miner's folks offered him everything if he would denounce the Mormons, but he would not. He died on January 3, 1848. Tamma met Enos Curtis on October 18, 1850, and they arrived in Springville in April 1851. Tamma had 14 children. She endured many hardships: being driven and burned out, mobs, and threats. She was with the saints in all their persecutions from Huron County to Kirtland, Ohio; from Kirtland to Missouri and back to Illinois; and across the desert. (Courtesy of the DUP.)

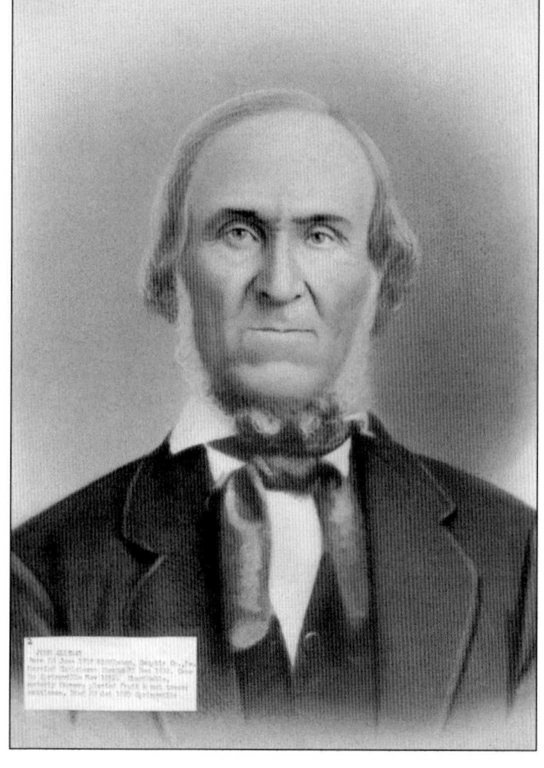

Pioneer Man. John Alleman and his wife Christeana arrived in Springville in November 1852. He planted fruit and nut trees and a garden. He raised cattle and horses, and his supplies of meat and grains kept many people from perishing during the town's lean growing years. John (Johannes) Alleman was born on June 28, 1808, in Middleton, Dauphin County, Pennsylvania, and married Christeana Stentz on December 11, 1832. He died on October 28, 1883, in Springville. (Courtesy of the DUP.)

Gideon Wood. Gideon Durfey Wood was the first mayor of Springville (Hobble Creek), and took office on April 4, 1853. He married Hannah Daley on December 30, 1830, and they had five children together. He was a farmer and a school teacher. He died on September 9, 1890, in Springville. (Courtesy of the DUP.)

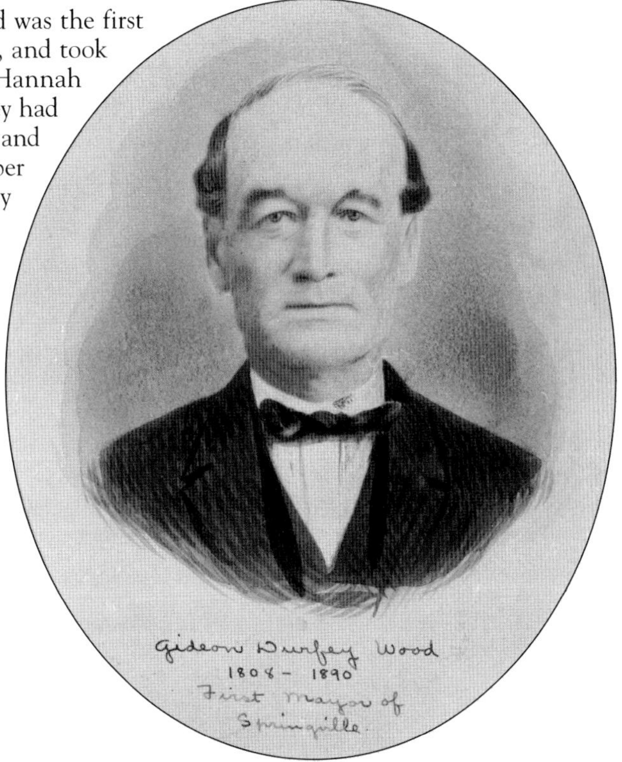

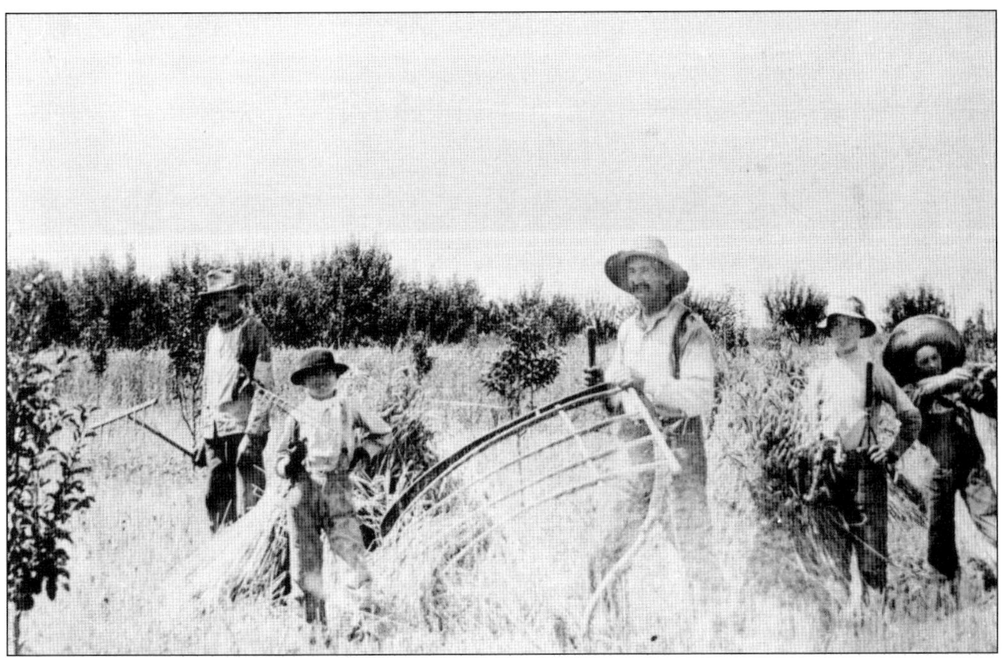

Haying. Ether Blanchard is pictured with his hand tool and helpers. He used a cradle scythe to harvest his 13 acres by hand around 1879. He is quoted as saying: "Ten thousand bushels, with might and main; have we reaped the golden grain." Boys were often kept out of school to help during the harvest. (GEA photograph, courtesy of the Springville Historical Society.)

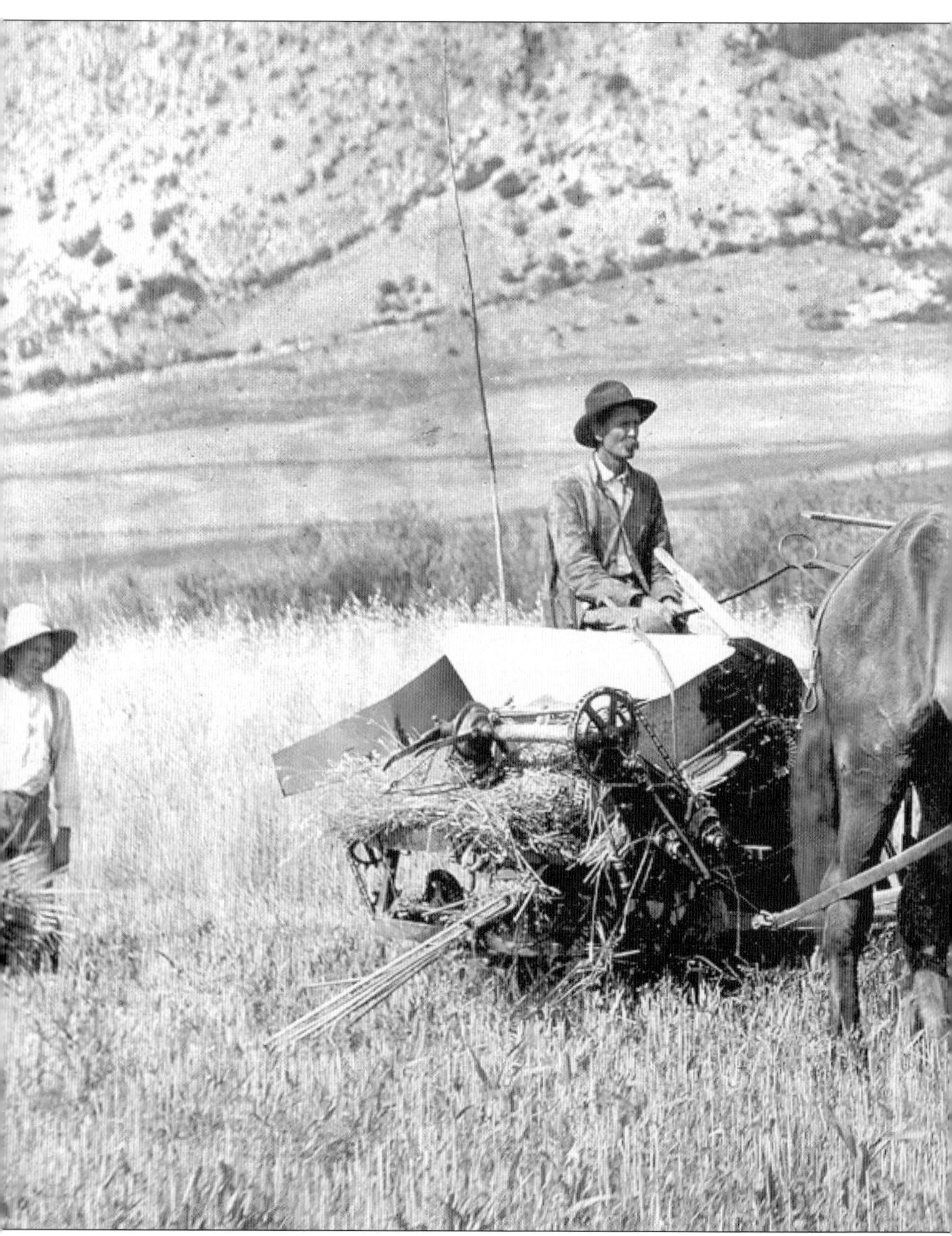

Haying with Team. Pictured around 1900 is the youngest son of Moses and Polly Childs, Archibald Orlo Childs, haying with his three-horse team and his grain binder. Following behind the binder is James B. Childs, his son. Archibald's mother, Polly, was a lovely seamstress and was hand-sewing

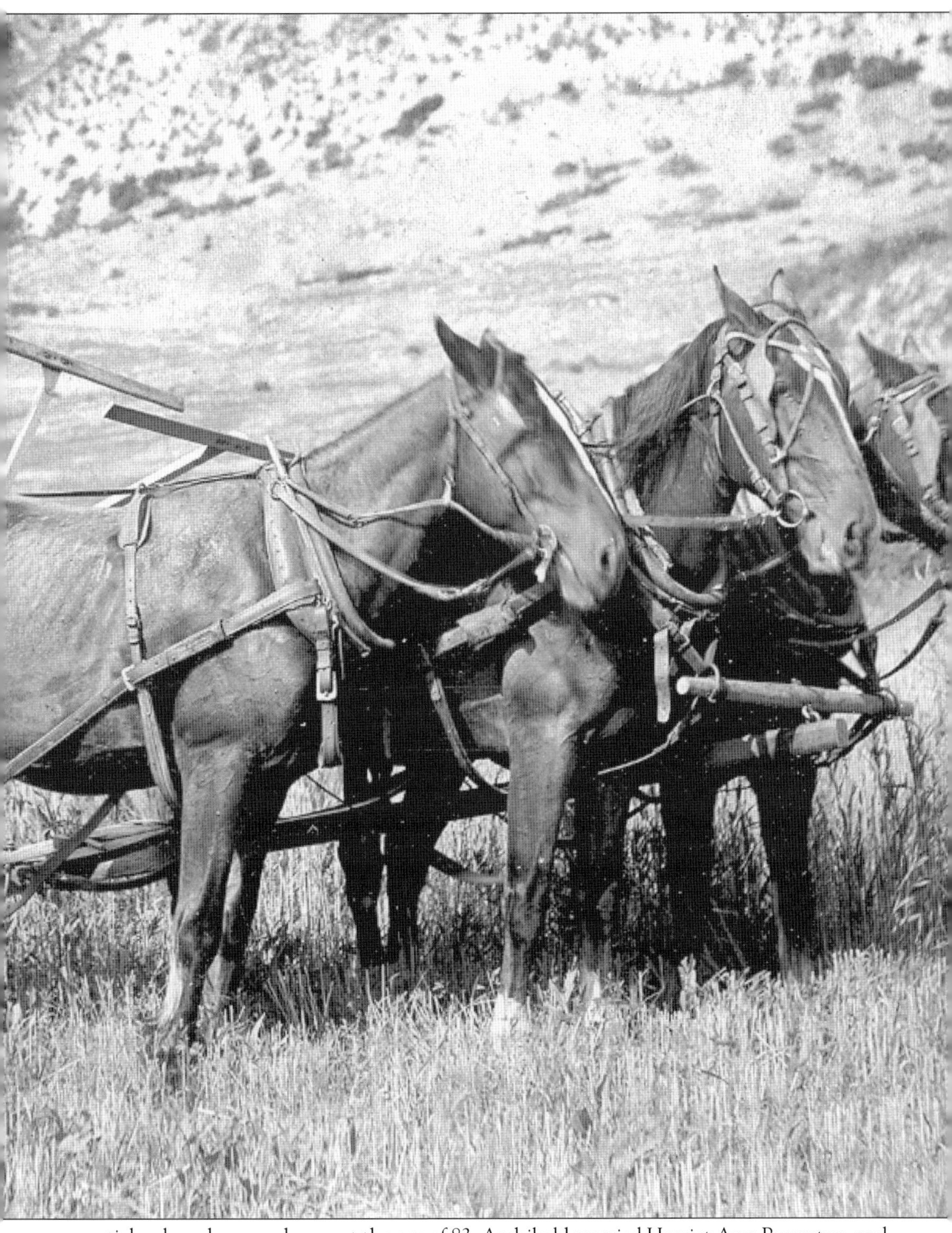

an article when she passed away at the age of 83. Archibald married Harriet Ann Burraston, and they had 11 children together. (Courtesy of the Springville Historical Society.)

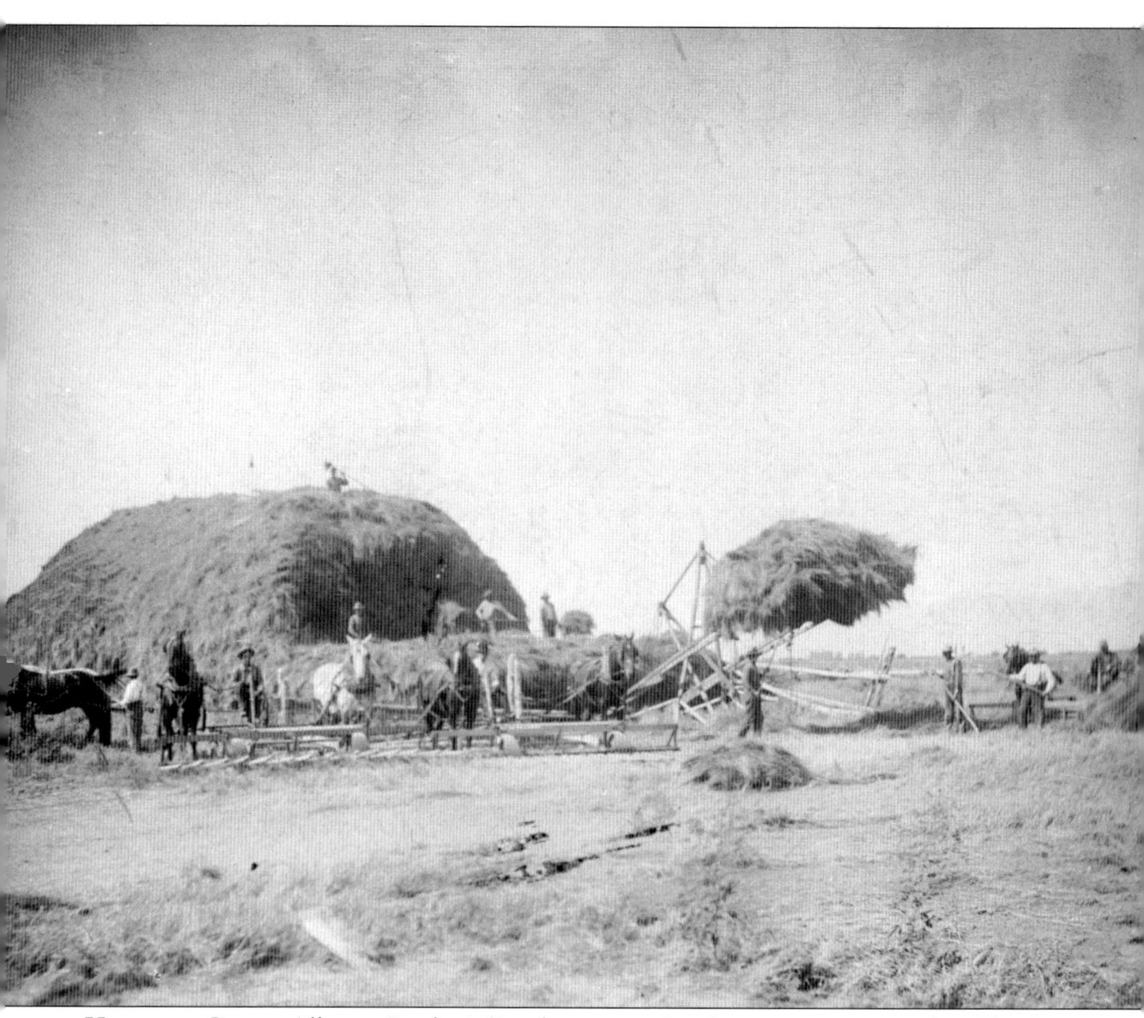

HAYING AS GROUP. Alleman Brother's Ranch is pictured with a group putting up hay. The farm was located west of Springville. The boys in the photograph were sons of Johannes (John) and Christeana Stentz Alleman of Springville. (Courtesy of the Springville Historical Society.)

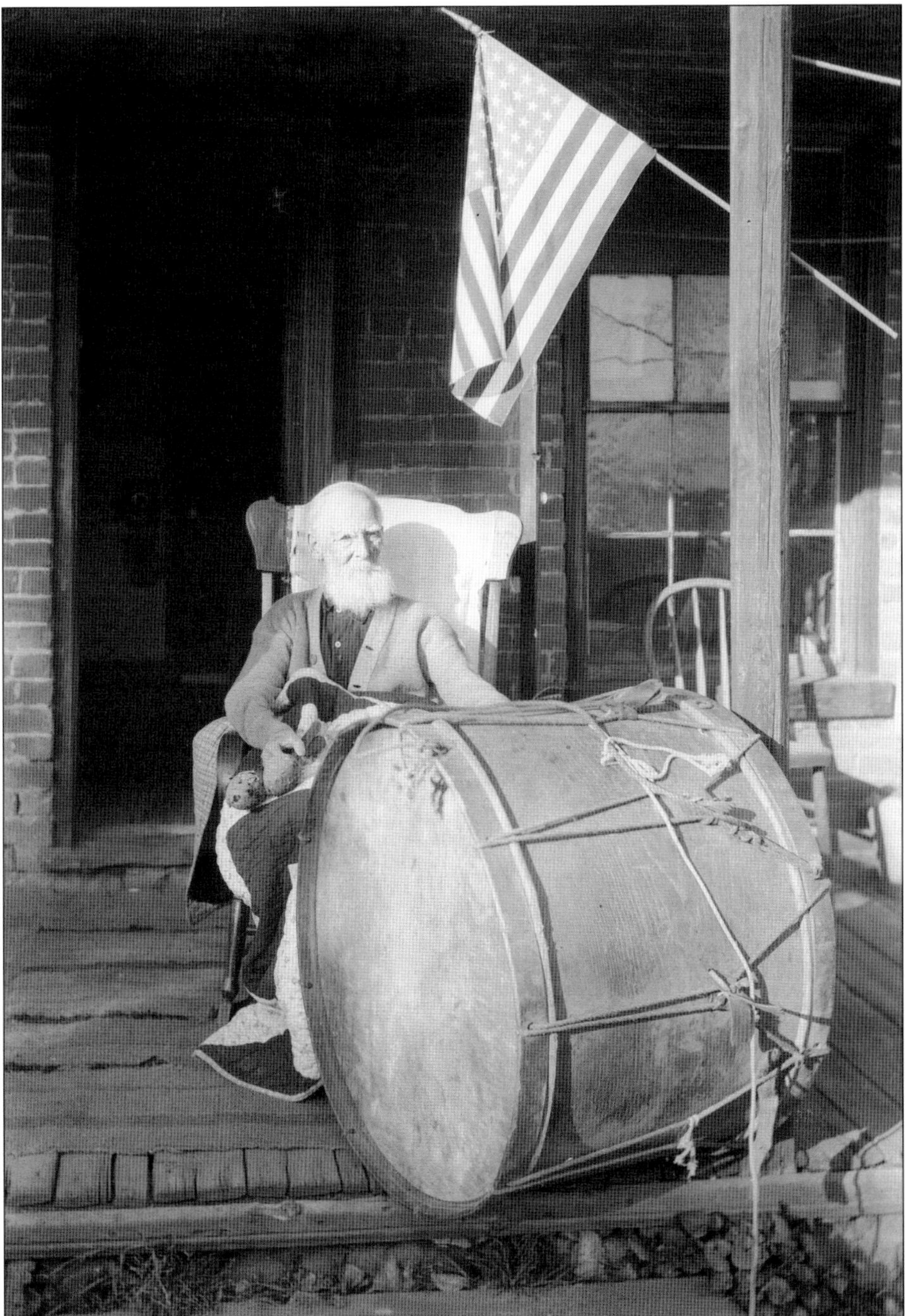

HANDMADE DRUM. William Morgan Clyde, pictured with his handmade drum, was known as the "Drummer Boy of Nauvoo," as he had played his drum as part of the Nauvoo Legion band. He was a member of the Springville Brass and Marshall Bands, and also entertained at town celebrations. He was born in Ogdensburg, New York, on April 8, 1829. He had been sick for several months when word came that the Armistice was signed ending World War I. At hearing this news, he asked to be taken out on the porch so he could beat his drum and wave the flag. He died a few months later, on January 22, 1919, at the age of 89. (Courtesy of the DUP.)

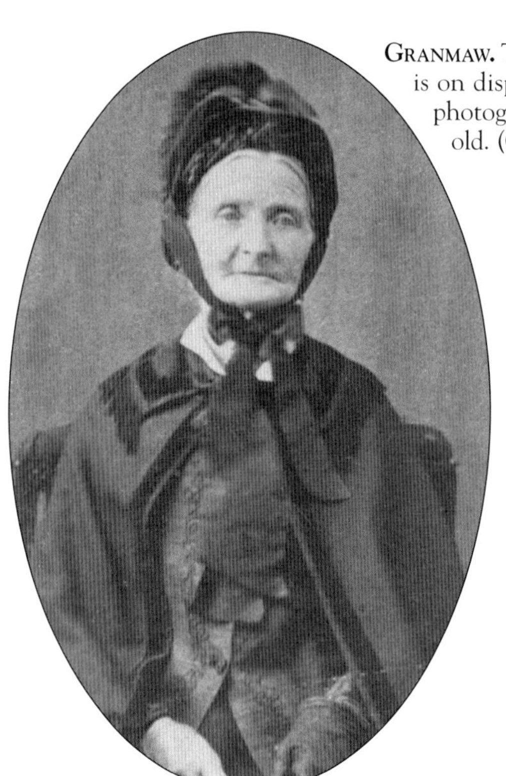

Granmaw. This photograph of Anna "Granmaw" Malmstrom is on display at the DUP museum. At the time of this photograph, she was 78 years, 3 months, and 15 days old. (Courtesy of the DUP.)

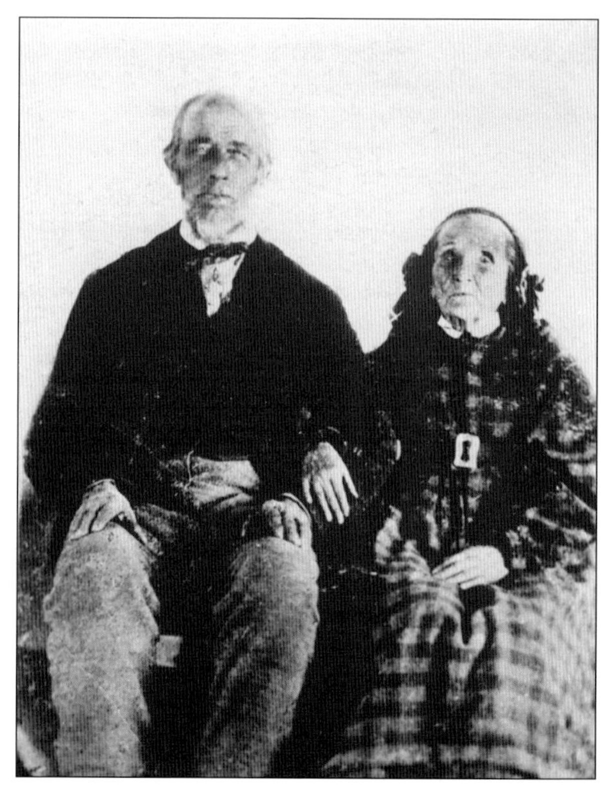

Smiths. Pictured are Richard and Diana O. Braswell Smith. Richard was born on September 19, 1792, in Holston River, Sullivan County, Tennessee. Diana was born on October 9, 1797, in Greenville County, South Carolina. They married on December 11, 1817, in Gibson County, Tennessee. Both are buried in the Heber City cemetery. The Richard and Diana Smith family helped to establish at least five pioneer settlements in four states and territories: Bradford, Tennessee; St. Albans, Illinois; Mount Pisgah, Iowa; Provo, Utah; and Heber City, Utah. They have many descendants in the area, as they were the parents of 13 children. (Courtesy of the DUP.)

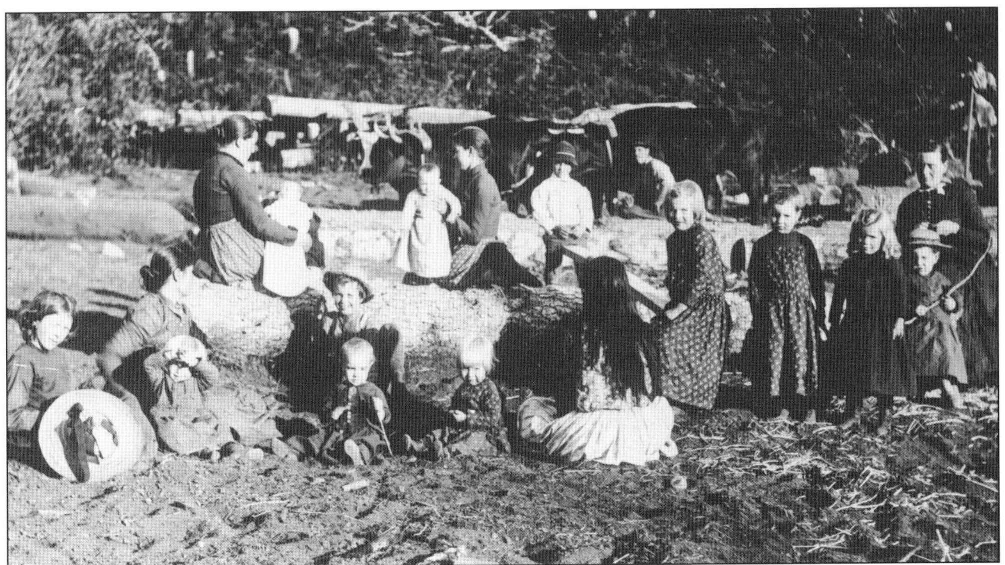

Canyon Camping. This 1870 photograph shows pioneers camping at the Edwin Whiting sawmill. This mill was located up the left fork of Hobble Creek Canyon. Pictured are Edwin's wives and children. From left to right are (first row) Bertha Johnson, Mrs. Arthur Whiting and baby, Lee Eddie Whiting, Louis A. Johnson at 18 months old, Mrs. Edwin Whiting's mother, May Whiting, Martha Whiting, Ernest Whiting, and A. Cox; (second row) Mrs. Edwin Whiting and baby, Will Whiting, and Edgar Whiting with the oxen. Aaron Johnson and Arth Whiting are back in the timber. The others are unidentified. (Courtesy of the Springville Historical Society.)

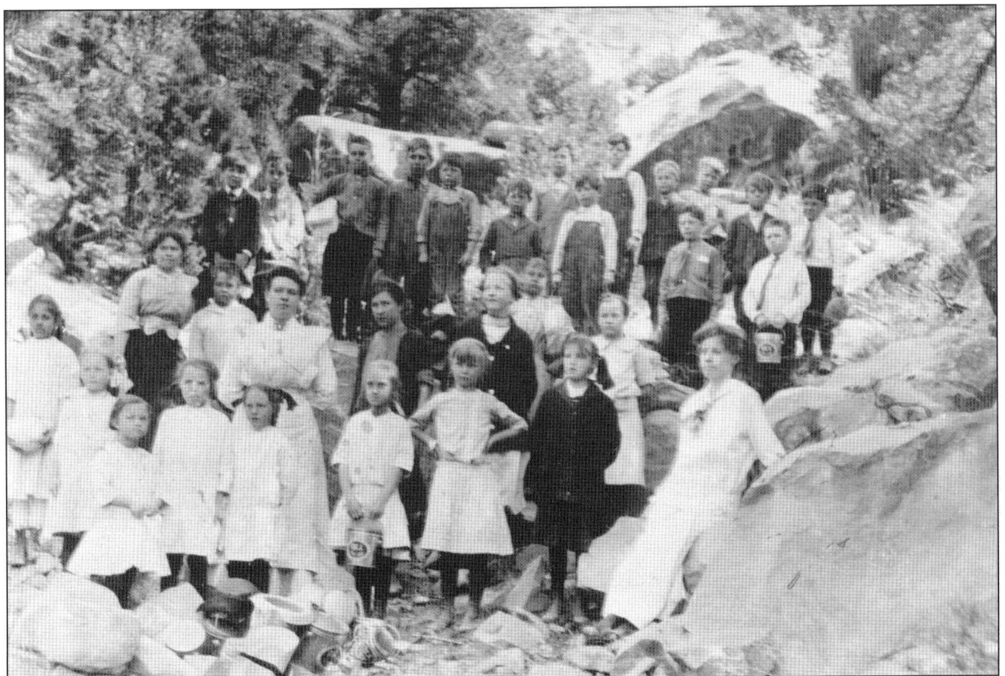

School Lunch. Children take a lunch break at a country school. No identifications are listed for this photograph, but it does show the schoolchildren and the teacher with their lunch pails. (Courtesy of the DUP.)

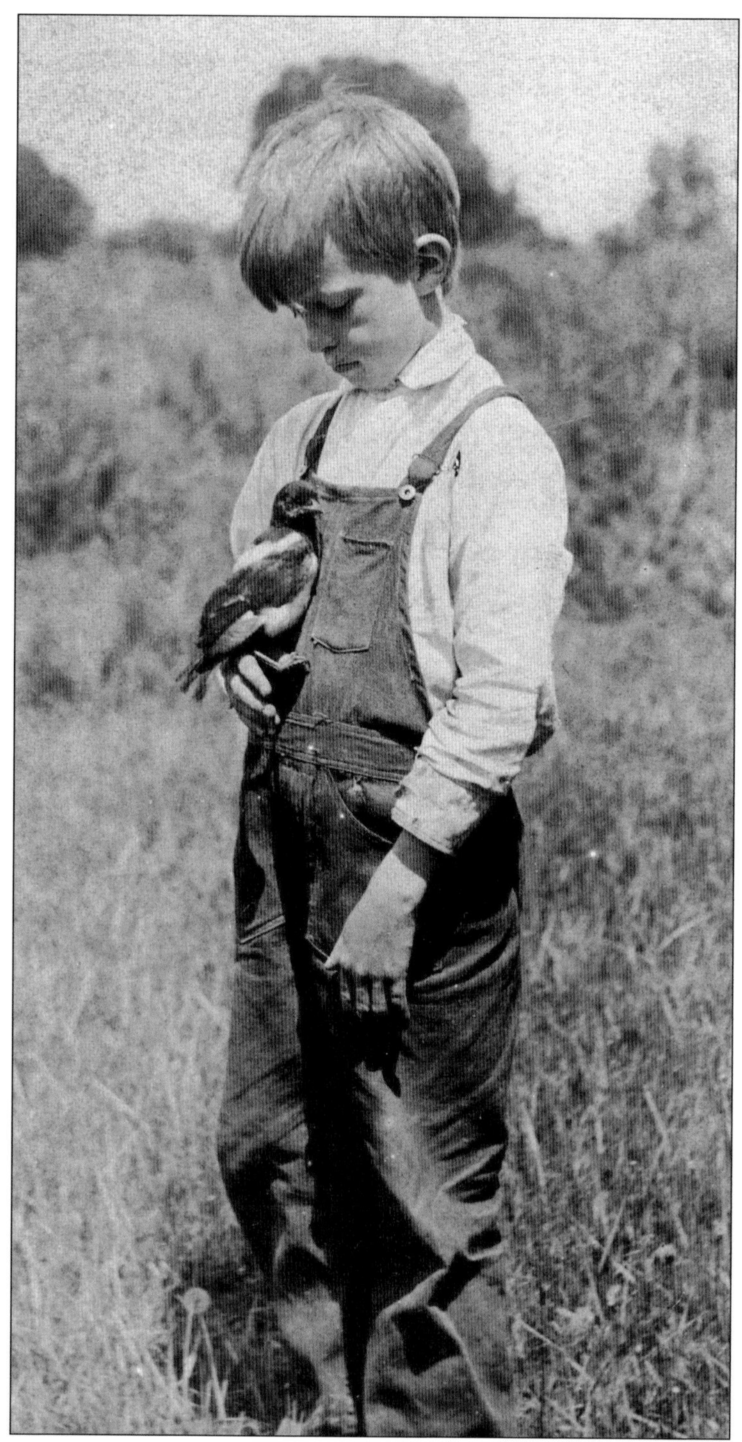

Horace Clark. Pictured is Horace Clark with a bird. He married Susannah Cole on May 5, 1855. Clark was a stage driver and a teamster. He died on November 7, 1900, she died on June 26, 1898, and both are buried in the San Bernardino, California, Pioneer Cemetery. (Courtesy of the DUP.)

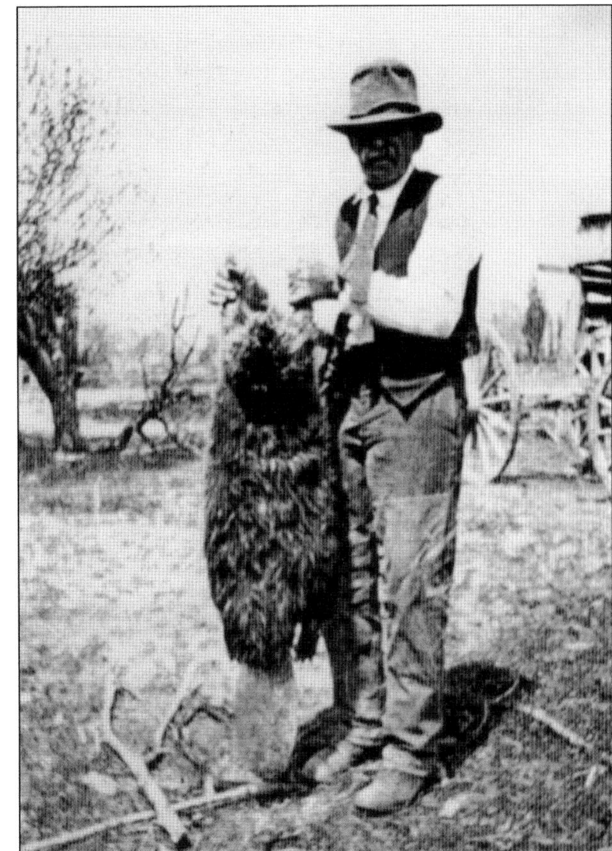

Beaver. George Marston Bartholomew is holding a beaver. With the creeks and ponds close by, beavers had lots of places to build their dams. (Courtesy of the DUP.)

Grading. The Cherrington/Miller Construction Company is grading for roads. Some of the men are Amyot Willard Cherrington, John Melvin Cherrington, and James Upton Cherrington. Horses were valuable animals and helped in many ways to make the cities and other areas accessible. (Courtesy of the DUP.)

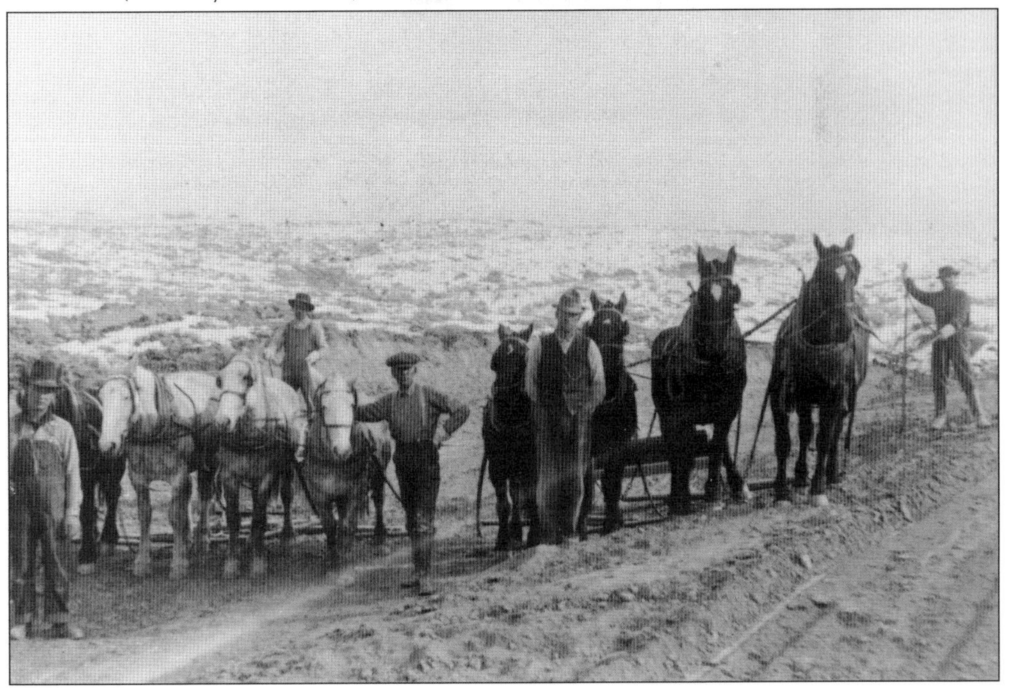

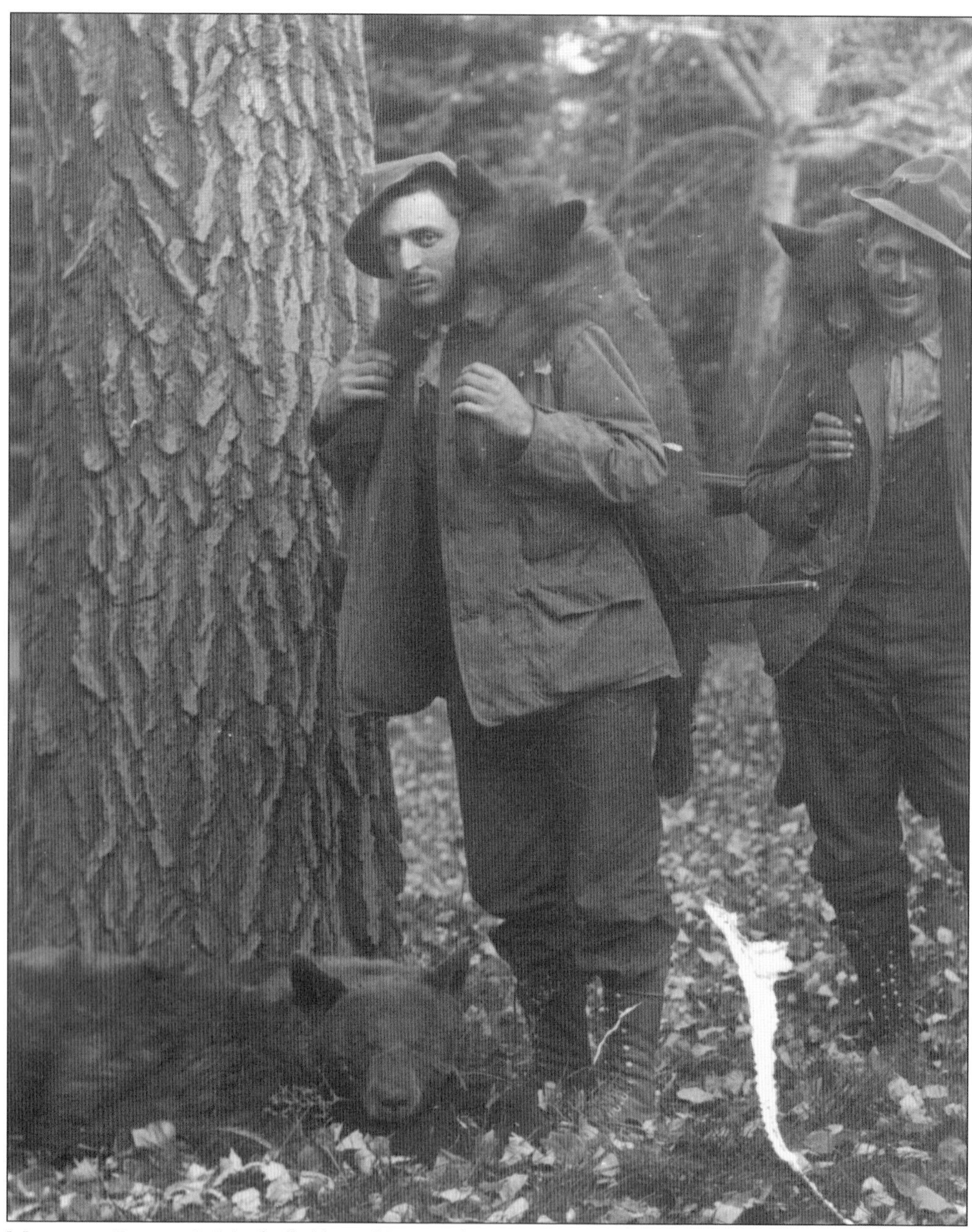

Men and Bears. J. Mock (left) and Joe Malmstrom are shown with a few dead bears after a successful hunt. Wildlife was plentiful in the area, and with the mountains close by, large game was frequently hunted. (Courtesy of the DUP.)

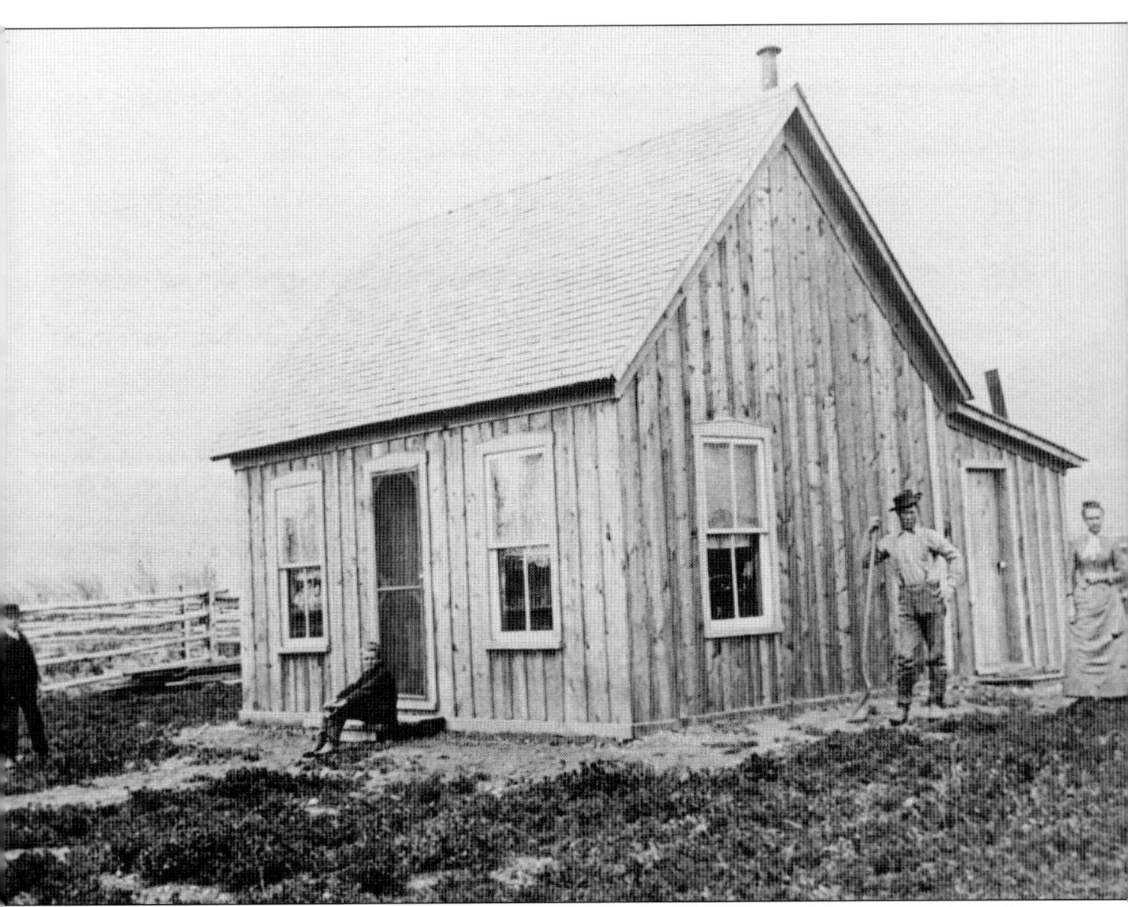

HOMESTEAD. William Daniel Coffman's Sage Creek homestead is pictured with William, his wife, and two children out front. Coffman was born in Springville on July 2, 1865. He married Mary Ann Bramall on May 28, 1886, in Logan, Utah. As a railroad construction foreman, he traveled all over the western states. Later in life, he farmed and raised livestock. His second child, Dora, was born in this home. Coffman died on February 26, 1943, in Salt Lake City. (Courtesy of the DUP.)

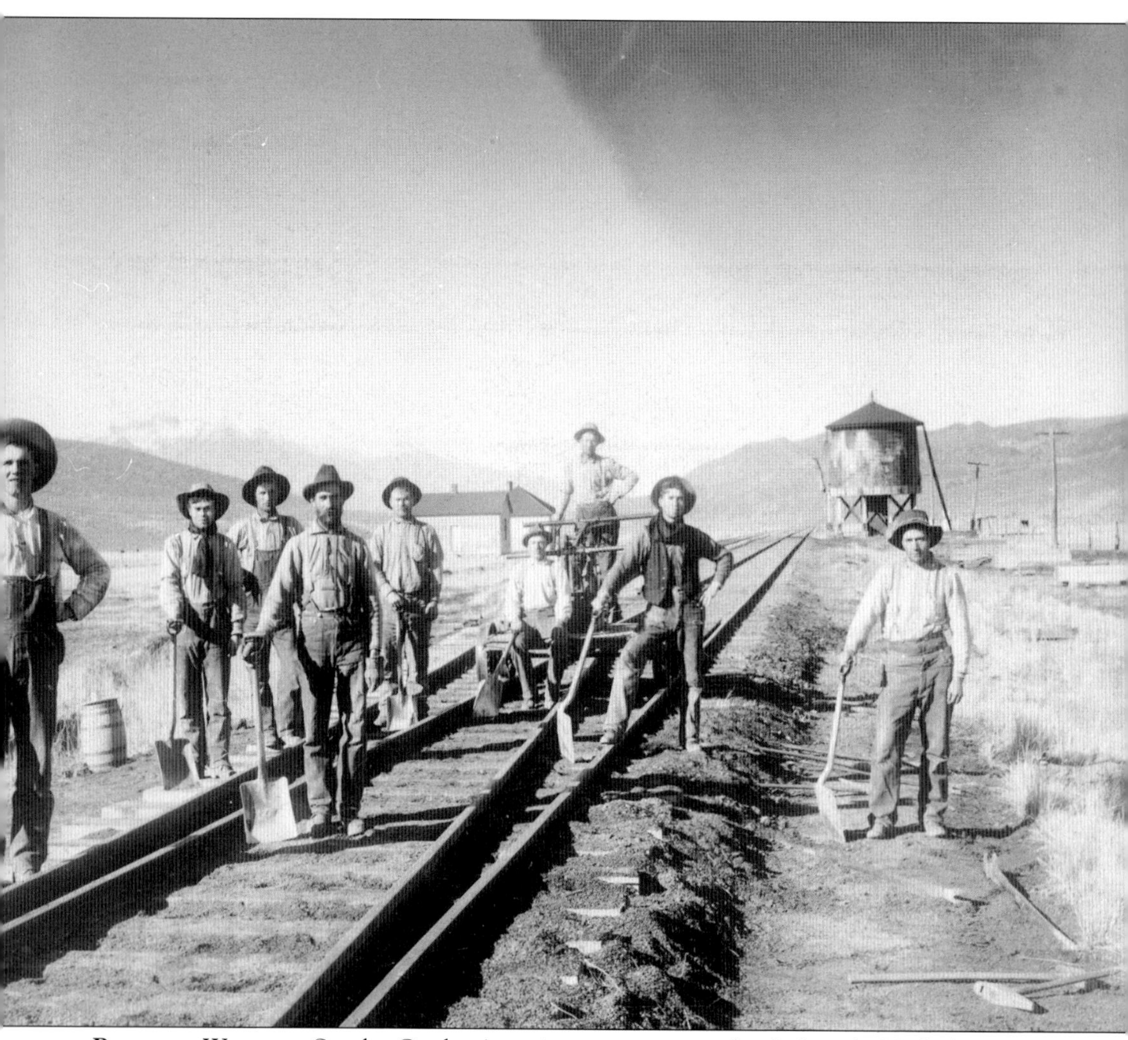

Railroad Workers. Stanley Gardner's section crew is pictured in Indianola, Utah, facing north toward Loafer Mountain around 1900. Twenty-one-year-old Stanley is at the left, apart from the crew. They are working on the Rio Grande Western Railway. Three years later, Stanley was killed when his handcar ran into an approaching locomotive. William White, next to Stanley, married his widow and raised his two children. The fifth man from the left is Butch Cassidy (Robert Leroy Parker), a notorious train and bank robber and the "Wild Bunch" gang leader of the Old West. His death remains a mystery. (GEA photograph, courtesy of the DUP.)

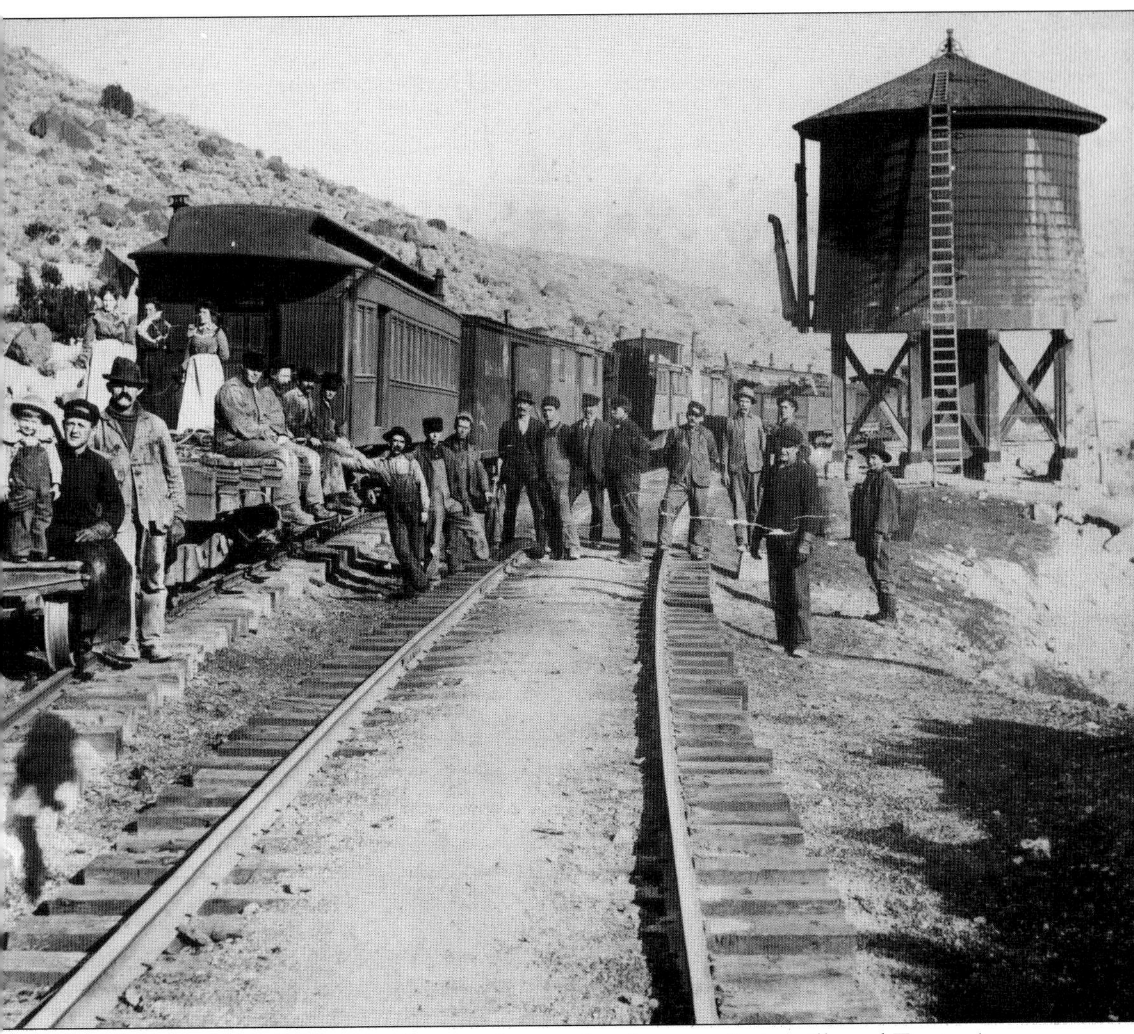

Train and People. This train photograph was taken between Springville and Tintic. A water tank is on the right. The only one identified is William Samuel Bramall, who is sitting on the platform at left in the foreground. Bramall was born and raised in Springville and is also buried here. He married Sarah Louisa Farr, and they had four children together: Franklin, Bert, Sarah, and Lois. (Courtesy of the DUP.)

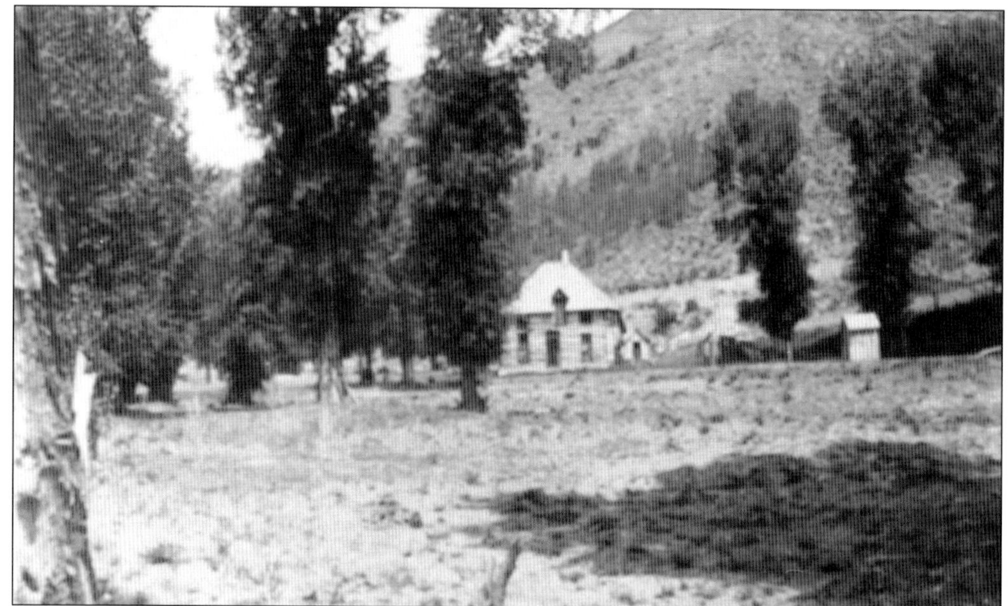

Homestead. The property is unidentified, but this photograph shows a typical scene from the American Old West: yard, trees, and an outhouse, with no neighbors close by. This image shows a lovely, quiet place to raise family and livestock. (Courtesy of the DUP.)

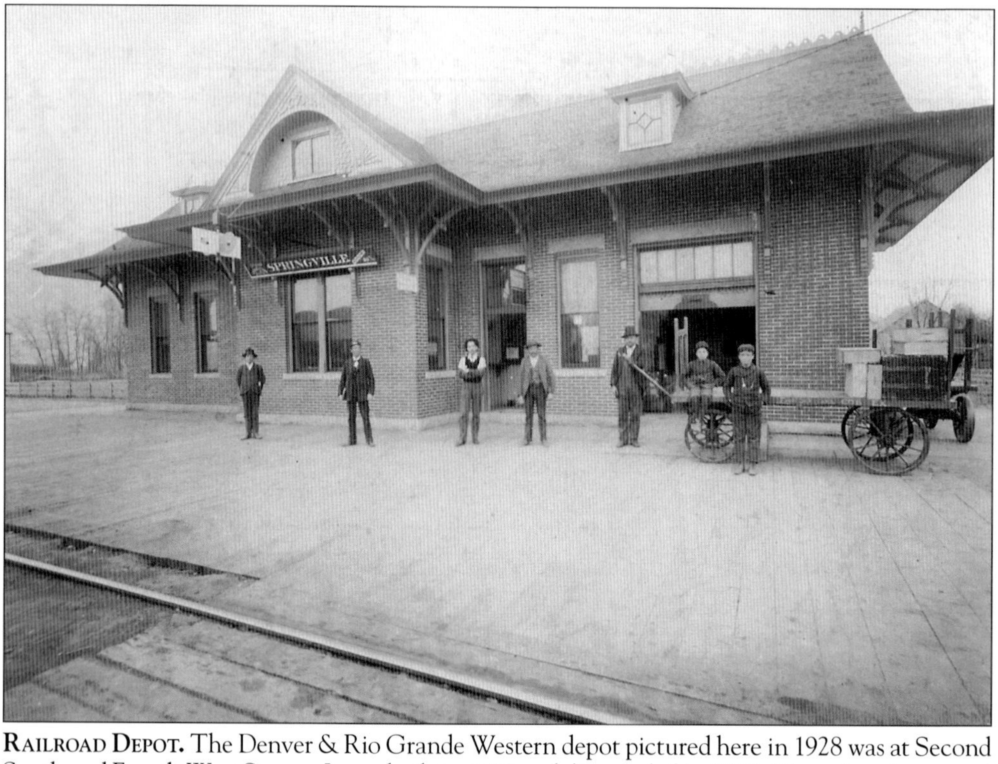

Railroad Depot. The Denver & Rio Grande Western depot pictured here in 1928 was at Second South and Fourth West Streets. It was built in 1909 and dismantled in 1964. The railroad operated in Colorado, Utah, and New Mexico from 1870 to 1988. The Southern Pacific and the Union Pacific Railroads now operate those lines. (Courtesy of the Springville Historical Society.)

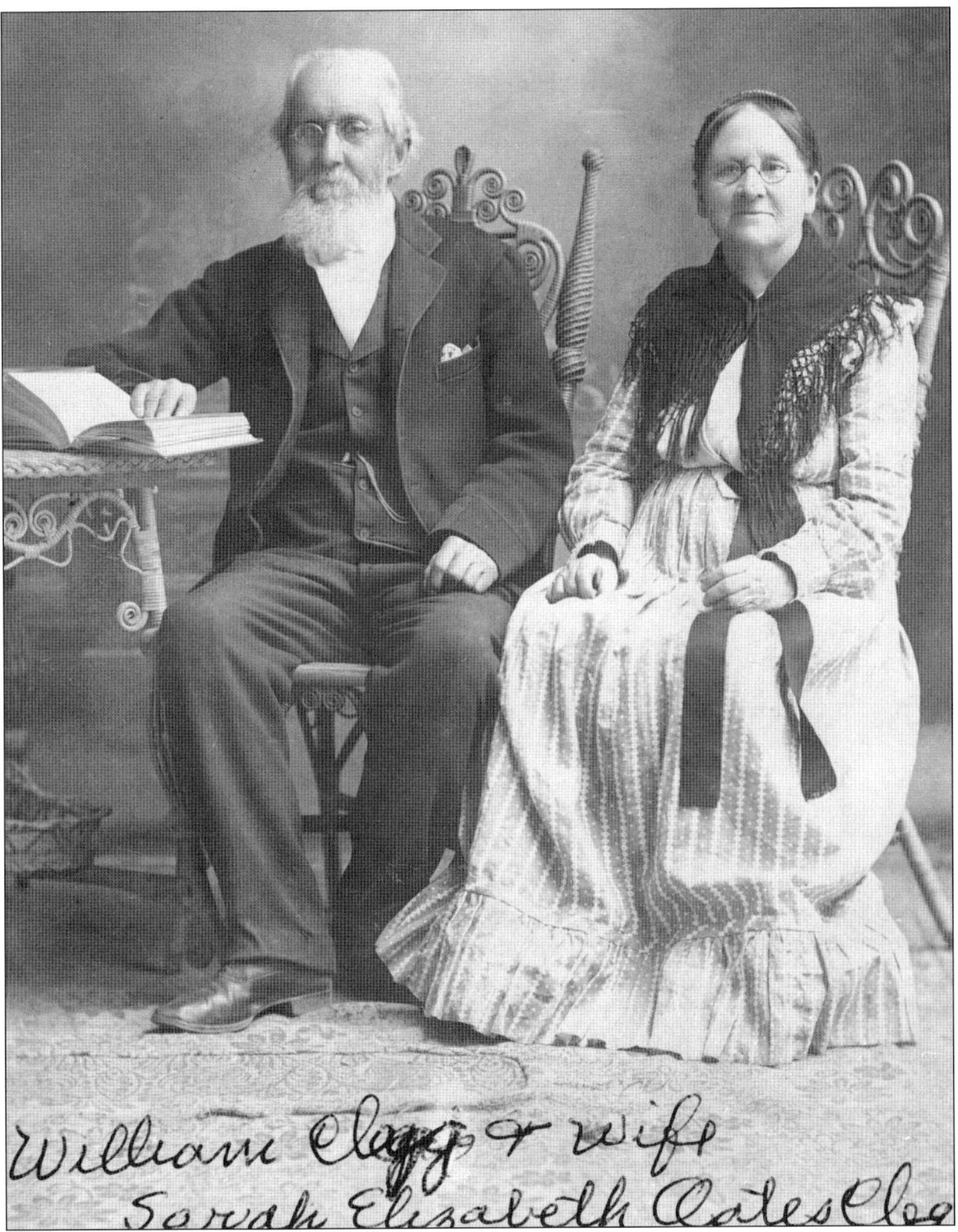

Cleggs. Pictured are William Clegg and his wife Sarah Elizabeth Oates Clegg. They came to Springville with meager means and stayed with friends until William could build a home for Sarah. He was very proud and happy when he took her to the new home. He had smoothed out the walls and the floor and had built a stone fireplace in a dugout-type cellar home. The furniture was made of split logs, and the steps were of cobblestone. Sarah immediately sat down on the bench and cried when she came in. William asked, "Sarah, why do you cry? I worked hard, and the house is nicer than some of our neighbors." She replied, "Yes . . . William, but I never thought I would have to go under the ground until I was dead." (Courtesy of the DUP.)

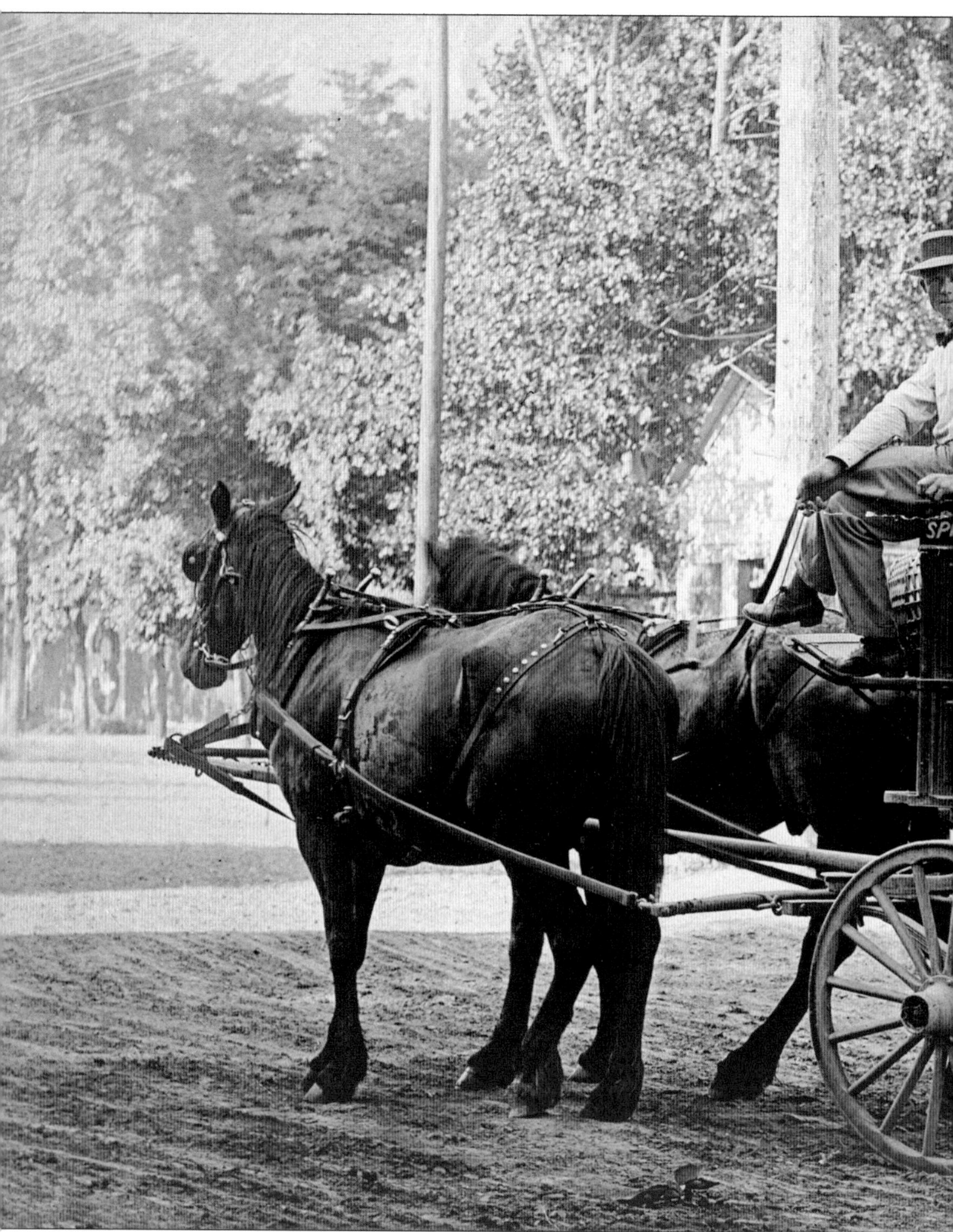

Robinson Bros. Music Dealers. This picture was taken on June 30, 1909. The Robinson Bros. Music Dealers business was downtown. The building still stands at 296 South Main Street, now home of Pier 49 Pizza. In this joyous scene, Floyd Miner and Margaret Johnson (standing at

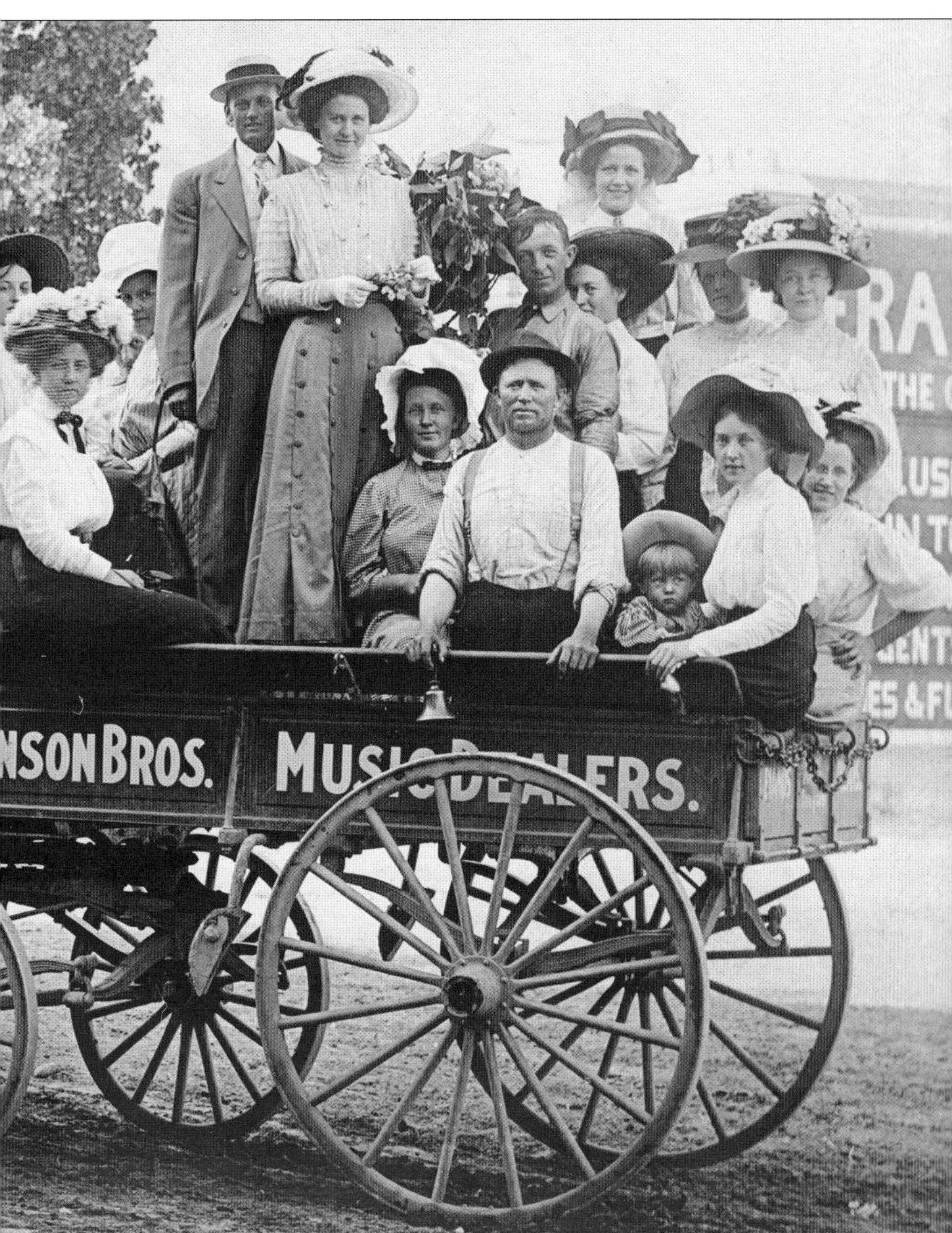

center) are being picked up and taken to the train depot. They were heading to Manti, Utah, to get married. Marian Francis "Med" Miner is seated in the carriage wearing suspenders. (Courtesy of the DUP.)

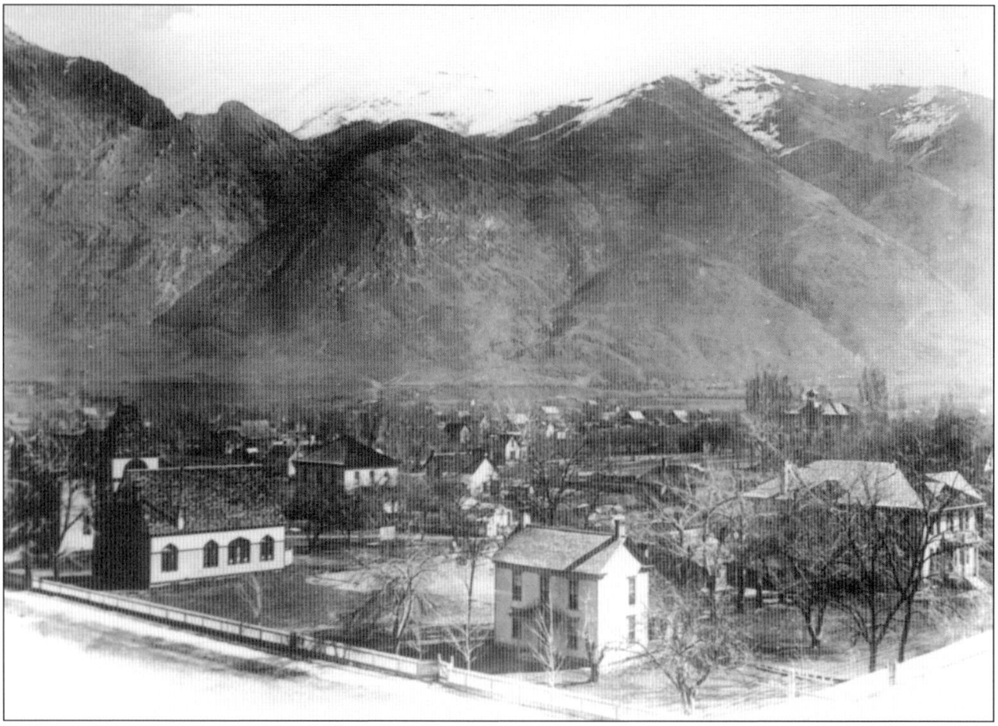

EARLY VIEW. Taken from the belfry of the Washington School, this is Springville in the early 1900s. From left to right are the Hungerford Academy, the Presbyterian church, the boys' dormitory, the reverend's home, and the girls' dormitory. The Washington School was at Third South and Second East Streets. (Courtesy of the DUP.)

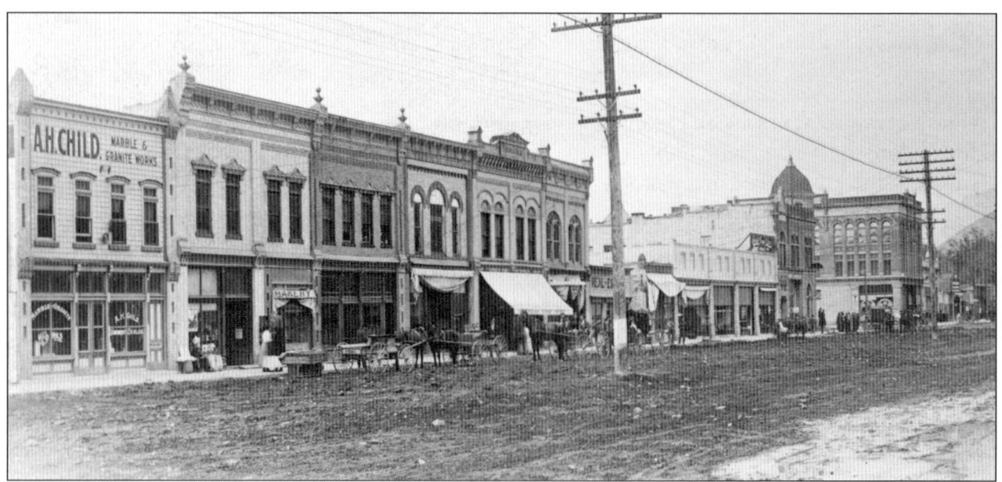

STREET VIEW. The town is becoming a city. Telephone poles have been installed, and businesses line the street. In the distance are the Springville Bank and the H.T. Reynolds building, which is pictured on the cover. Horses and carriages await their owners as they shop and conduct business. (Courtesy of the DUP.)

Two

The Arts and Beyond

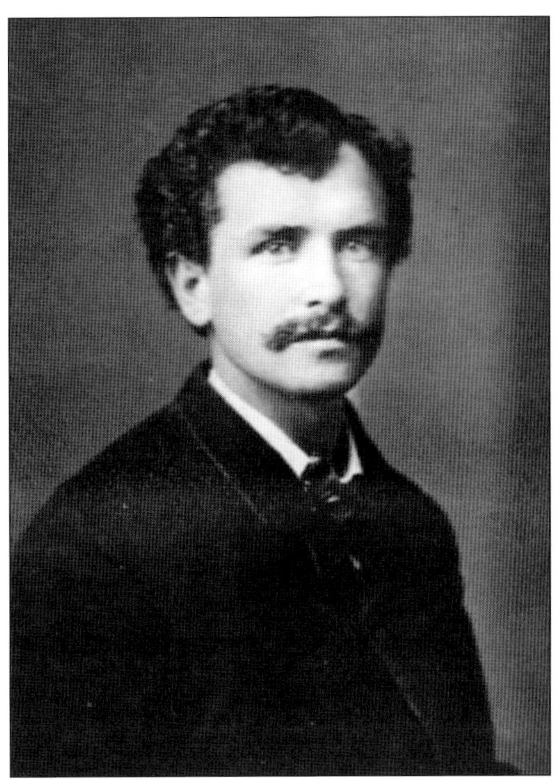

George Edward Anderson. George Edward Anderson is shown at about 24 around 1884. He loved art, history, and his religion. Anderson was a traveling photographer, and it has only been within the last 50 years that his photographic work has been widely acknowledged as phenomenal for his day. His popularized artistry is now being shown by the remaining known prints in existence, with exhibits and publications being held around the globe. His half-remembered world is shown by the remarkable photographs that have graced the pages of the books *Mapleton* and *Springville*. (Courtesy of the Springville Historical Society.)

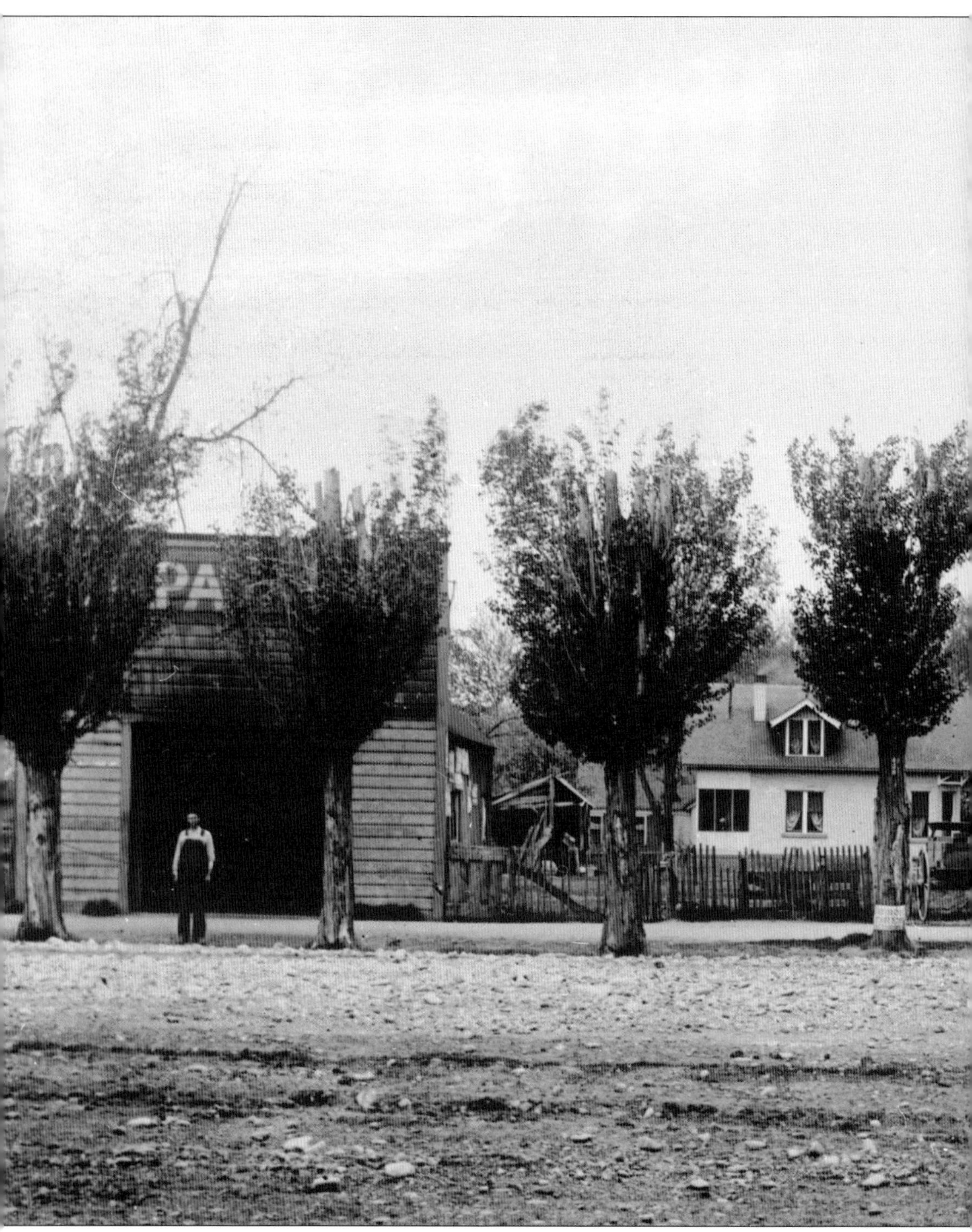

Anderson Studio. Anderson's large studio gallery, pictured here, was built around 1906. The first floor was devoted to the arts, and the second floor held the studio. The basement was fitted for developing and storage purposes. The gallery was not the financial success he anticipated, and eventually the different floors had to be rented out to meet financial obligations. At left, John Patrick

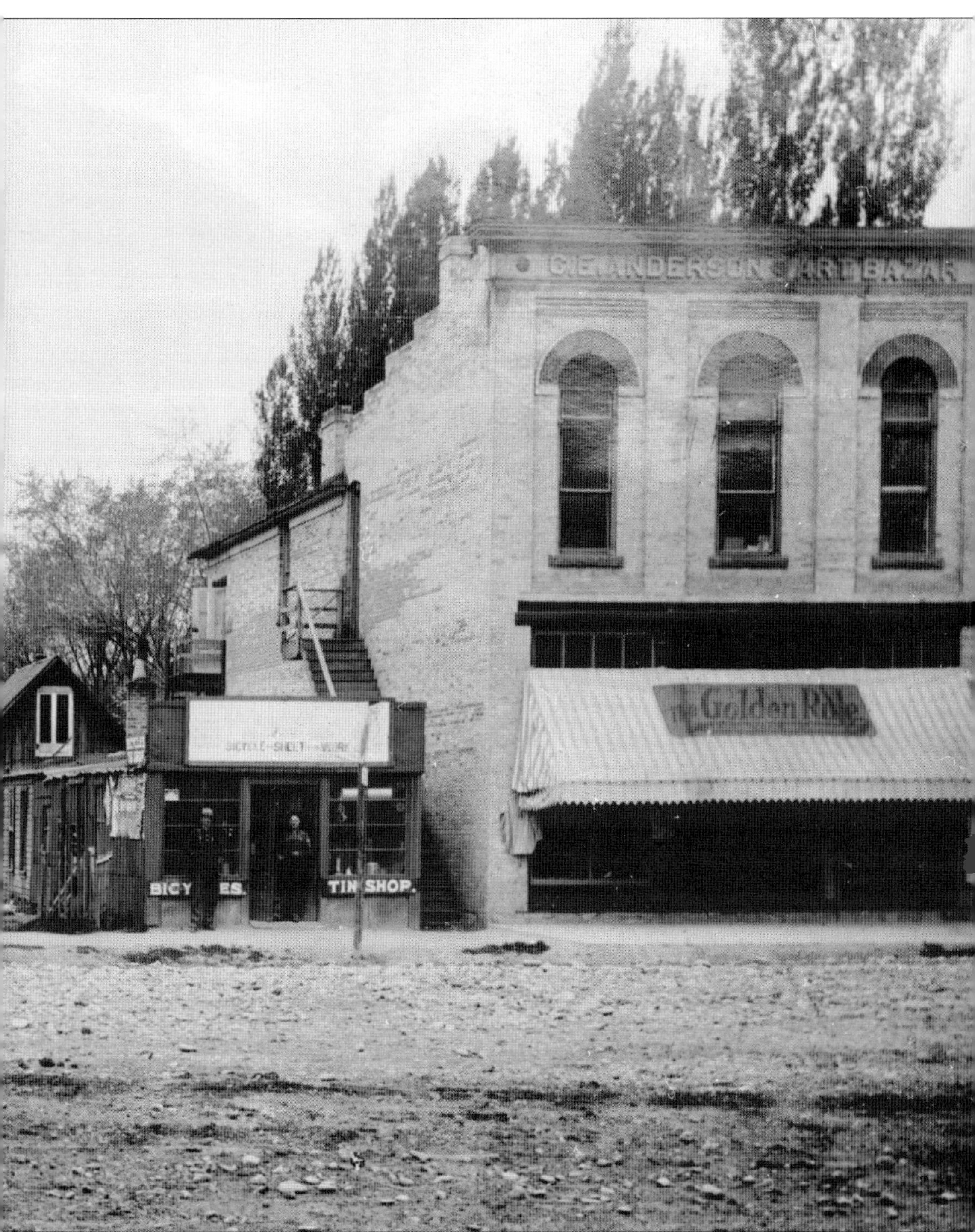

stands in front of his blacksmith shop. The awning on the right says "Golden Rule," which was the original name of the J.C. Penney chain. This was one of the businesses that eventually rented space from Anderson. (GEA photograph, courtesy of the Springville Historical Society.)

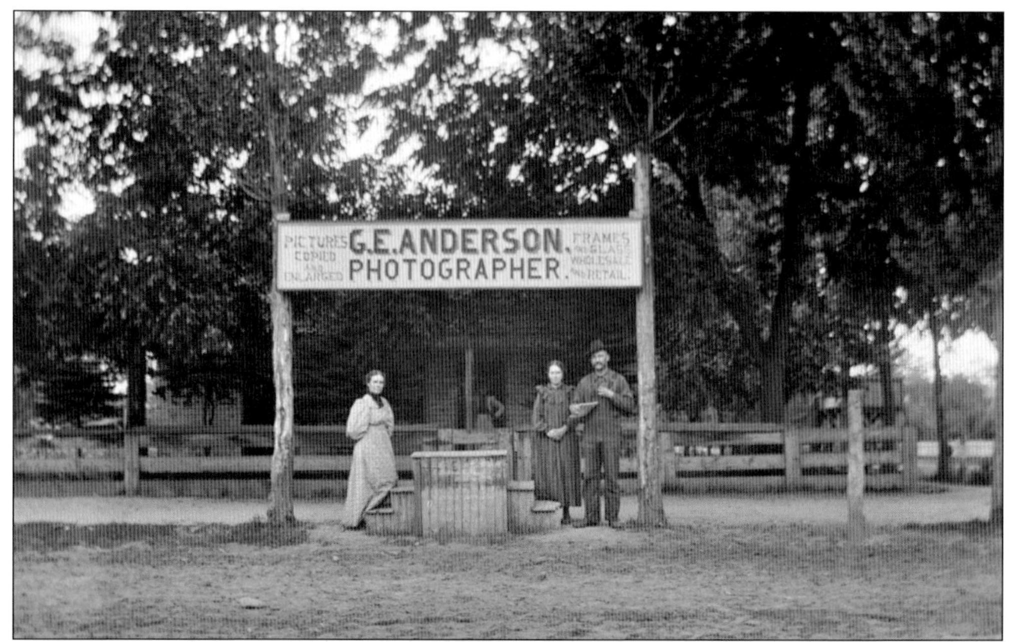

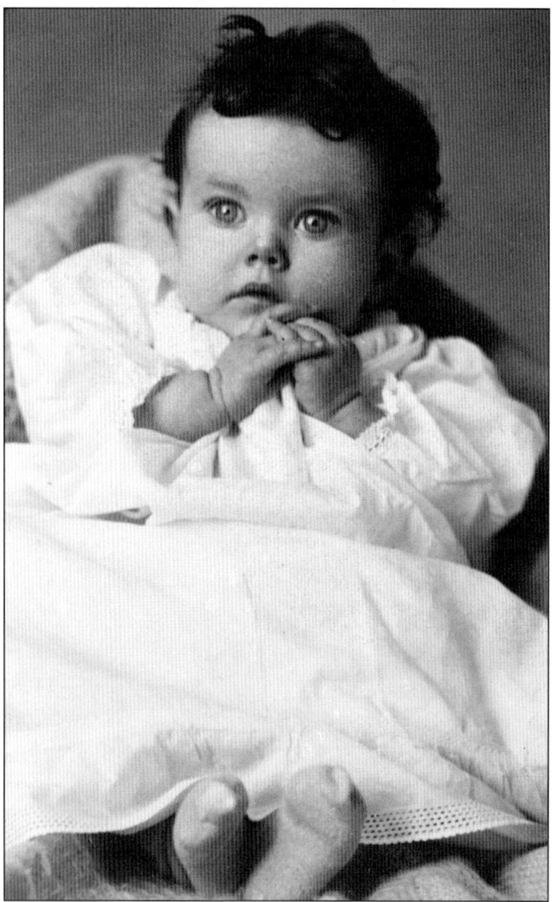

ORIGINAL ANDERSON STUDIO. This is the original G.E. Anderson photo studio at 310 South Main. The raised platform in the center was used to assist people getting out of horse-drawn wagons. This was in the same location as the building that replaced it, shown on the previous pages. (Courtesy of M. Lee Taylor.)

ANNA ELECTRA MCKENZIE. Anna Electra McKenzie was born on June 17, 1872, and lived only a few days. "Little Eva," as she was called, was the most beautiful child her father had ever seen. The family was heartbroken at her sudden passing. Her parents were blessed with 11 children. George McKenzie brought back to his wife, Elizabeth, the most beautiful linens, china, silver, and furniture that he could find as he traversed the countryside on freight trips. (Courtesy of the DUP.)

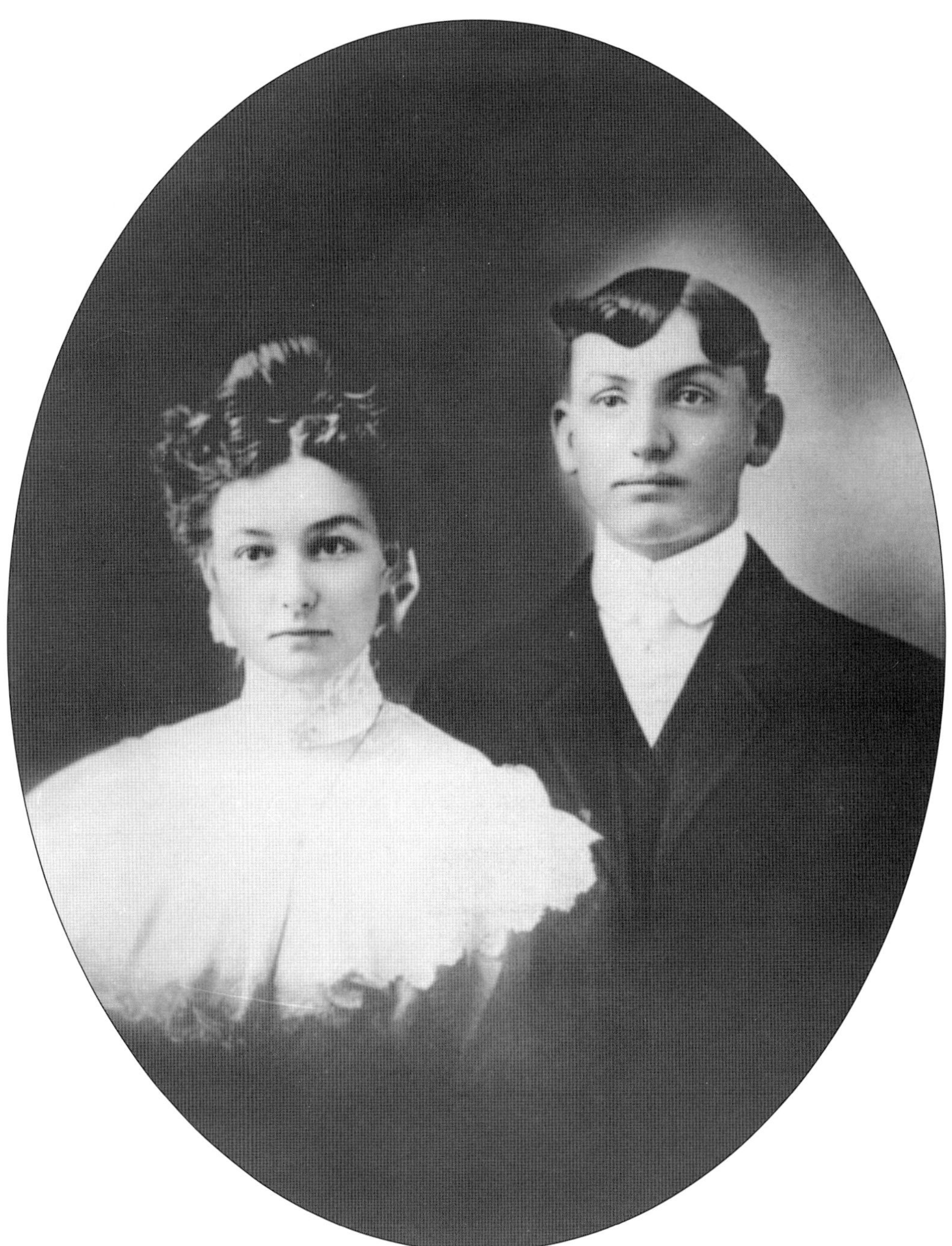

THORNS. Pictured are Maud Laurine Barnett Thorn and Adelbert "Bert" Glines Thorn. They were married on April 6, 1905, in Springville. Their son Norman "R" Thorn was a twin to Scott Lee Thorn, and they were born on August 5, 1918. R was a boxer and a pharmacist's mate third class in the US Navy. He was said to be a jack of all trades and a master of none. (Courtesy of the Springville Historical Society.)

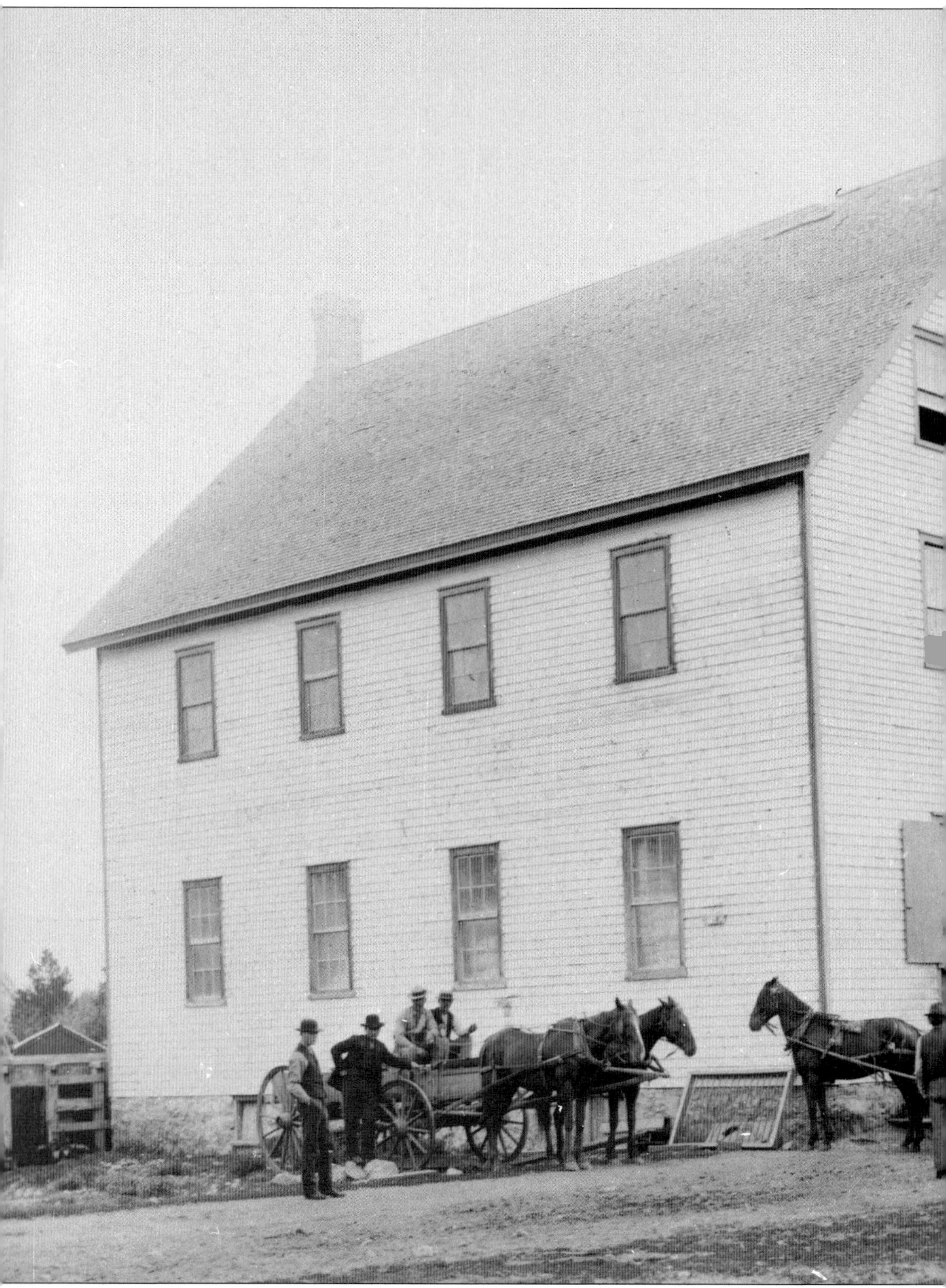

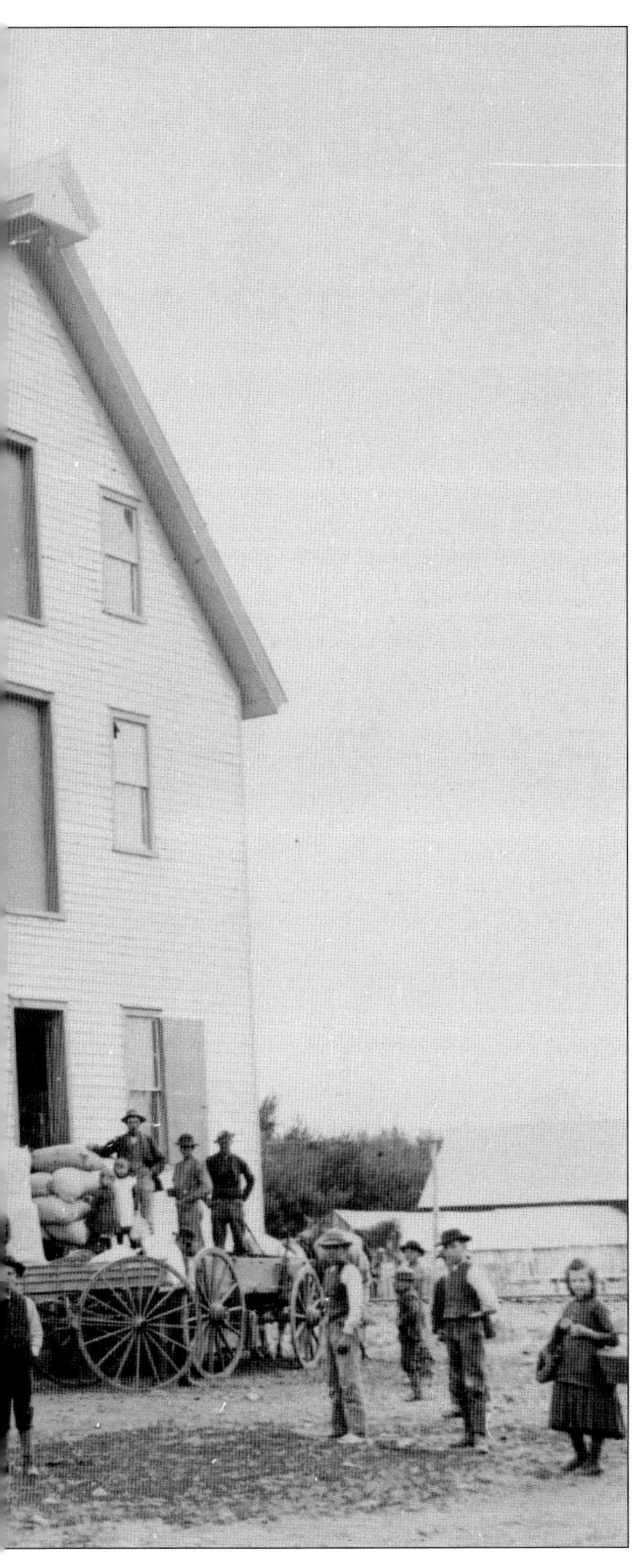

Flour Mill. In this early 1900s photograph by GEA, the Springville Co-Op Flour Mill is shown with residents gathering and loading their goods. This mill served the community for 65 years. It was east of Hobble Creek at 70 West 100 North (Johnson Street). At first the mill ran on waterpower diverted from the creek, then electricity was installed. It continued to operate until competition forced it to close in 1936. (Courtesy of M. Lee Taylor.)

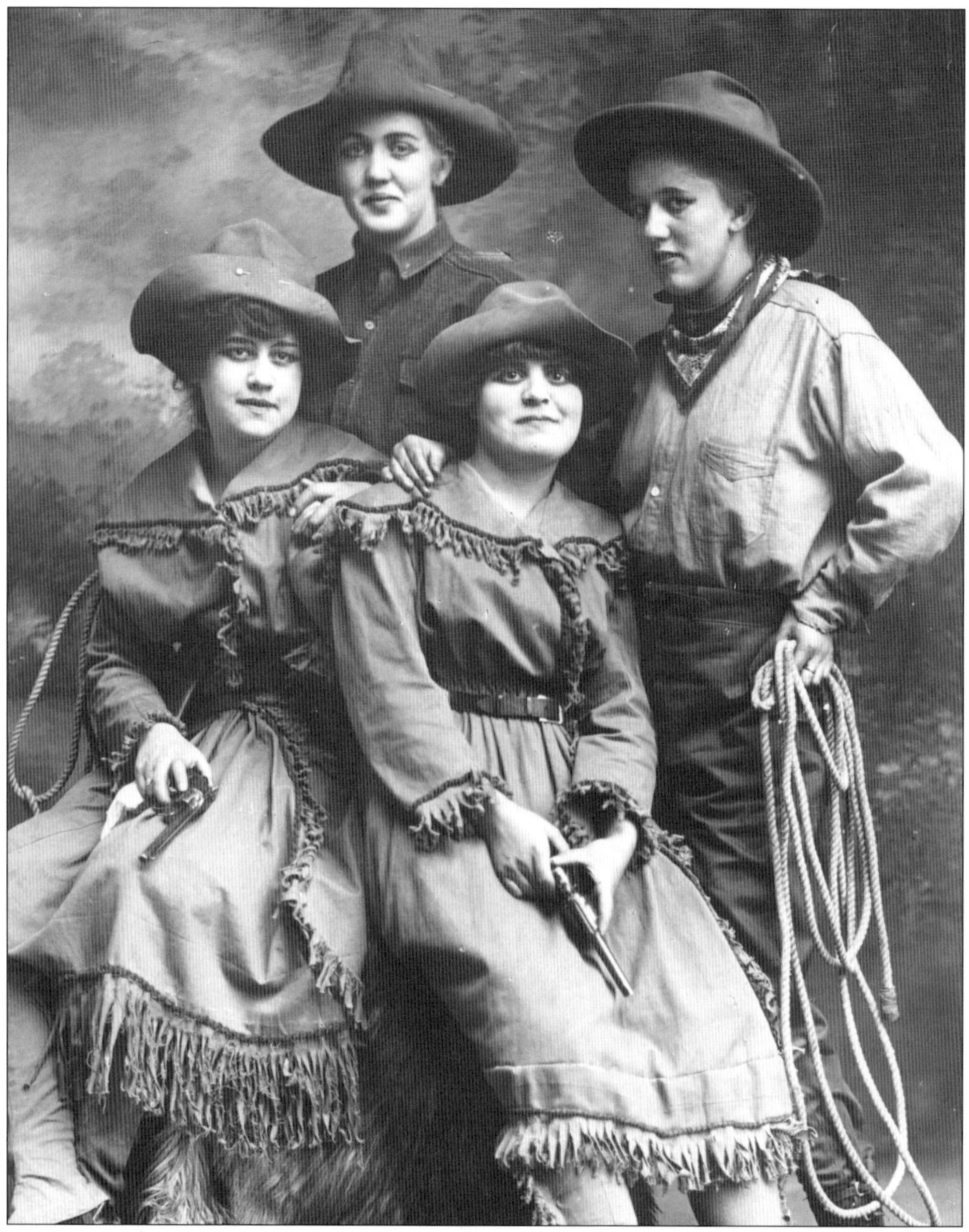

Cowgirls. This photograph shows the Cowgirls of Springville in 1917. During World War I, these gals entertained residents with songs and fun. In the center is Belle Anthon (Sumsion), and from left to right are Velma Blackett (Jarvis), Elsie Munn (Thyret), and Julia Alleman (Caine). (GEA photograph, courtesy of the Springville Historical Society.)

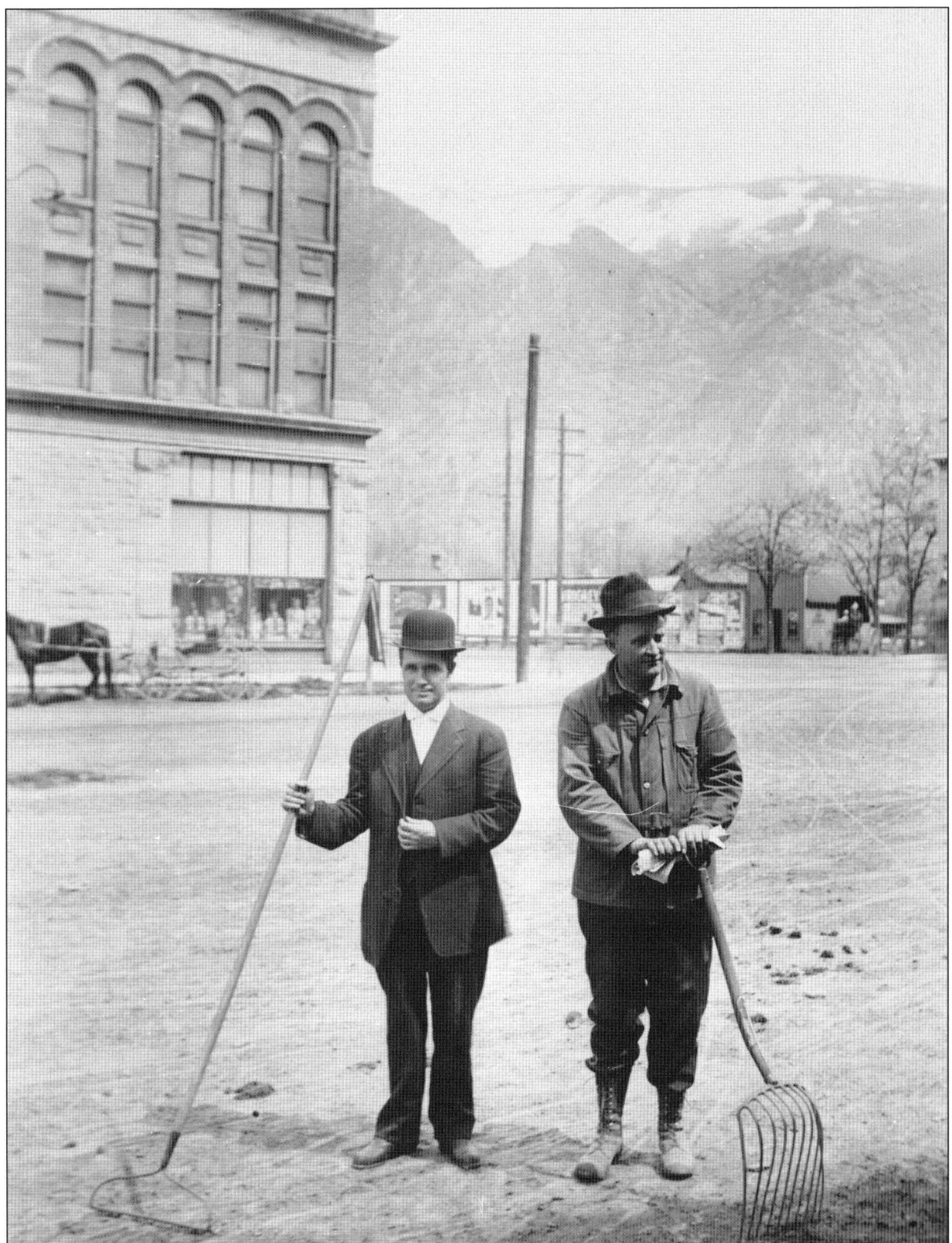

CLEAN-UP DAY. The annual clean-up day is still celebrated in the early springtime. This historic April 18, 1914, picture of the downtown area includes Mayor Harold Alleman (left) and Springville High School principal N.K. Nielson. Nielson was one of the founders of the Springville Museum of Art, which now houses one of the most valuable art collections in the United States. (GEA photograph, courtesy of the Springville Historical Society.)

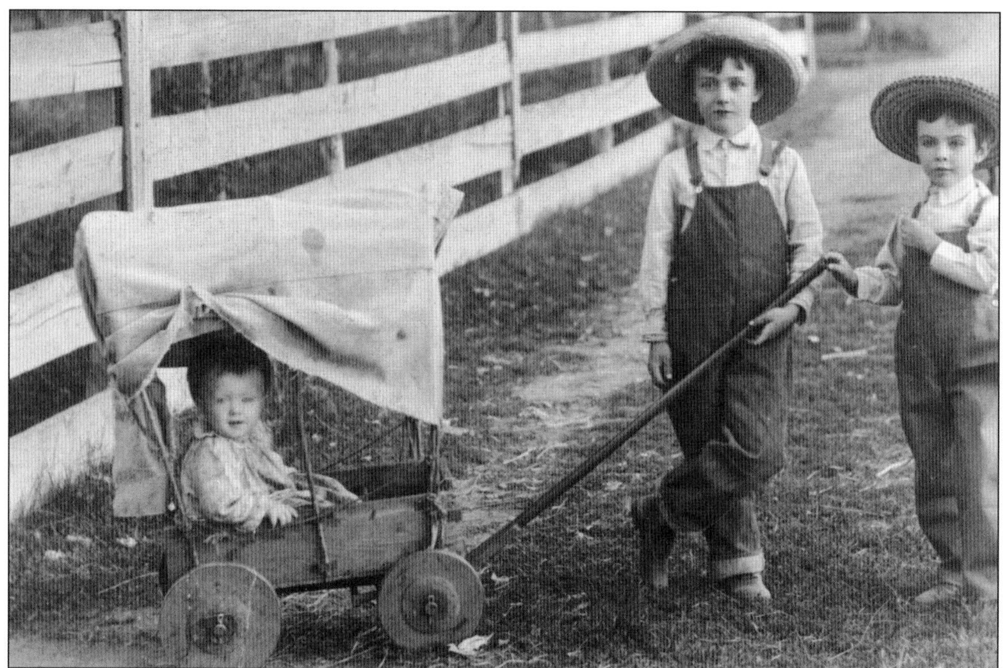

THREE BROTHERS. From left to right around 1905 are George (in the covered wagon), Glenn, and Elmo Coffman. George passed away at 16 years old in 1919. Glenn lived to be 92, and Elmo lived to be 90. Their father, William Daniel Coffman, was born in Springville on July 2, 1865. He married Mary Ann Bramall on May 28, 1886; they had seven children together, three boys and four girls. (Courtesy of the Springville Historical Society.)

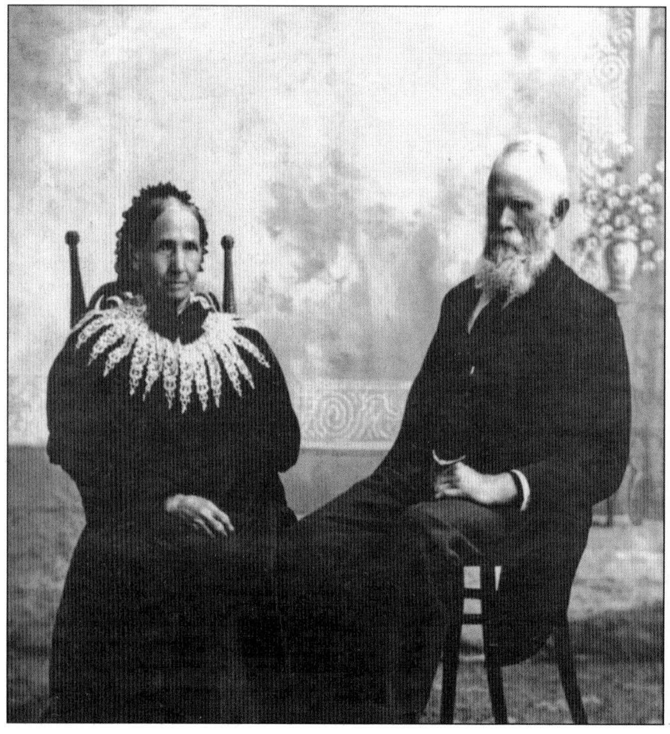

SISTER AND BROTHER. Zina Diantha Huntington Smith Young and Oliver Boardman Huntington are pictured here. Zina was the third general president of the Relief Society of the LDS Church. Oliver returned to Springville in 1852, having previously scouted the area. It was his horse that lost its hobble and ran off, giving the area the name Hobble Creek. He was a school teacher and a farmer. In 1892, he was chosen to serve as the president of the Utah Bee-Keepers Association. He is credited with teaching the first class with books in Utah, in 1847. (GEA photograph, courtesy of M. Lee Taylor.)

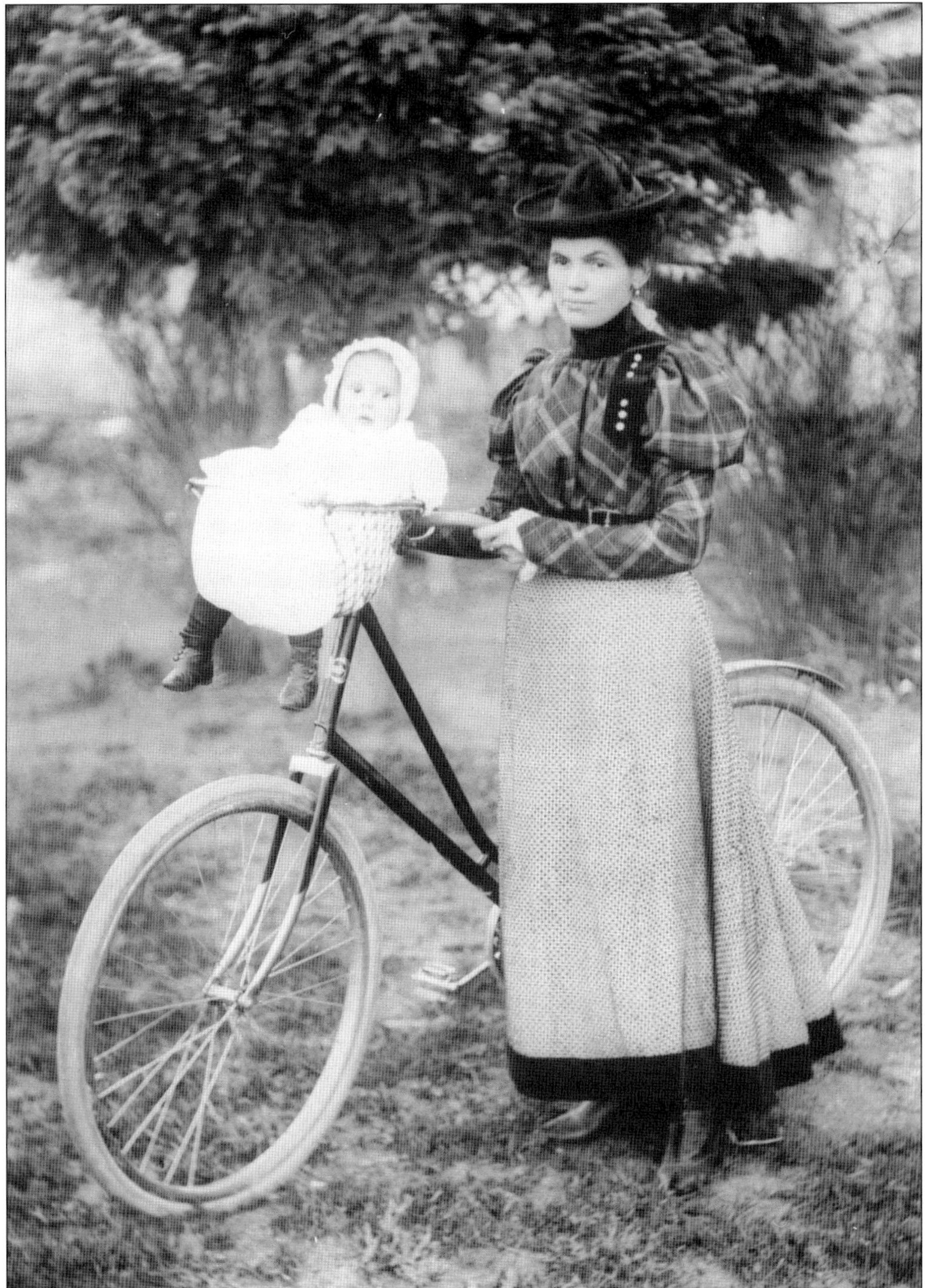

Baby in Bicycle Basket. In this c. 1895 photograph, Adeline Harris Spiers Felt is pictured with her bicycle and her baby Norma Louise in the basket. David Pile Felt, the husband and father, owned and edited the *Springville Independent* newspaper. In 1901, he was elected president of the Utah Press Association and served seven terms. (GEA photograph, courtesy of the Springville Historical Society.)

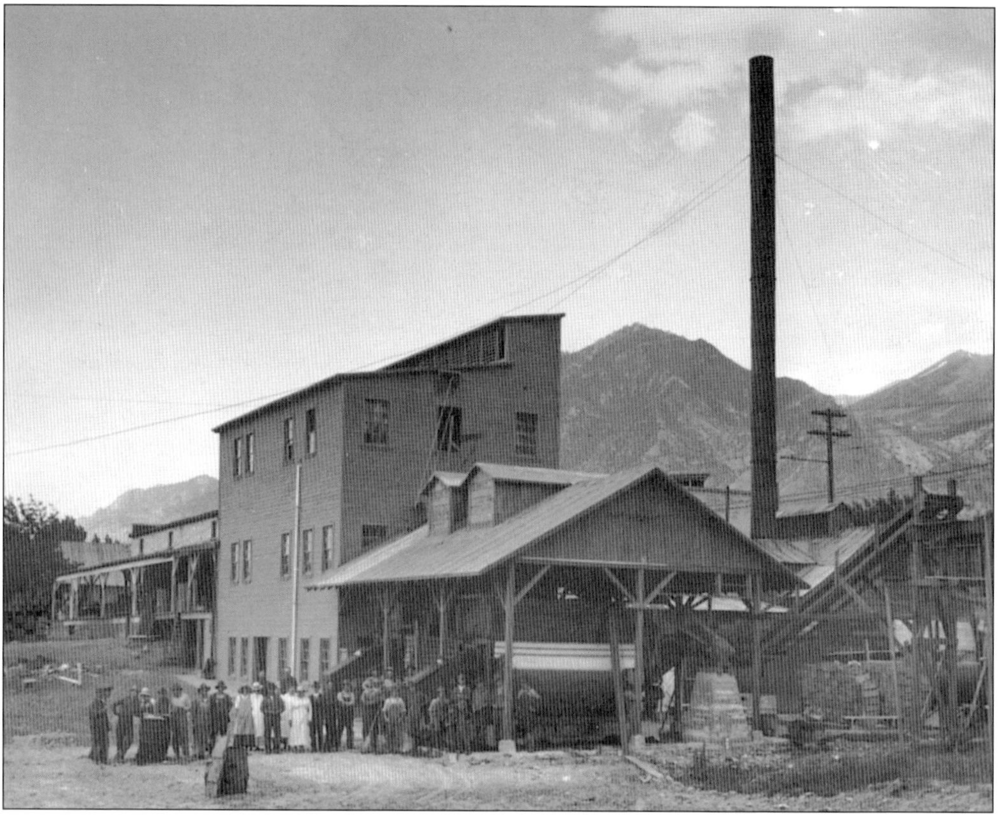

CANNERY & CANNING LABEL. The Springville Cannery is pictured above in 1919. A 1926 label is below. Mapleton and Springville both grew crops for this cannery. The Del Monte company also canned some area crops at a plant in nearby Spanish Fork. The demand for canned goods was high following the end of World War I. (Above, GEA photograph; both, courtesy of the Springville Historical Society.)

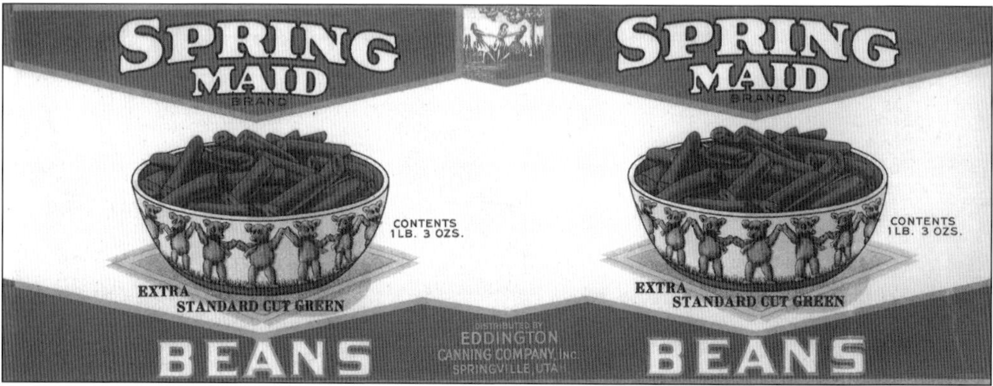

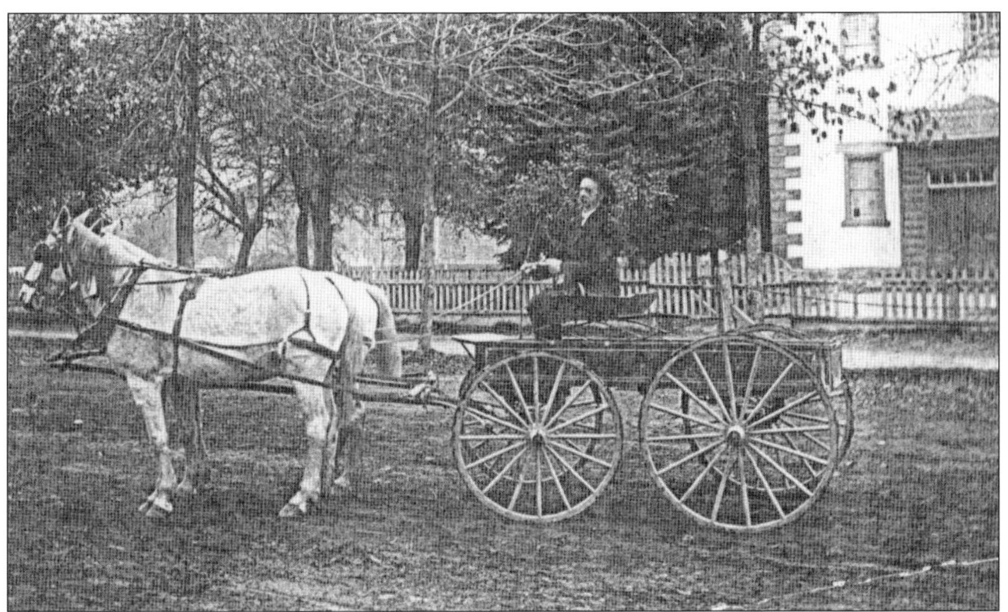

Walter Wheeler and Business. Above, Walter Wheeler is shown with his carriage and horses with the White Meeting House on the right in the background. Wheeler was proud of his teams and would take his family for rides in his wagon or sleigh. Wheeler Mortuary, founded in 1888 by Walter Wheeler, has been in business for more than 118 years. Wheeler was the first embalmer licensed in the state. The mortuary added a facility in Mapleton in 2004. Pictured below with the business sign are Walter Wheeler (left) and Thomas Child with many headstones. This photograph was taken on July 5, 1888. Headstones were hand cut and hand carved and placed on display for the customers. (Below, GEA photograph; both, courtesy of the DUP.)

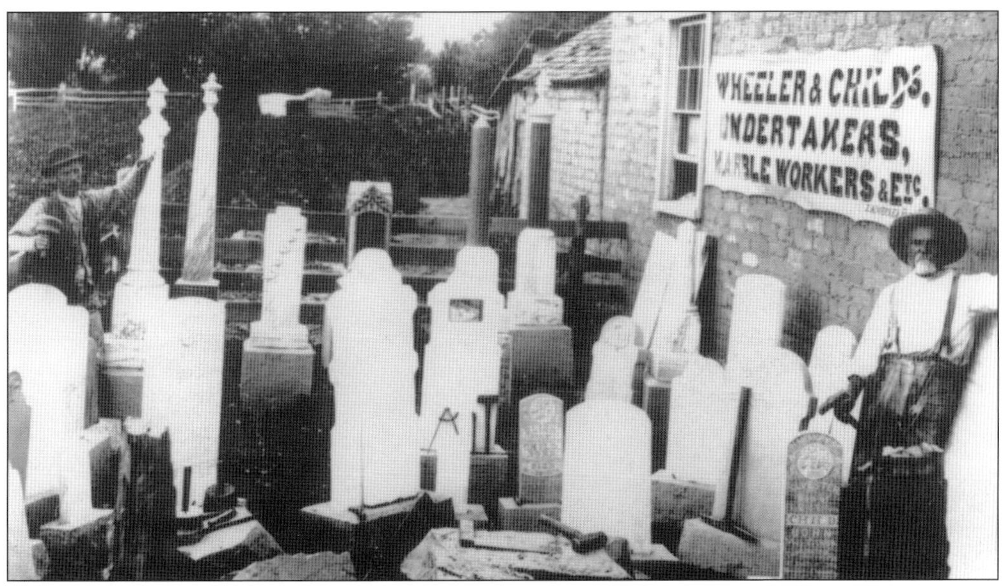

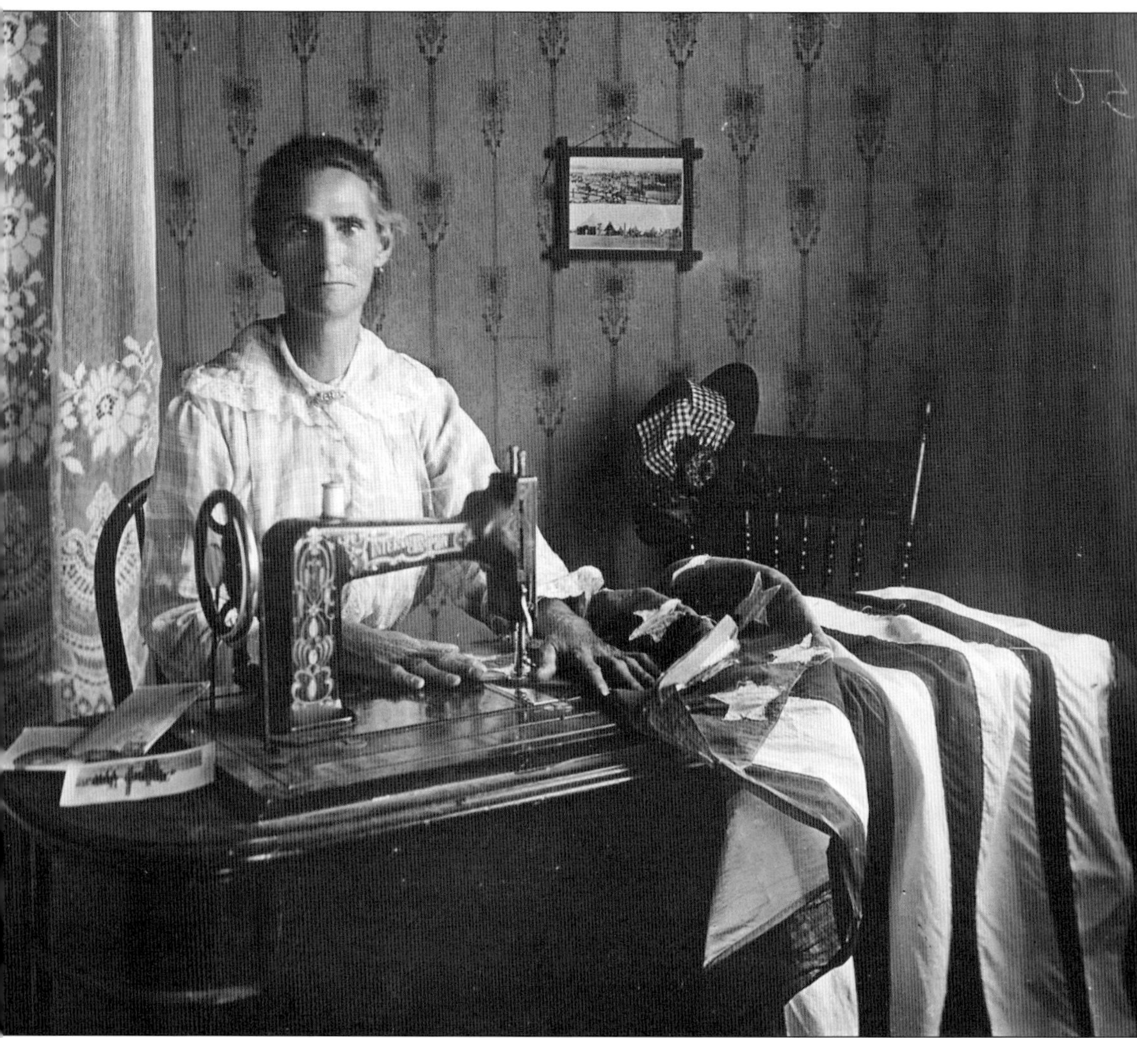

Seamstress and American Flag. Laura "Alice" Dean Horton Jasperson is shown in this c. 1918 photograph sewing an American flag to support her son Calvin, who was serving in the cavalry in Nogales, Arizona. One of her flags was sent to the governor of Utah and another one to the president of the United States. (GEA photograph, courtesy of the Springville Historical Society.)

Martha and George. Martha and George Washington are celebrated in a July 24 Pioneer Day parade photograph taken around 1896. Emma Dougall and John Crandall are dressed as the Washingtons. Anderson made this portrait in his tent gallery; absolute stillness was required to produce the best exposure. (Courtesy of the Springville Historical Society.)

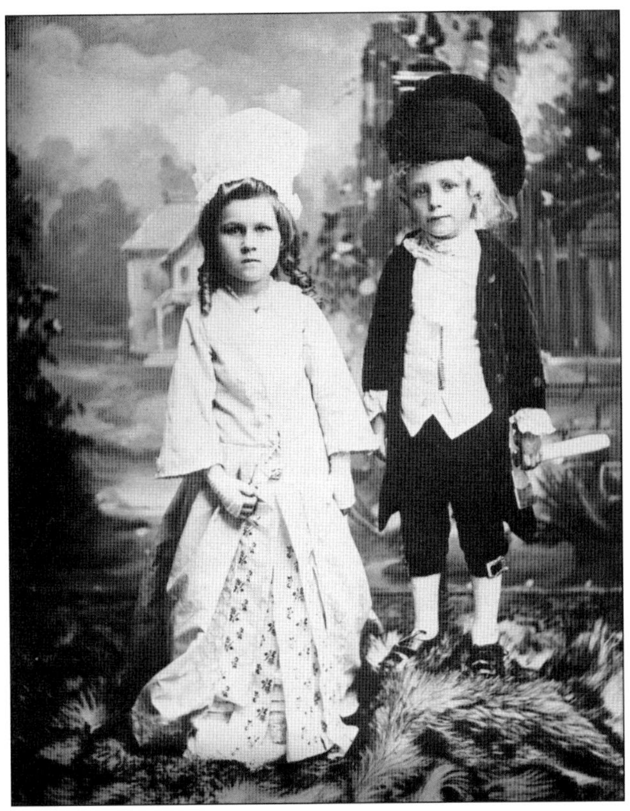

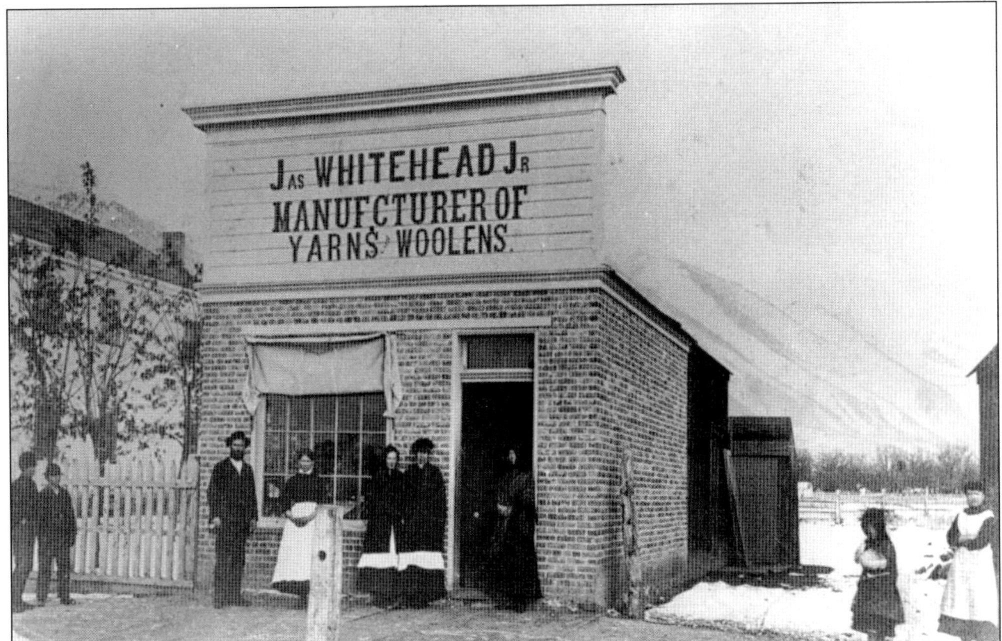

Business. This little building was later the home of the Child Monument Company. It was located at about 45 South Main, and was in business there until about 1964. (Courtesy of M. Lee Taylor.)

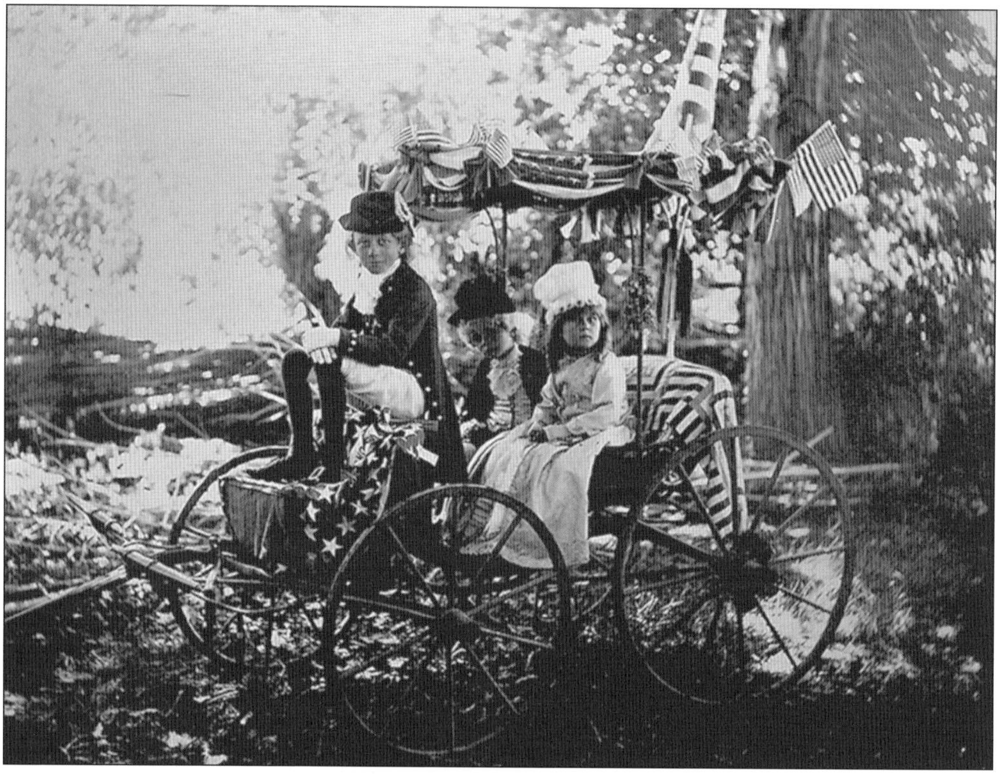

Martha and George in Buggy. In a ceremonial picture for the 1896 Pioneer Day celebration, the Washingtons are ready to be escorted in the parade. The driver is unidentified. (Courtesy of the Springville Historical Society.)

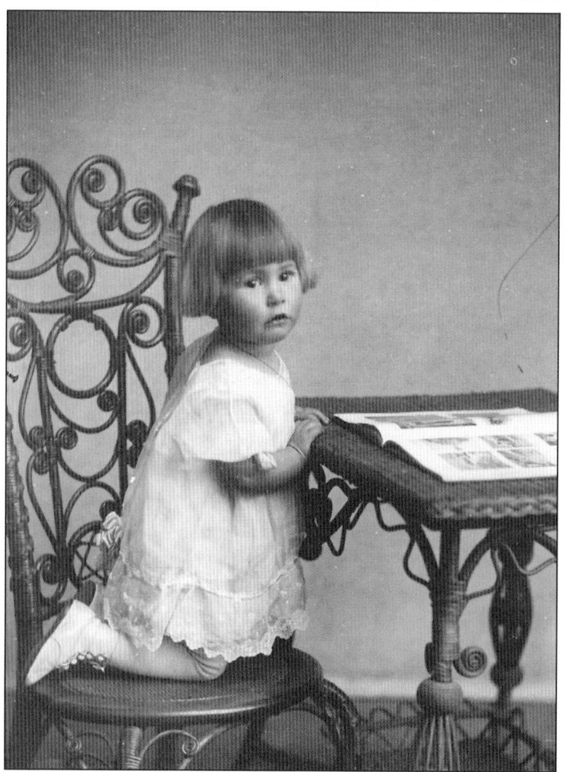

Tess. Young Tess Child poses with her book. She was born on January 1, 1914. Her father, Ivan, was on the committee that helped secure the funds for the Pioneer Mother Monument, sculpted by Cyrus E. Dallin and located in Springville City Park. Ivan Child and his brother Arvil inherited a shop in the downtown area. They ran the store until Arvil's daughter and son-in-law took ownership of it. Her mother, Violet Moore Child, was a young Maori girl brought to Springville/Mapleton at age six by missionary Parley Afton Waters in 1896. (GEA photograph, courtesy of the Springville Historical Society.)

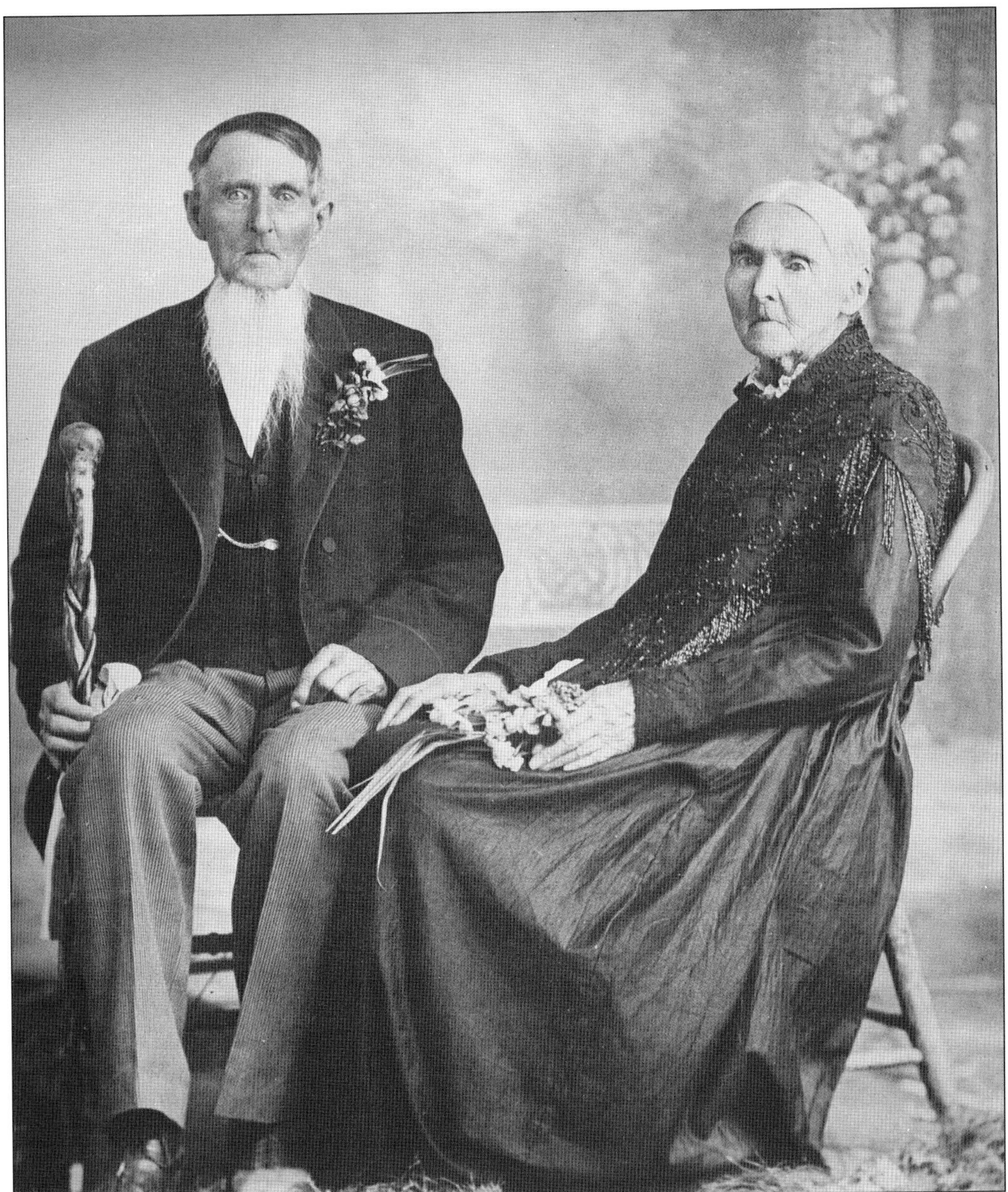

Dibbles. Philo Dibble, a Danite lieutenant colonel, and his wife, Hannah Ann Dubois Dibble, are pictured around 1890. "Father Dibble," as he was called, arrived in Springville in 1858 with his family. He held art exhibitions in his home, the first art shows to be held in Springville. His vision of an art gallery in town finally came to fruition years after his death; the Springville Museum of Art was completed in 1937. The museum has quite the reputation and is one of the reasons Springville was listed in 2015 as one of the best places to live in the state of Utah. (GEA photograph, courtesy of the Springville Historical Society.)

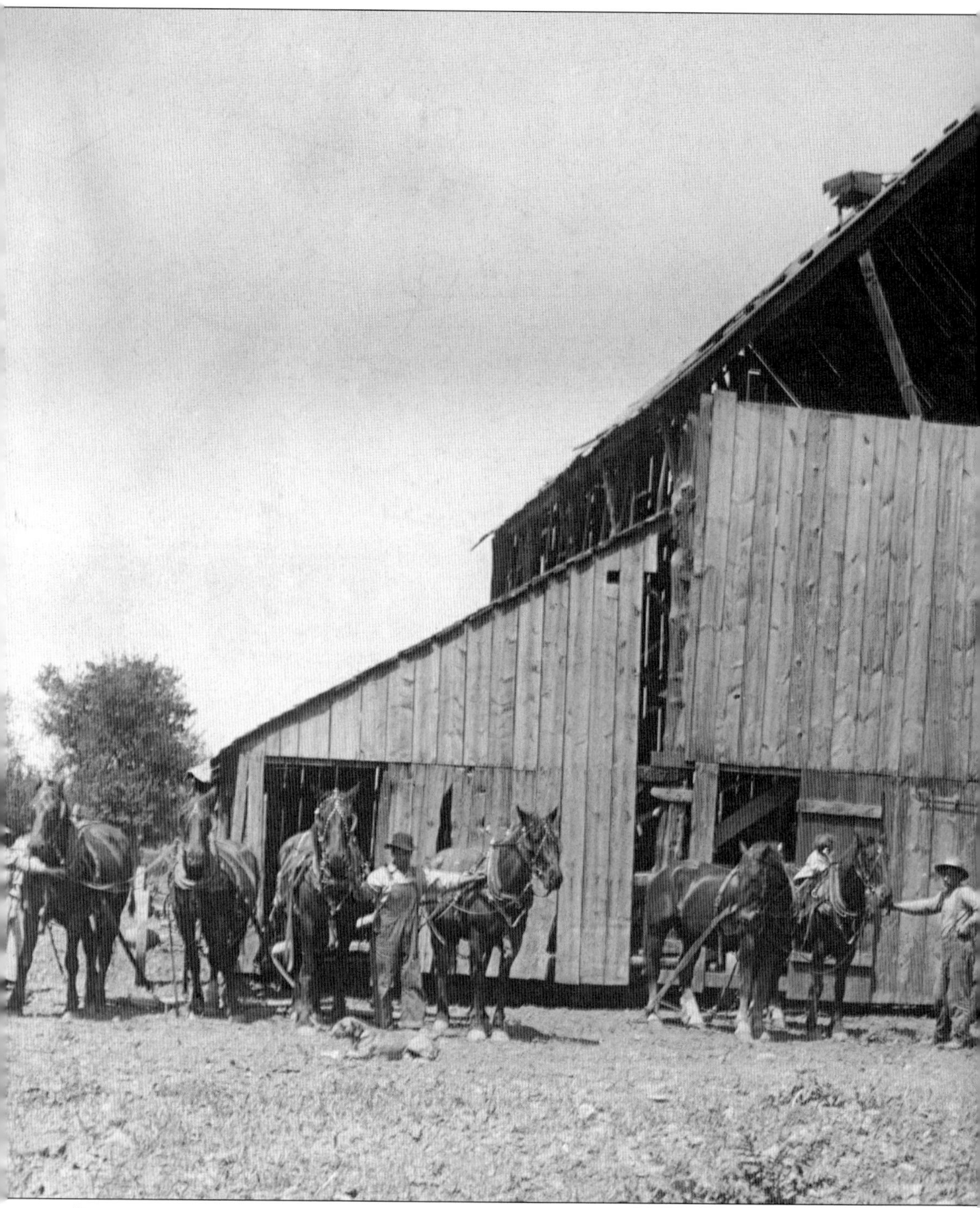

"Tobe" Averett Barn Moving. In this Huntington Bagley photograph taken at 700 East Center Street are, from left to right, (at left) Charles Averett, Frank Averett, and George Averett; (in front of the barn) Billy Peterson and Bill Childs (wearing high-top shoes); (at right) Jay Averett, Ruphas Averett, Jeduthun "Tobe" Averett, and John Averett. The barn belonged to Jeduthun "Tobe" Averett, the father. It was being turned to face east to get it off the property line because

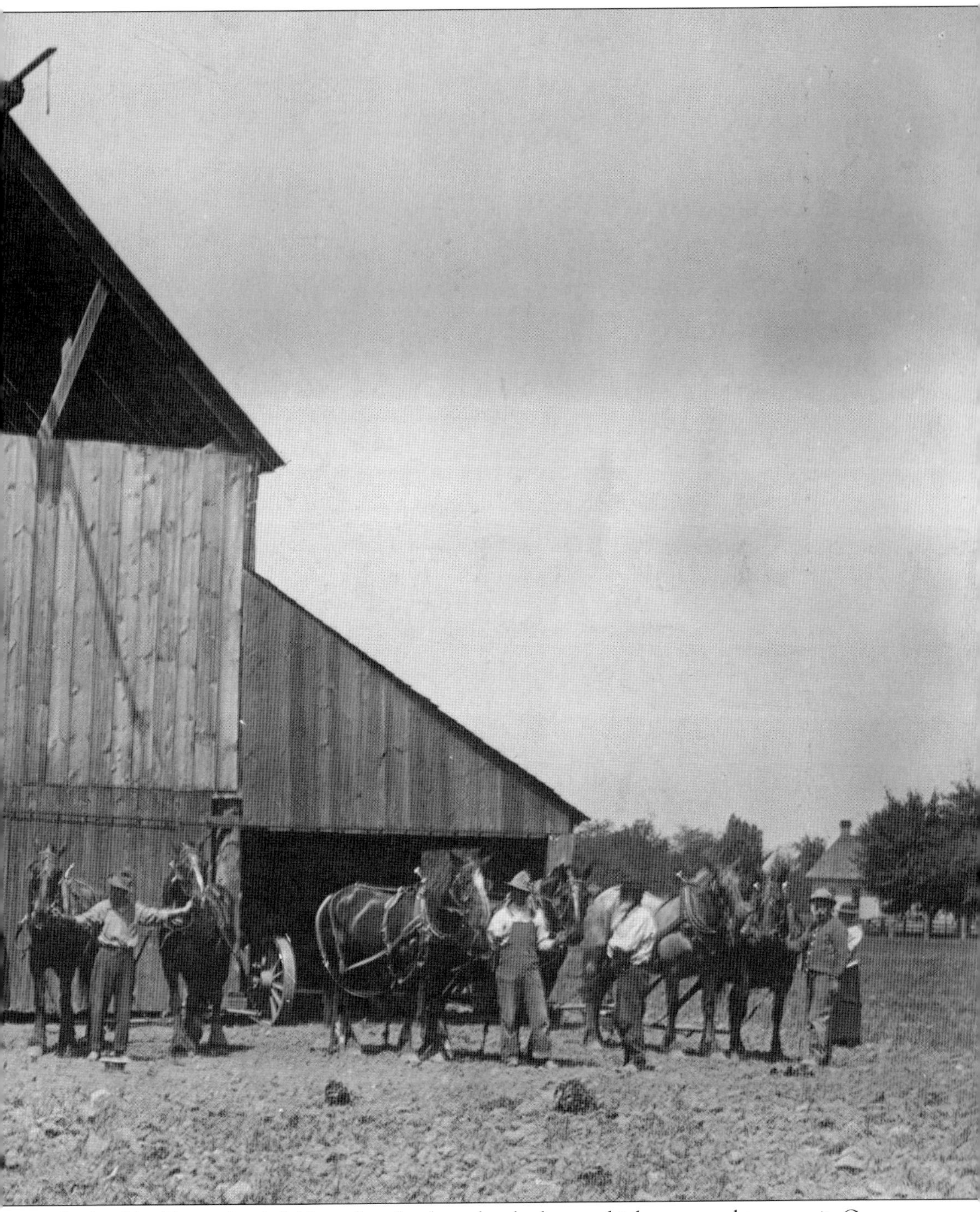

the land had been divided. Note the wheels under the barn, which were used to move it. George Averett was known as a house mover. The horses in the picture were Belgian. The first Belgian stallions were brought into Springville around 1900, and were used to breed bigger horses in the area. Jeduthun "Tobe" Averett was born 1842 in Alabama and died 1913 in Springville. (Courtesy of the Springville Historical Society.)

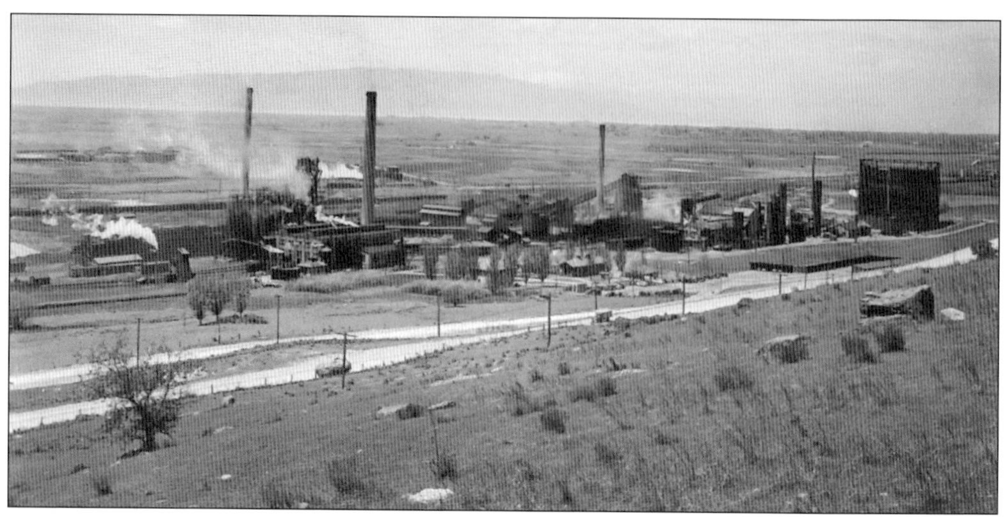

Steel Mill. The Ironton Steel Mill, pictured above around 1922 and below in an aerial view looking south, was on Ironton Hill at the north end of Main Street. A blast furnace at the site manufactured pig iron. It employed quite a few men until the late 1950s. The Ironton Works, as it was known, was one of the largest pig iron plants in the West. Springville gained the nickname "The Steel City" during this time. (Both, courtesy of M. Lee Taylor.)

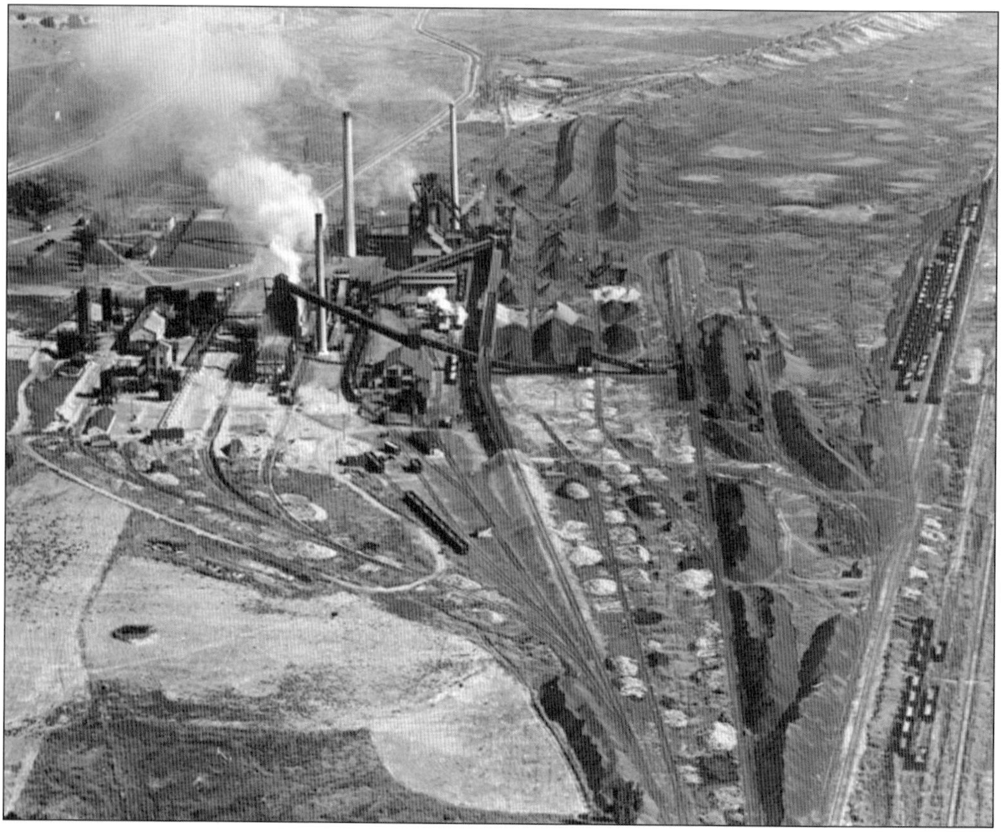

BEATRICE. Beatrice Hatfield (Glazier) is pictured at Christmastime in 1912. The photographers were Olsen & Griffith of Salt Lake City. Beatrice was a lifelong Springville resident. Her father, William Hatfield, was in the mining business and is known as the first man to strike ore in the Bullion-Beck mine. He also helped discover the Swansea mine. Throughout his life, he mined in Utah, Idaho, and Nevada. (Courtesy of the Springville Historical Society.)

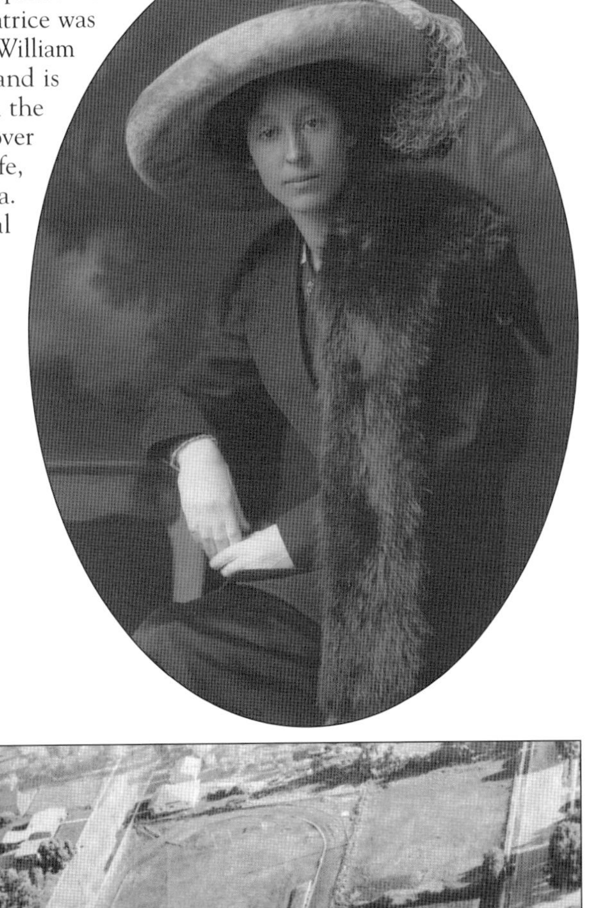

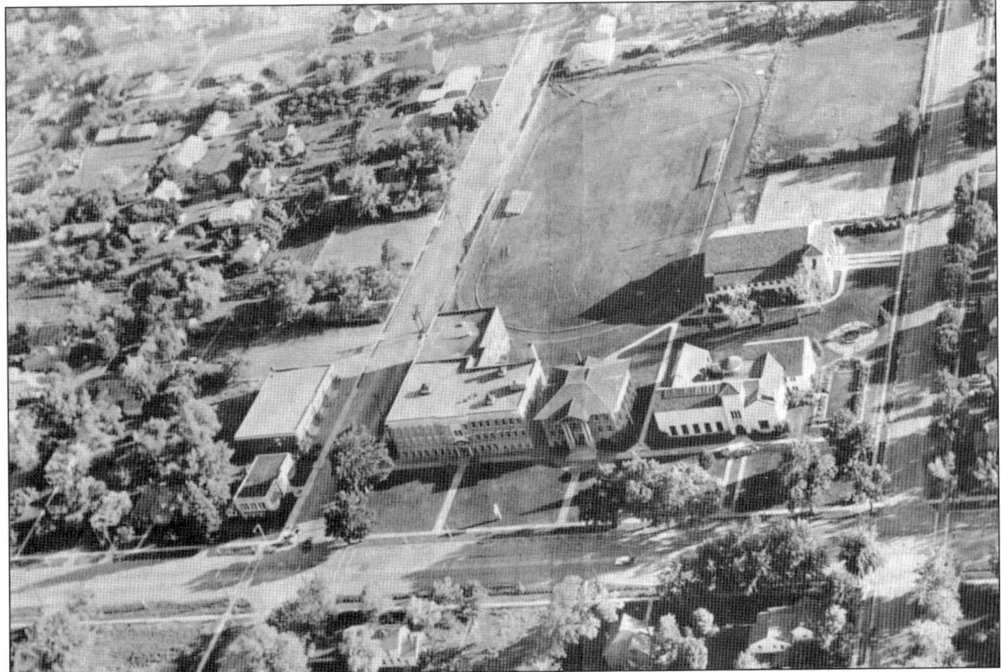

HIGH SCHOOL. Here is an aerial photograph of the complete high school campus in 1962. Note the original Springville Art Museum building at lower right. (Courtesy of M. Lee Taylor.)

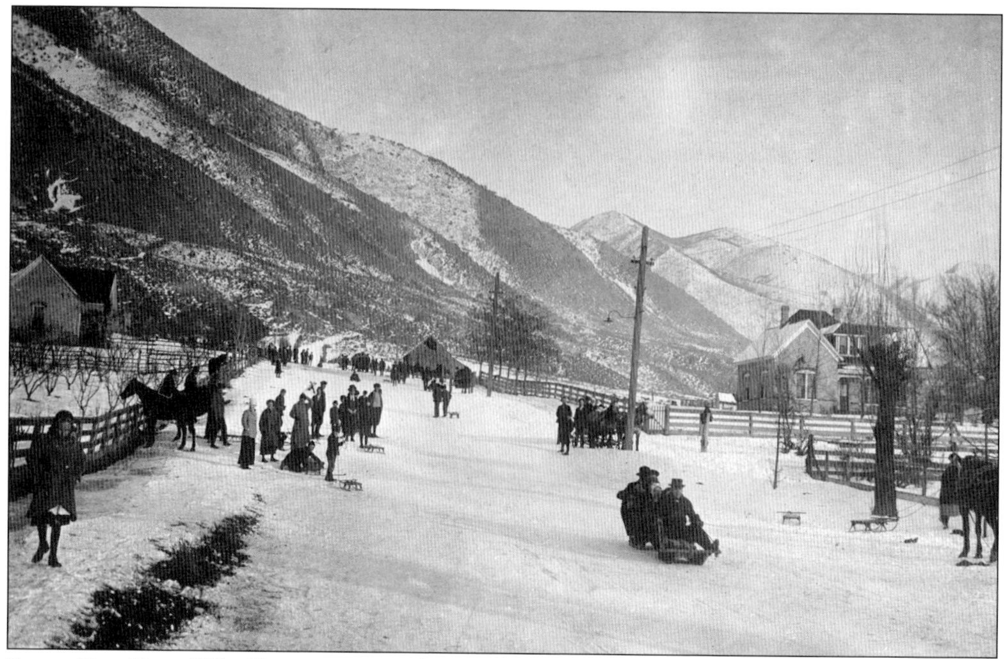

Snow Day Fun. Elfie Huntington took this picture of sleigh riding on Weight Hill (Center Street) around 1915. In the front sleigh are, from back to front, Victor Frandsen, Mr. Boyer, and Clifford Fullmer. In the back on the right waiting to sleigh are Miss Packard, Clara Jensen, Marie Cranmer, Cornel "Pete" Mendenhall, Vesta Anderson, and Donald Holley. (Courtesy of Lois Bartholomew.)

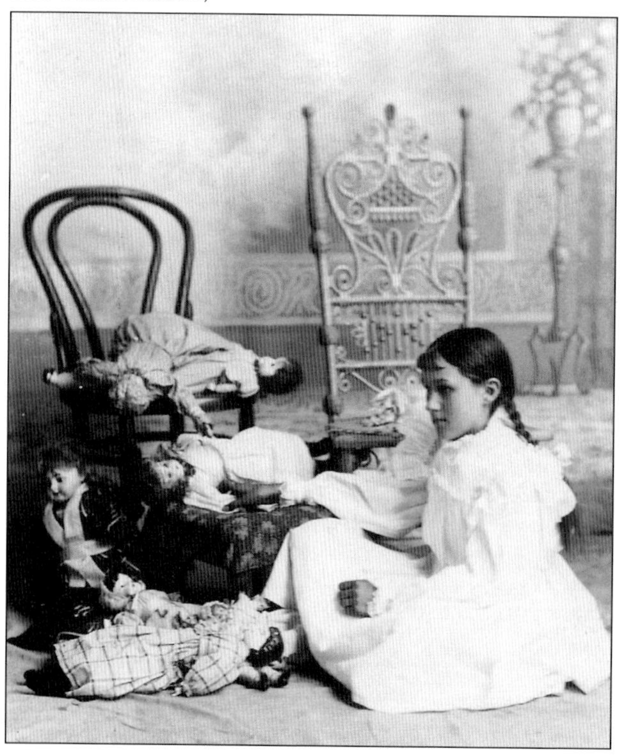

Emma and Her Dolls. Mary "Emma" Dougall (Gardner) is pictured with her dolls. She was born on November 13, 1883. Her father, Hugh, was the postmaster in Springville for 25 years and a contractor on the Union Pacific Railroad. Her mother, Mary, was instrumental in bringing the silkworm industry to the town until it failed due to Utah's climate. (GEA photograph, courtesy of the Springville Historical Society.)

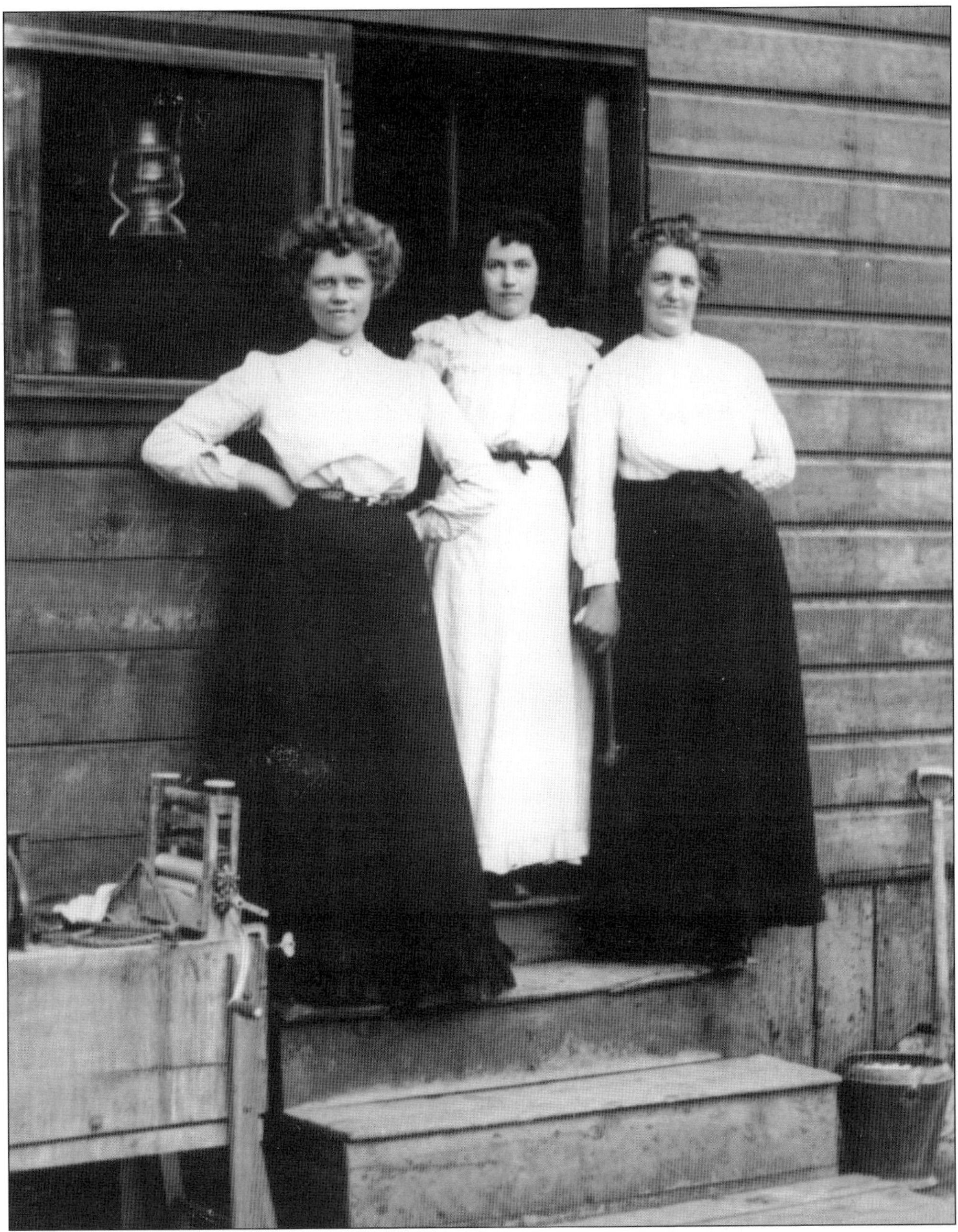

Women in Doorway. Pictured from left to right around 1914 are Springville women Sarah Anderson, Nell Starr, and Ida Alleman Taylor, who was a school teacher. On the left is a Great Western washing machine. This early hand-powered washing machine looks different from modern machines; notice also the old lantern in the left window. (GEA photograph, courtesy of the Springville Historical Society.)

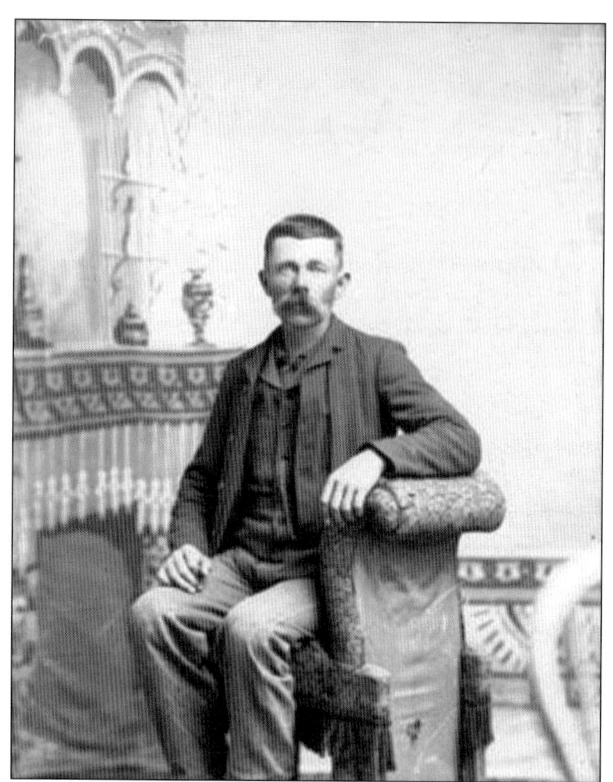

Moses Clawson. Pictured is the author's husband's great-great-great-grandfather Moses Clawson. He lived in Springville for a while, and three of his children were born here. Clawson presided over the LDS immigrant ship *Ellen Maria*, which left England for America. There were 299 LDS saints aboard it; he then served as captain over a company of 56 wagons that crossed the plains to Salt Lake City, arriving in September 1853. He died in Toquerville on June 14, 1879. (GEA photograph, courtesy of the Springville Historical Society.)

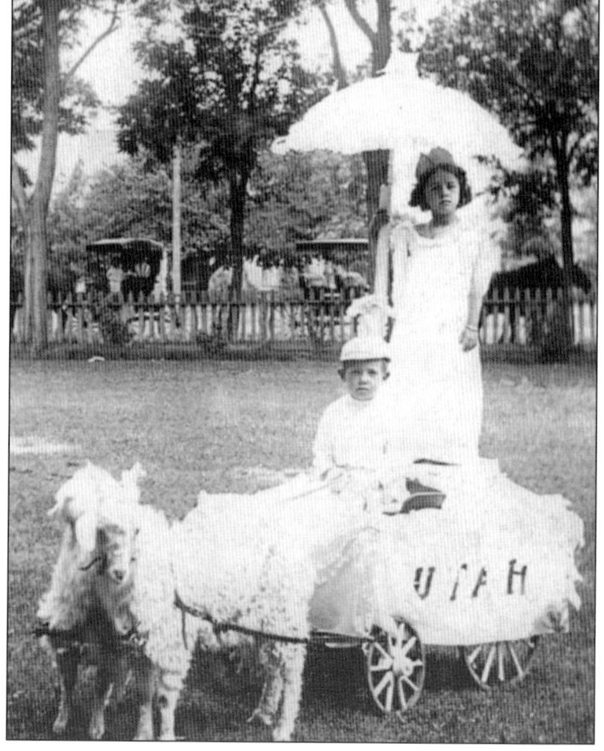

Goats on Parade. Pictured are Corine Robinson (Booth) as the queen and Edward Boyer as the driver, along with two goats, in this entry in the Children's Parade on July 24, 1916, a Pioneer Day celebration held throughout the state of Utah each year. Even today, various cities have their own parades and all-day activities. Edward Boyer was a founding member of the Springville Historical Society in 1983, and its first president. (Courtesy of the Springville Historical Society.)

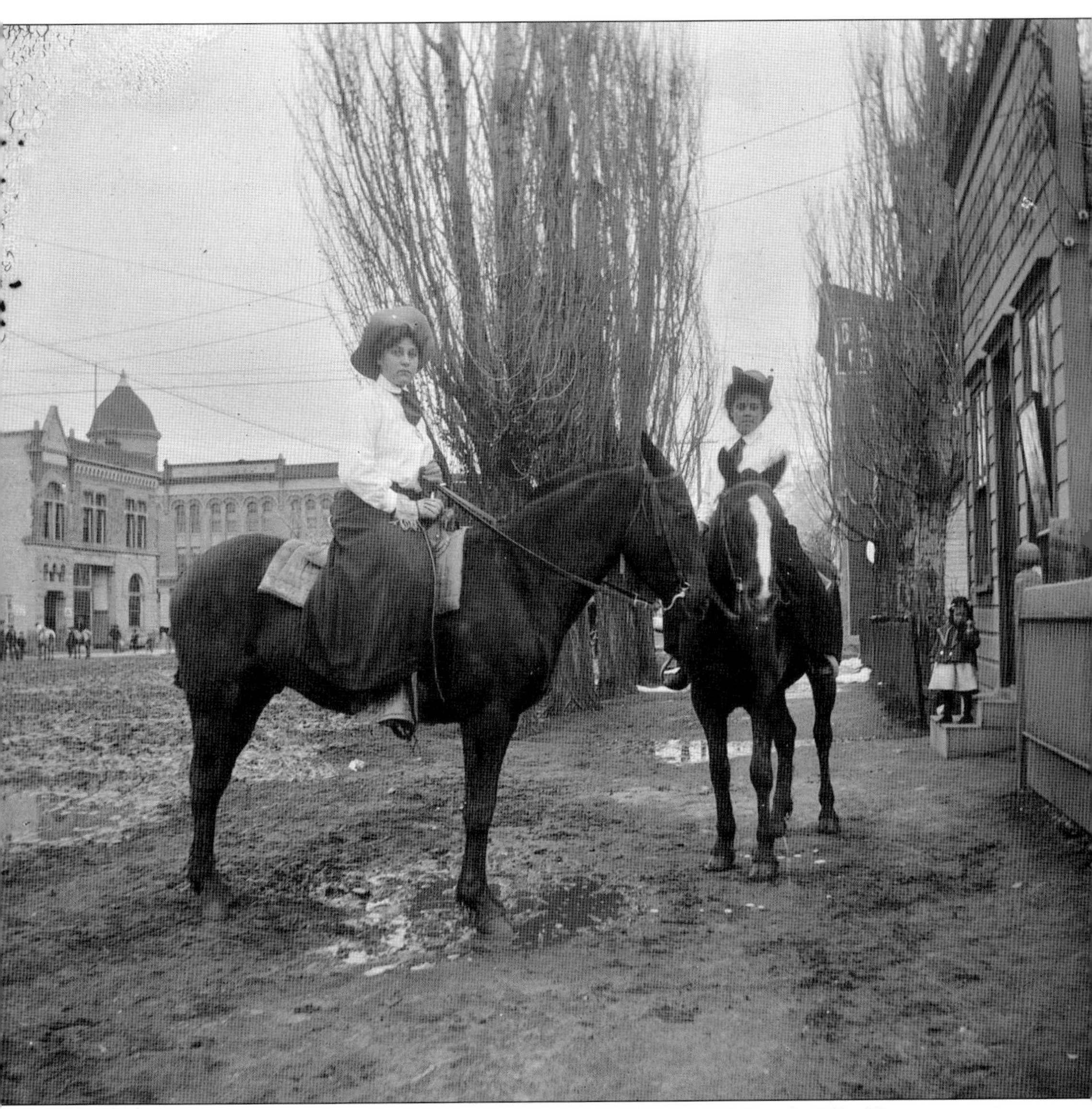

Early Main Street. Main Street is pictured looking north near 300 South. Elfie Huntington is on the left on the horse. In the left background is the Springville Bank and the top of the H.T. Reynolds building. Notice the absence of sidewalks and how wet and muddy everything is. Elfie Huntington was an early photographer in the area and co-owned the Huntington Bagley studio. (Courtesy of the Springville Historical Society.)

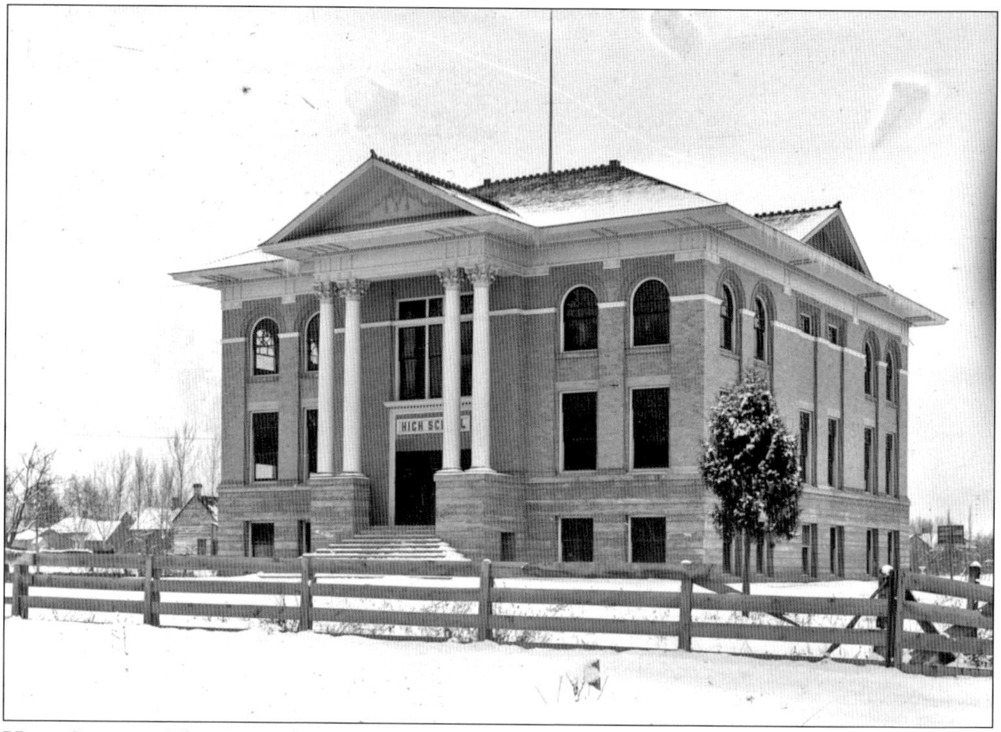

HIGH SCHOOL. The original Springville High School building is pictured above shortly after its completion around 1909 and below in 1913. (Both, GEA photographs, courtesy of M. Lee Taylor.)

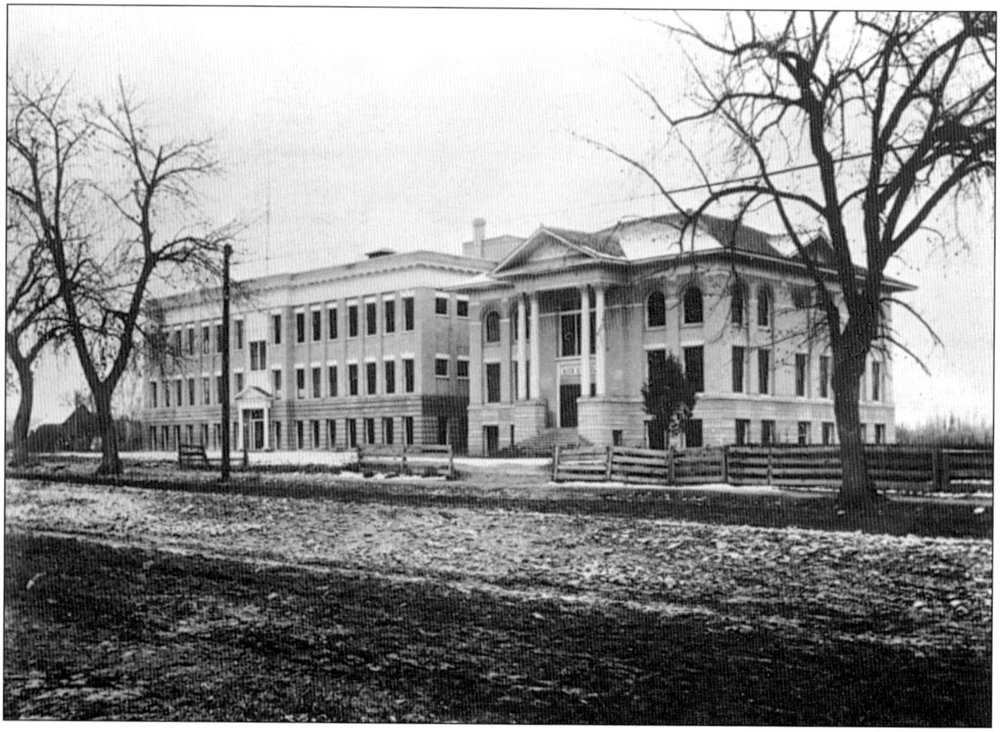

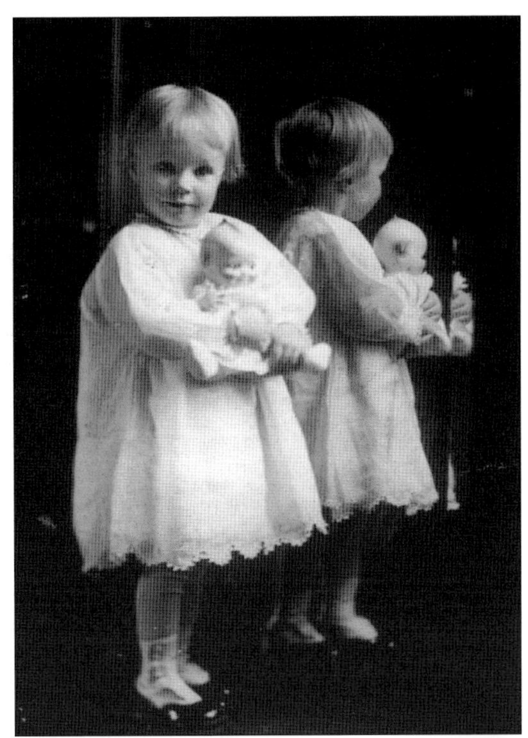

Child and Doll. Josephine Bagley was photographed by her father, Joseph. She was born on December 10, 1913, and died on September 20, 1917. She is buried in the historic Springville City Cemetery. Joseph Bagley was an early photographer in the area. After the death of the mother of his first wife, Josephine, he and his partner and future wife, Elfie, co-owned the Huntington Bagley photography studio. (Courtesy of the DUP.)

Donkey Rider. Posed in front of the Springville bank is famous American author Robertson Pitcher Woodward. He rode this donkey from New York to San Francisco in 1896–1897 to settle a bet. He was to start traveling without a dollar in his pocket, and he had to make the journey in a year. Woodward had to wear the same Prince Albert coat the entire journey, and had to document his travels. (GEA photograph, courtesy of the Springville Historical Society.)

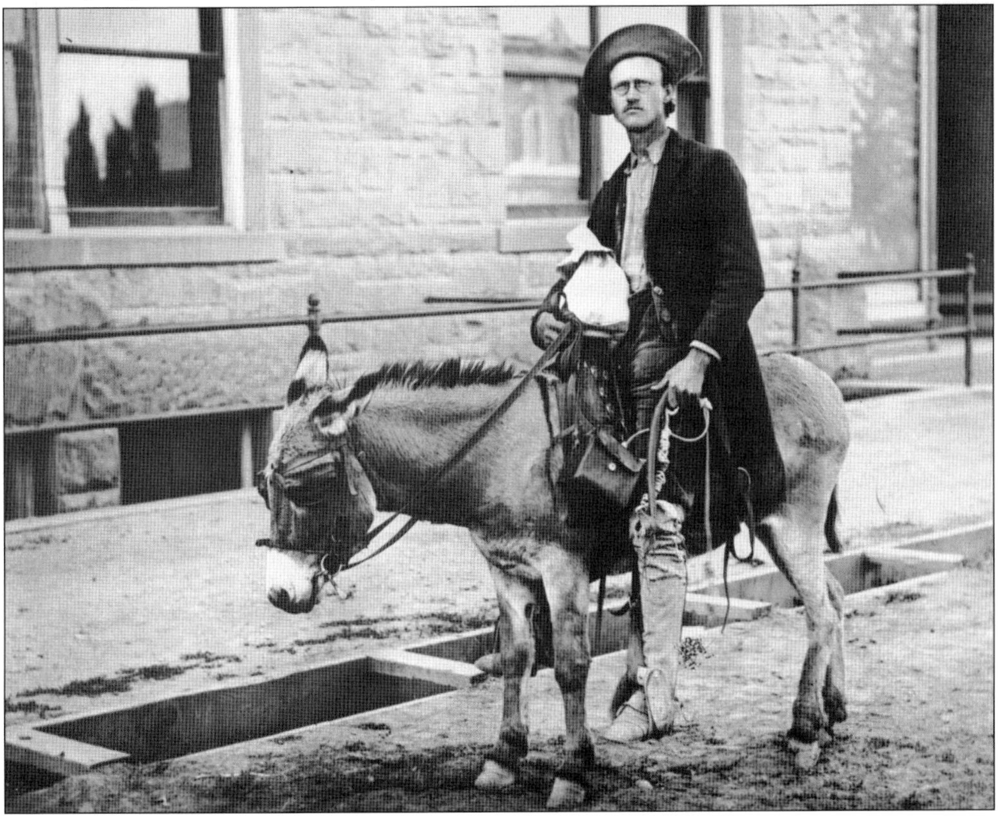

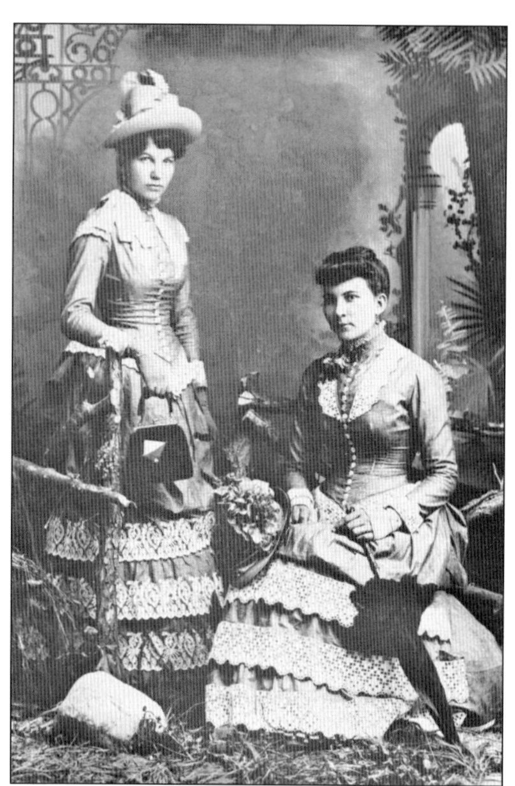

DRESSMAKERS. Pictured are two of the daughters of William Morgan Clyde, Elva Jane Clyde Houtz (left) and Mary Loretta Clyde Thorn. They were early dressmakers in Springville and are wearing their stunning sewing creations. Parents William and Eliza McDonald were married on January 24, 1851, in Mountainville, now Alpine, Utah. They were the first couple married there. Elva and Mary were two of 11 children. The family arrived in Springville in February 1851. (GEA photograph, courtesy of the Springville Historical Society.)

HAYMOND'S. Haymond's Cash Exchange, originally the home of the first H.T. Reynolds store, was at 164 South Main Street. The woman in front is owner Luella Wood Haymond. Her husband, Thomas, died on January 1, 1900, leaving her with six children to raise. She learned the mercantile business from her father, Gideon Durfey Wood. Haymond opened another store in 1904 that was also located downtown on Main Street. (Courtesy of the DUP.)

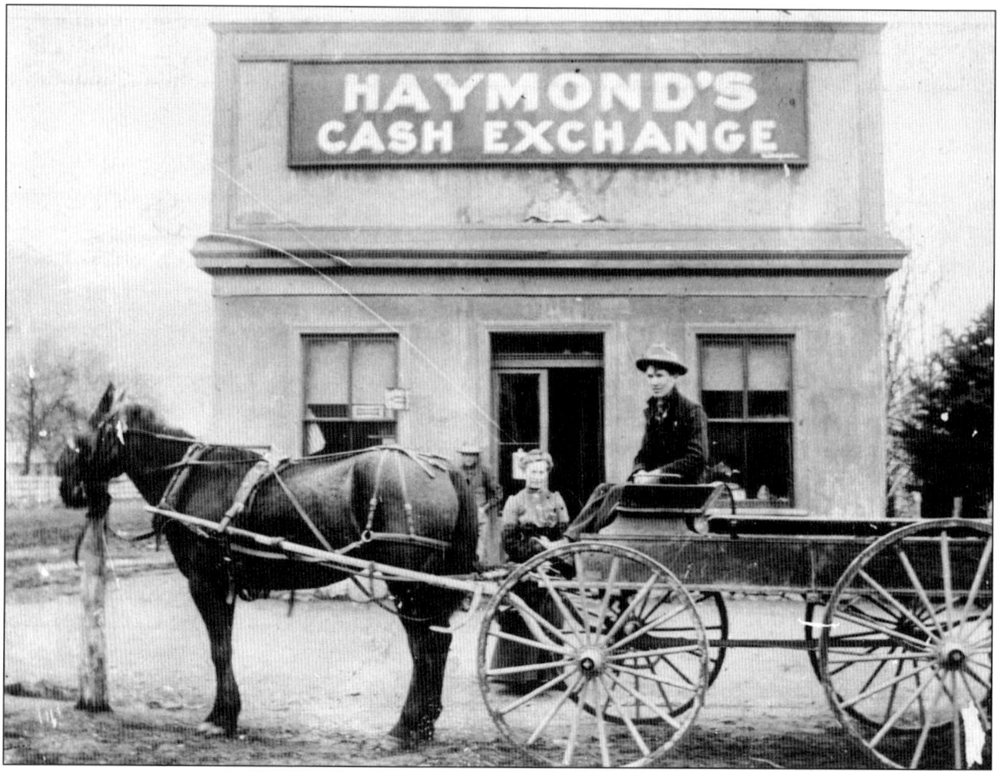

Brothers. A.W. Bursman took this photograph of Charles Frederick Marshall (left) and James Marshall with a toy horse. (Courtesy of the DUP.)

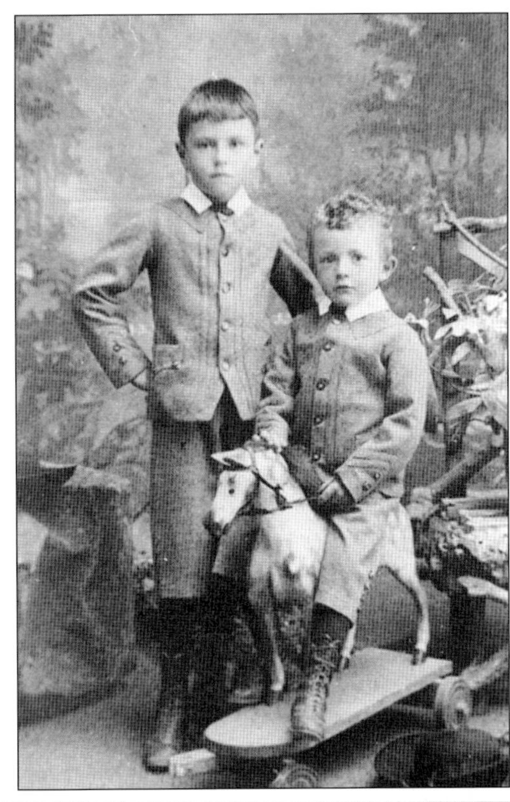

Cemetery. An unidentified mourner is pictured on her knees at the Springville City Cemetery. (GEA photograph, courtesy of the Springville Historical Society.)

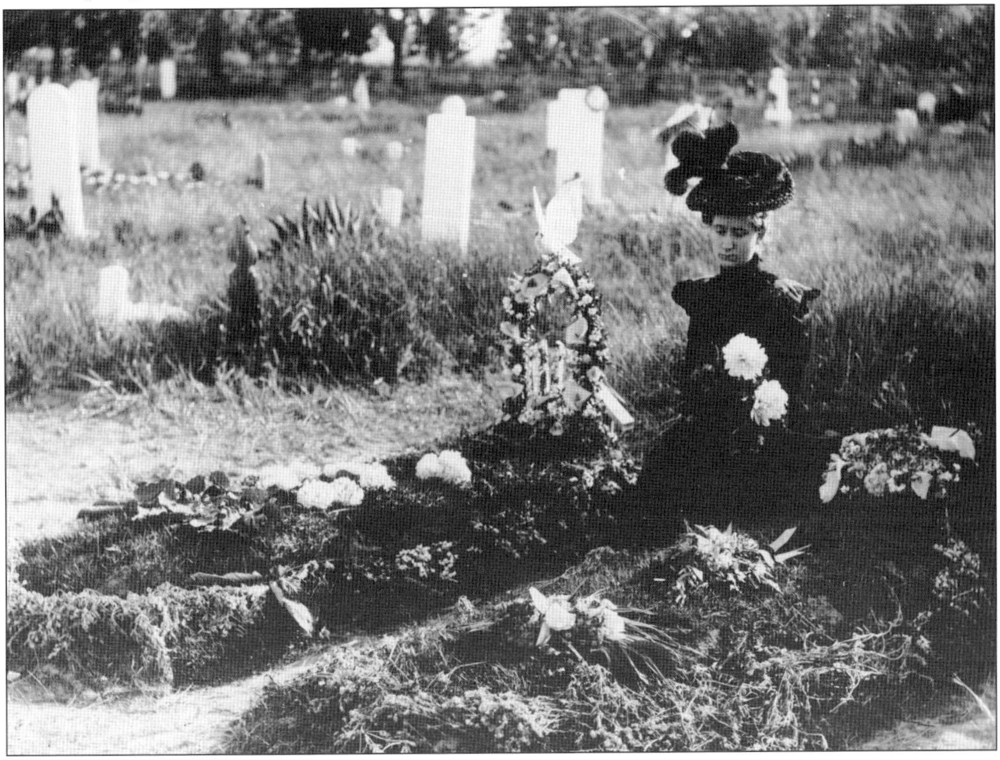

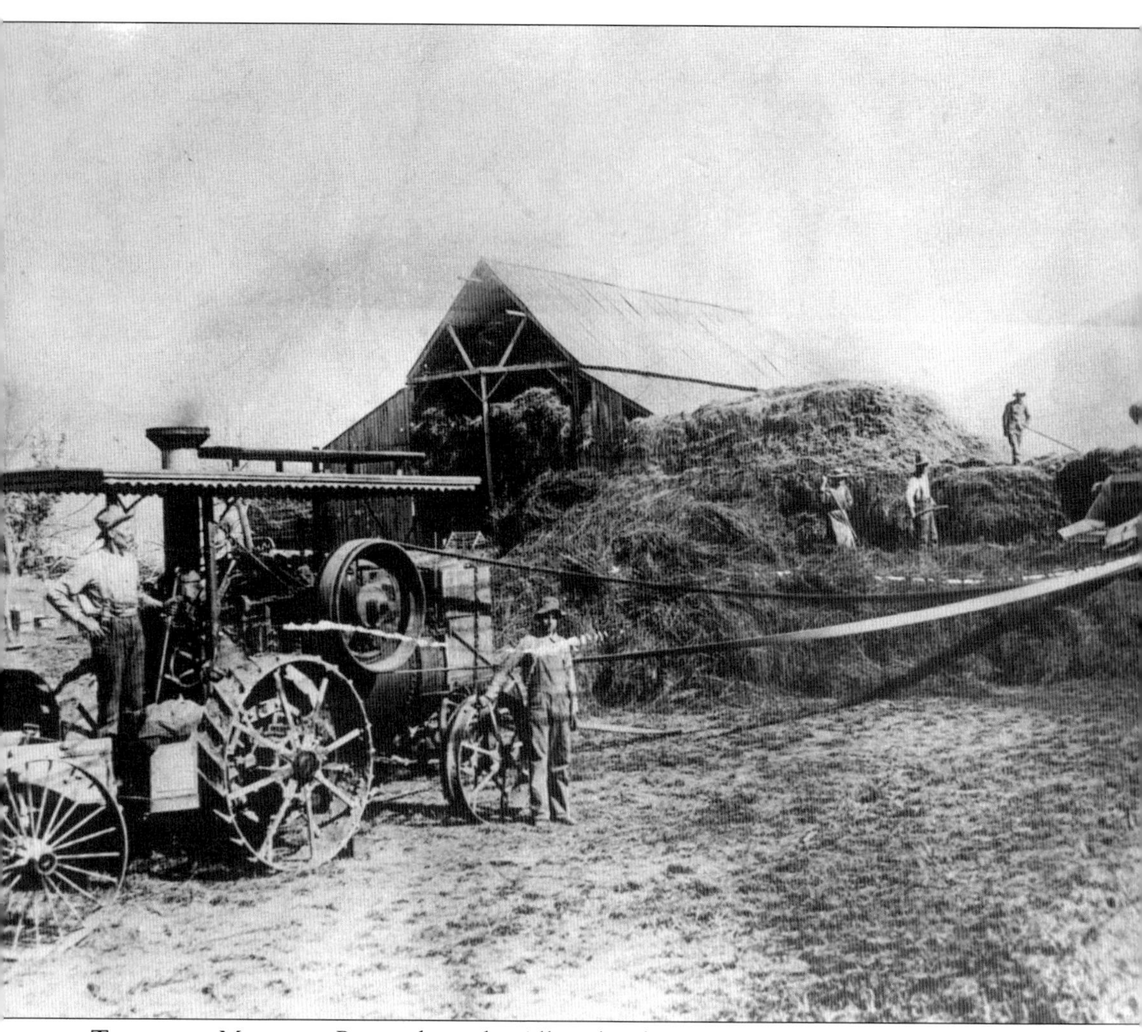

THRESHING MACHINE. Pictured are the Allan threshing crew: from left to right are Charles Allan, James Allan, Mary Allan, Henry Allan, Joseph Allan, Charles Allan Jr., and William Allan underneath the long strap. It was a huge blessing to have a grain harvester. With the older handheld tools, it took all day for one man to lay down and harvest just an acre of grain. (Courtesy of the DUP.)

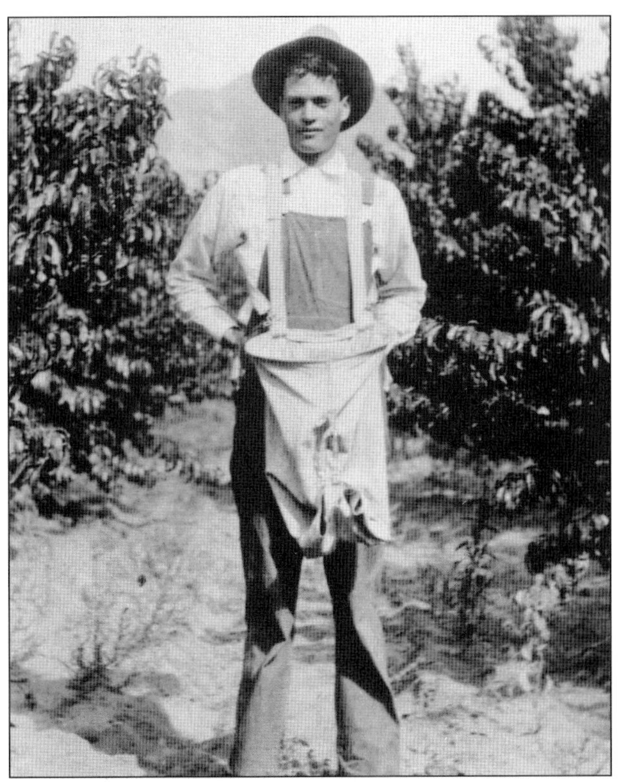

Peaches. Aaron Bruce Mendenhall is picking peaches in Bishop William T. Tew's orchard around 1920. The trees were north of Mapleton. The bag unhooks from the bottom, which allows the peaches to drop carefully into larger containers, and it has shoulder straps to help it stay on. (Courtesy of the Springville Historical Society.)

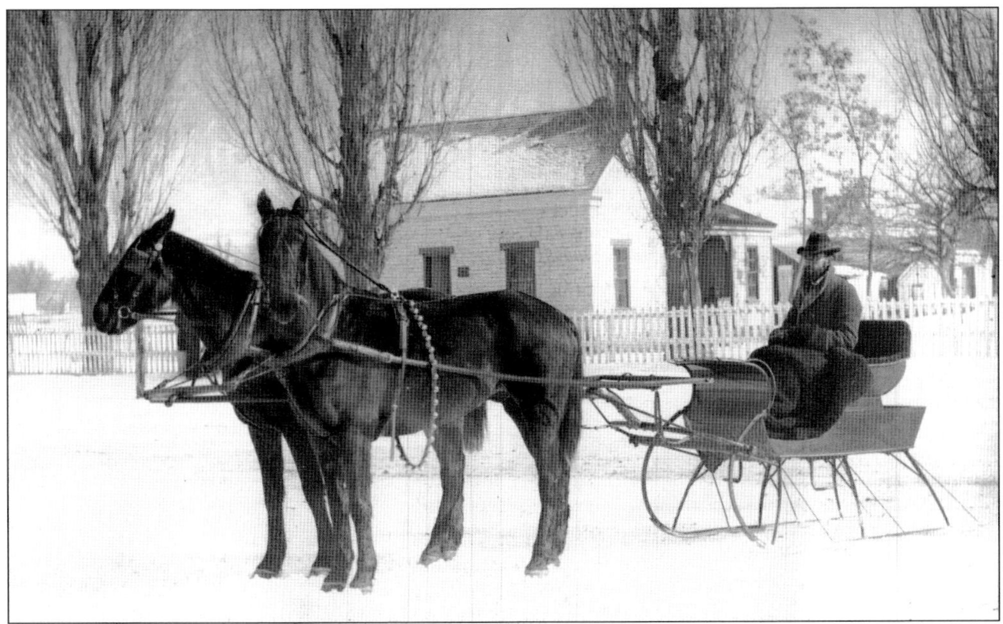

Dr. George L. Smart. Dr. Smart is pictured in his horse-drawn buggy around 1900. Dr. Smart and his wife, Emma, became essential figures in the art awakening of the area. They collected fine art, and she was an amateur painter who studied under John Hafen, an American landscape artist. In 1925, they donated 65 works of art to the Springville Museum of Art. (GEA photograph, courtesy of the Springville Historical Society.)

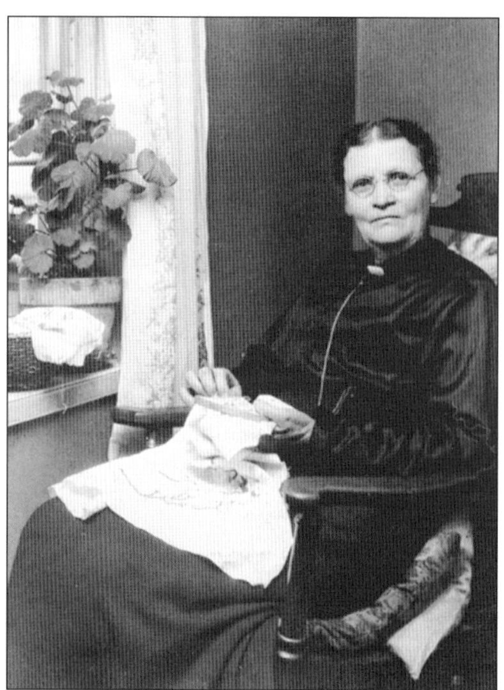

EVA STARR. Evangelina "Eva" Happylona Sanford Starr is in her chair, doing needle work. After her husband died, she took up sewing to help make a living for herself and the children. When she was 16 years old, she was on an excursion to Utah Lake when a sudden gale descended upon the water, capsizing the boat. She and 21 others were all safely rescued. Five hundred people on the shore watched and waited and were terrified by this unpleasant boating incident. (Courtesy of the DUP.)

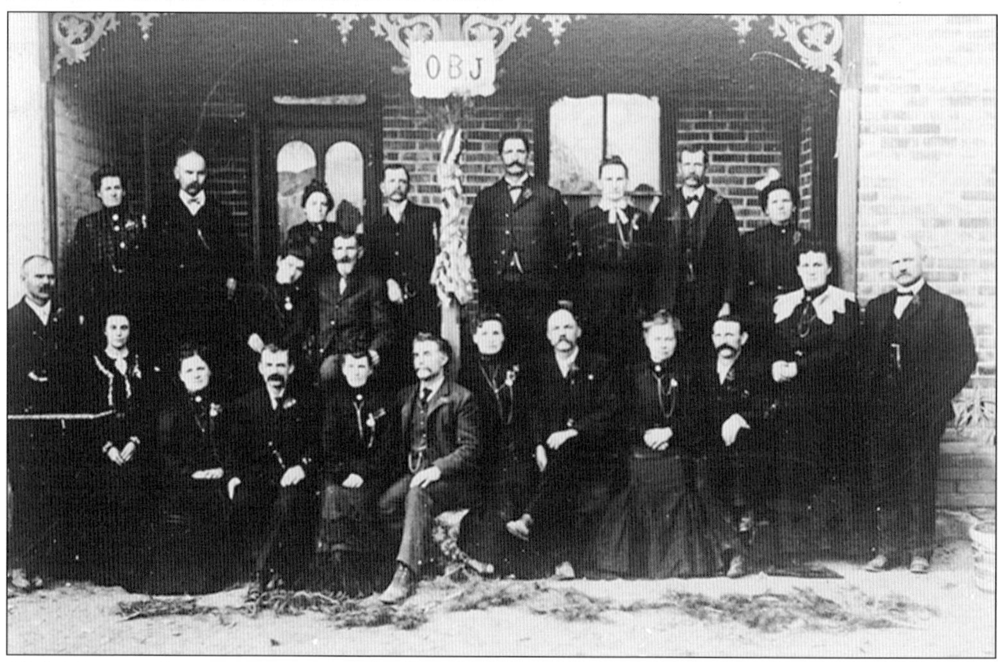

OBJ. The social entertainment couples' group known as OBJ (O Be Joyful) is pictured here. These married couples gathered regularly to promote entertainment. From left to right are (first row) Mr. and Mrs. Edwin Johnson, Mr. and Mrs. Hardy Averett, Mr. and Mrs. John Averett, Mr. and Mrs. Frank Gammell, Mr. and Mrs. Dennis Palfreyman, Mr. and Mrs. John Bryan, Mr. and Mrs. Joseph Hall, Mr. and Mrs. James Weight, Mr. and Mrs. Alfred Weight, and Mr. and Mrs. Joseph Weight. Sitting in the center are Mr. and Mrs. Ed Child. This photograph was taken in July 1902 on Thomas Edward Child Sr.'s front porch at 1300 East and 400 South. (Courtesy of the DUP.)

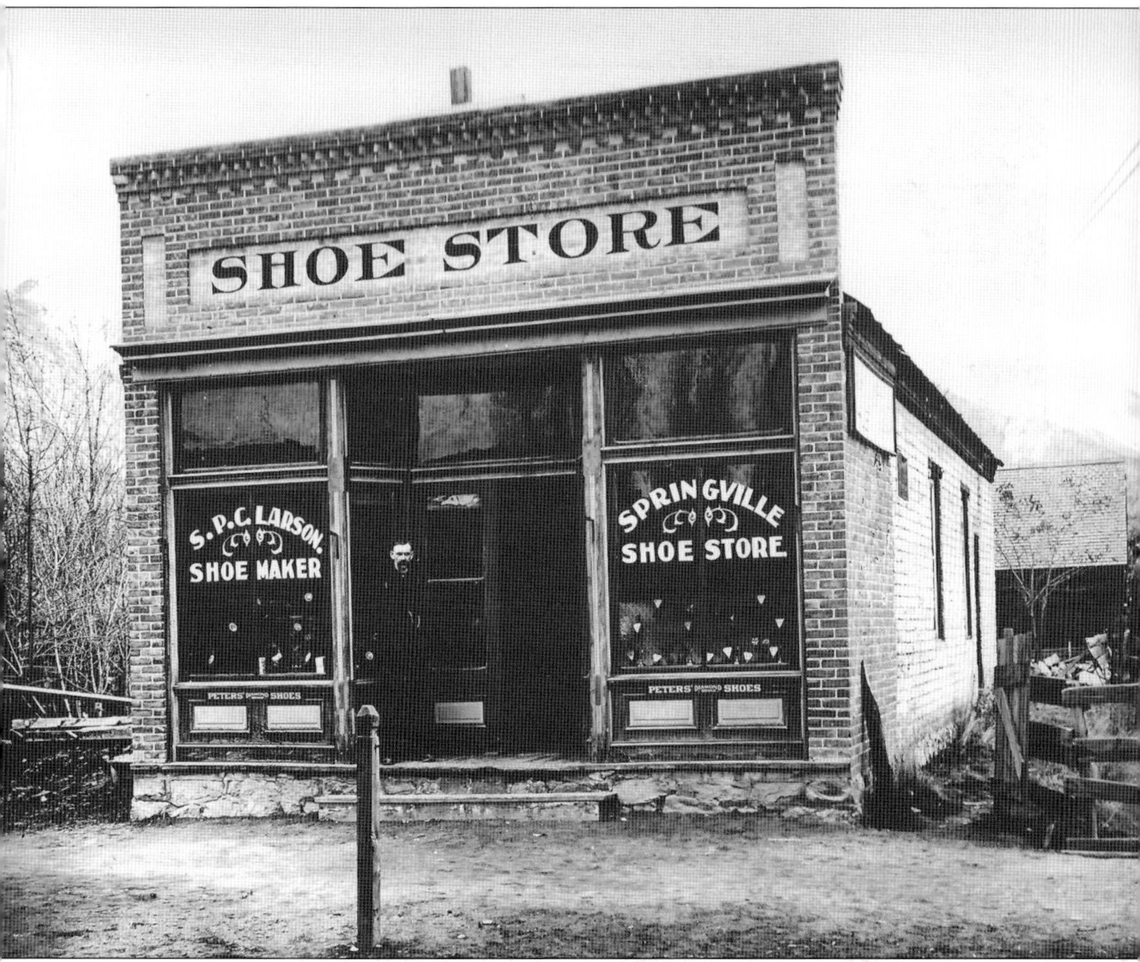

Larson Shoe Store. S.P.C. Larson's shoe store, seen around 1909, was on Main Street across from the Wood Mercantile Company. Larson made and mended shoes, and the store was a great place to purchase shoes. Larson sold Peters Diamond Brand shoes. This building at 139 South Main Street housed Independent Print and is now H&R Block. (GEA photograph, courtesy of the Springville Historical Society.)

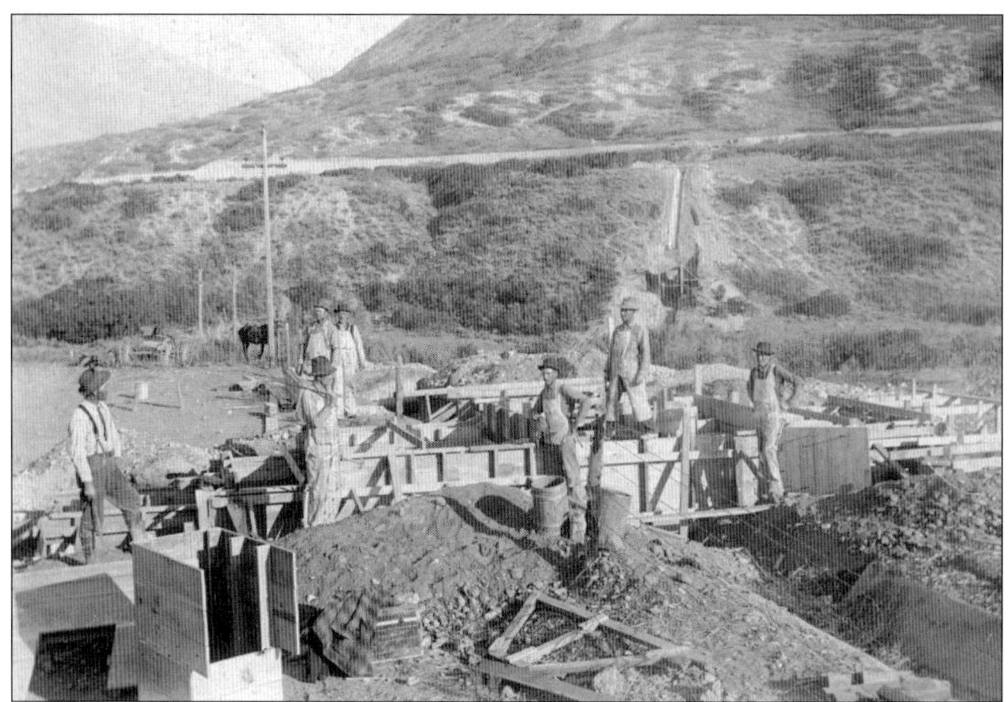

Strawberry Canal. These two pictures show the construction of the Strawberry High Line Canal around 1912. The development stores water and brings it to some of the arid sections of Utah. The Strawberry Tunnel, nearly four miles long, brings water from the Colorado River Basin to the Great Basin through the Wasatch Divide. (Both, courtesy of the Springville Historical Society.)

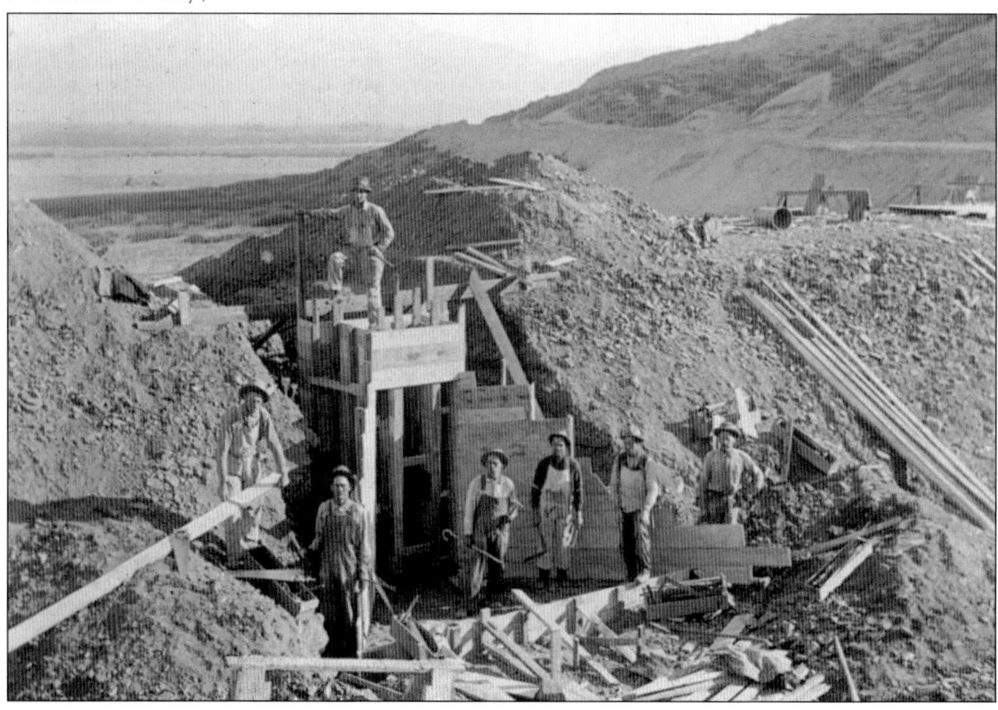

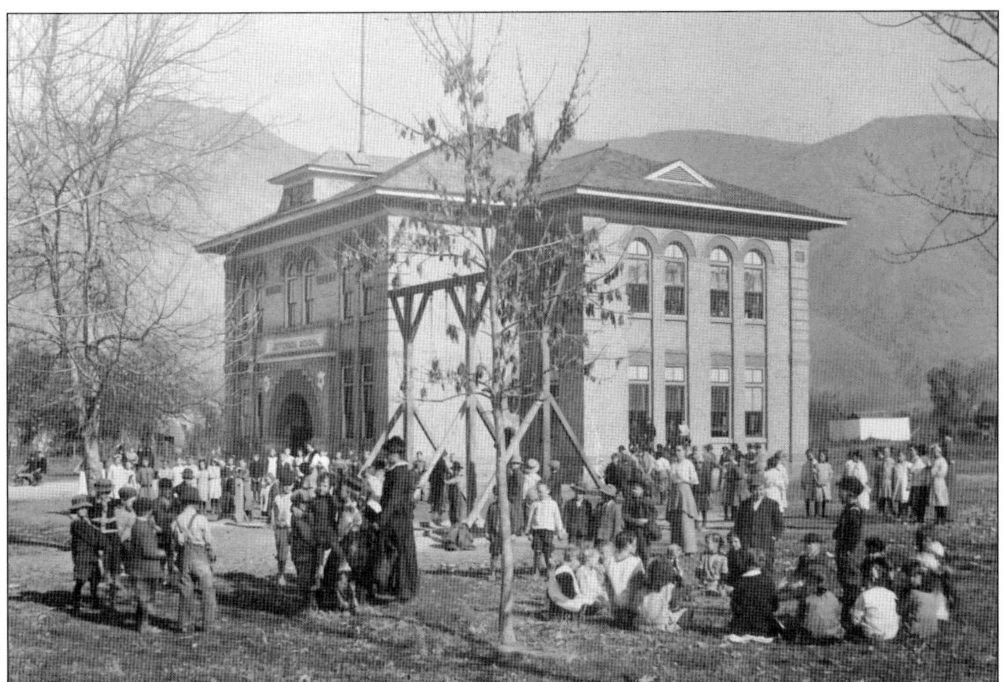

Jefferson School. The Jefferson School is pictured around 1905 at 757 South Main Street. It opened in 1902, and the last classes were held in 1967. In 2004, the school was listed in the National Register of Historic Places. It is part of the Springville Historic District. It has been renamed the Jefferson Center, and helps at-risk youth, specializing in outdoor activities. (GEA photograph, courtesy of the Springville Historical Society.)

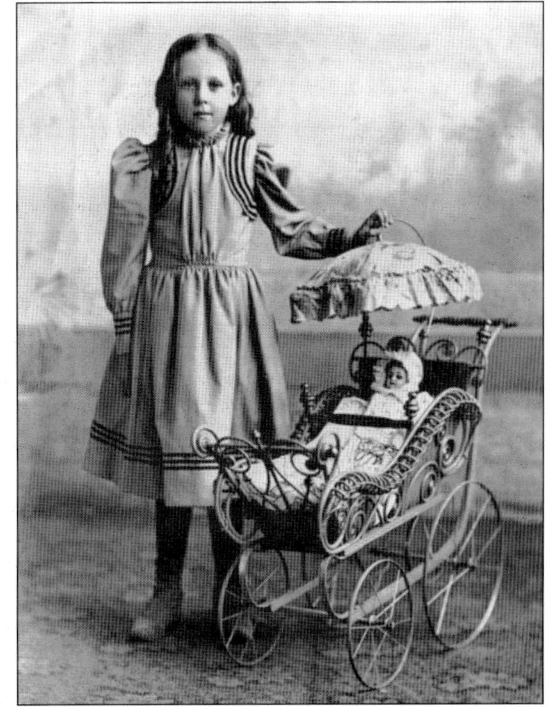

Hepsy Berry and Buggy. Hepsy Orilda Berry Burch is pictured around 1896 with her doll and buggy. She was born on July 23, 1890, in Springville. Her parents were Charles Alma Berry and Eliza Jane Lydia Harmer. Hepsy married Dallas Stockwell Burch, and they are buried in Whittier, Los Angeles County, California. (GEA photograph, courtesy of the Springville Historical Society.)

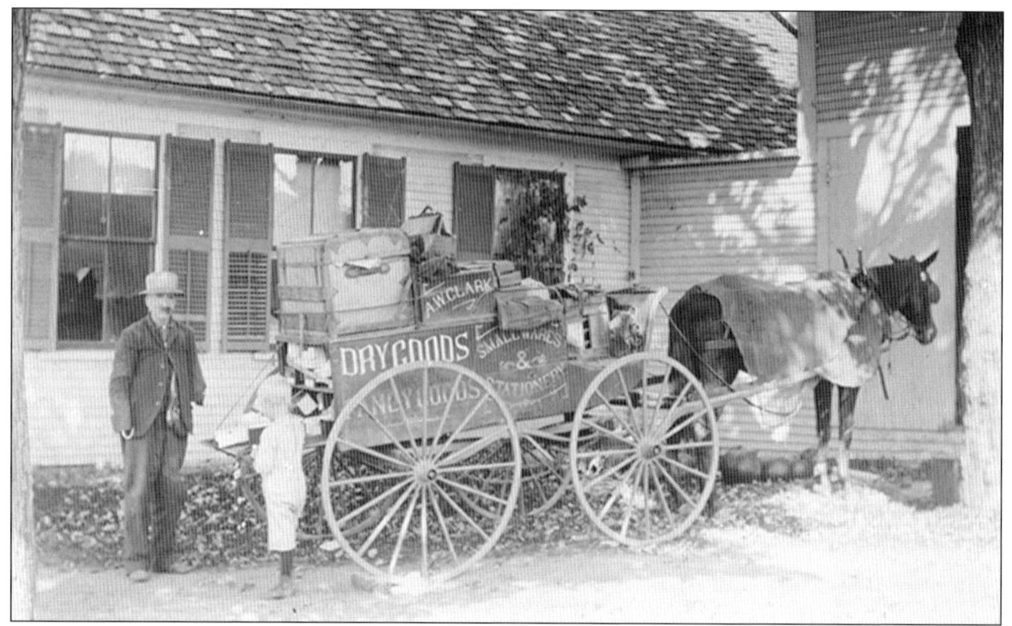

Traveling Peddler. A.W. Clark, a traveling salesman, is selling his dry goods to a young boy in this photograph. His horse-drawn wagon or small box store would have been stocked with handy tools, practical merchandise, and wares for the settlers. (GEA photograph, courtesy of the DUP.)

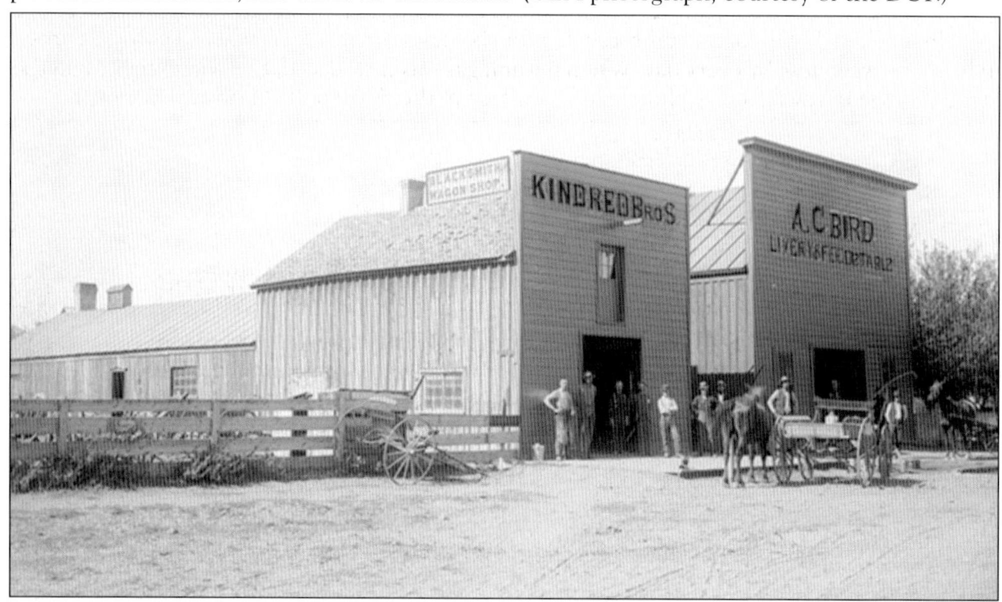

A.C. Bird Livery and Kindred Bros. A blacksmith shop operated by Edward Haymond was the first store to set up operations inside the fort when the pioneers first arrived. In this 1895 photograph, the A.C. Bird Livery and Feed Stable and the Kindred Bros. blacksmith and wagon shop are still standing. The businesses were on the south side 200 South, between Main and 100 West. The town was growing, and the demand for livestock feed and services and blacksmithing kept these two businesses busy. Blacksmiths were very valuable at the time, as they repaired wagons and scrapers and shoed horses. The Kindred Bros. store also had a showroom for Studebaker wagons. (GEA photograph, courtesy of the Springville Historical Society.)

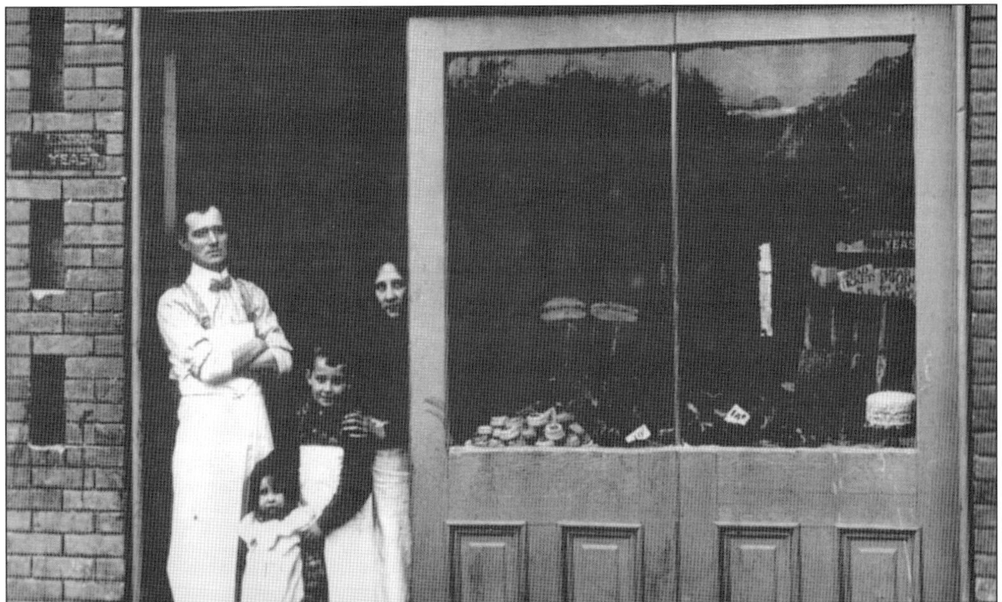

BAKERY. Wainwright Bakery is pictured at 274 South Main Street around 1906. In the doorway are William and Loisa Wainwright and their two children. On January 13, 1906, Wainwright opened the first modern bakery with a European atmosphere in Springville. As an incentive to buy his goods, he put a $5 gold piece in the bread mix. Cinnamon rolls and doughnuts were 25¢ a dozen, cookies 10¢ a dozen, and bread 25¢ for six loaves or 5¢ a loaf. Water had to be carried in from the well close by every day. When natural gas was introduced, the Wainwrights had the first gas range in town. (GEA photograph, courtesy of the Springville Historical Society.)

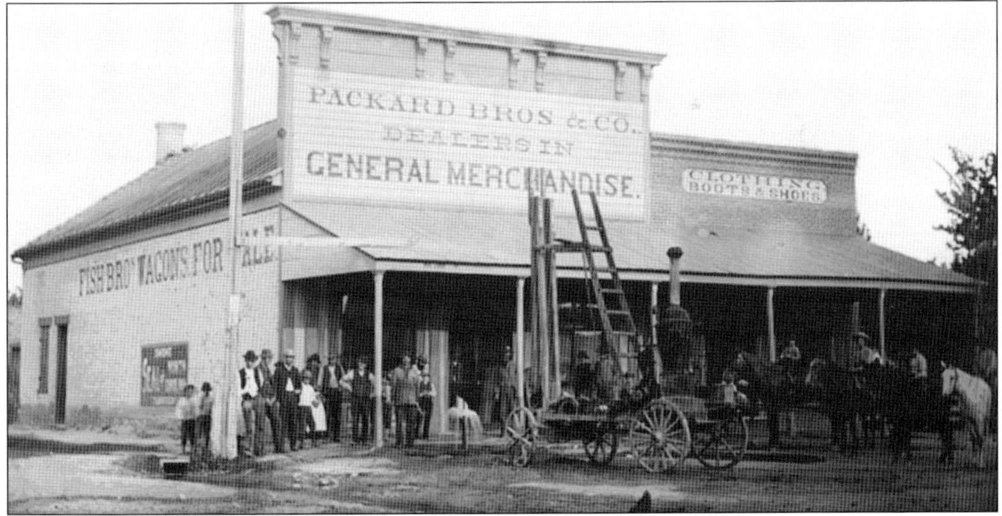

PACKARD STORE. Packard Brothers and Company dealt in general merchandise, clothing, boots, shoes, and wagons at 96 North Main Street. It was established in 1873 and is still standing. James E. Hall, in front, is driving a new artesian well digger. An artesian well had been discovered on the east bench of town. Flowing water was found at a depth of 180 feet, and the water rose within eight feet of the surface. Springville was named for the many water sources the pioneers had access to, which helped the area grow into what it is today. (GEA photograph, courtesy of the Springville Historical Society.)

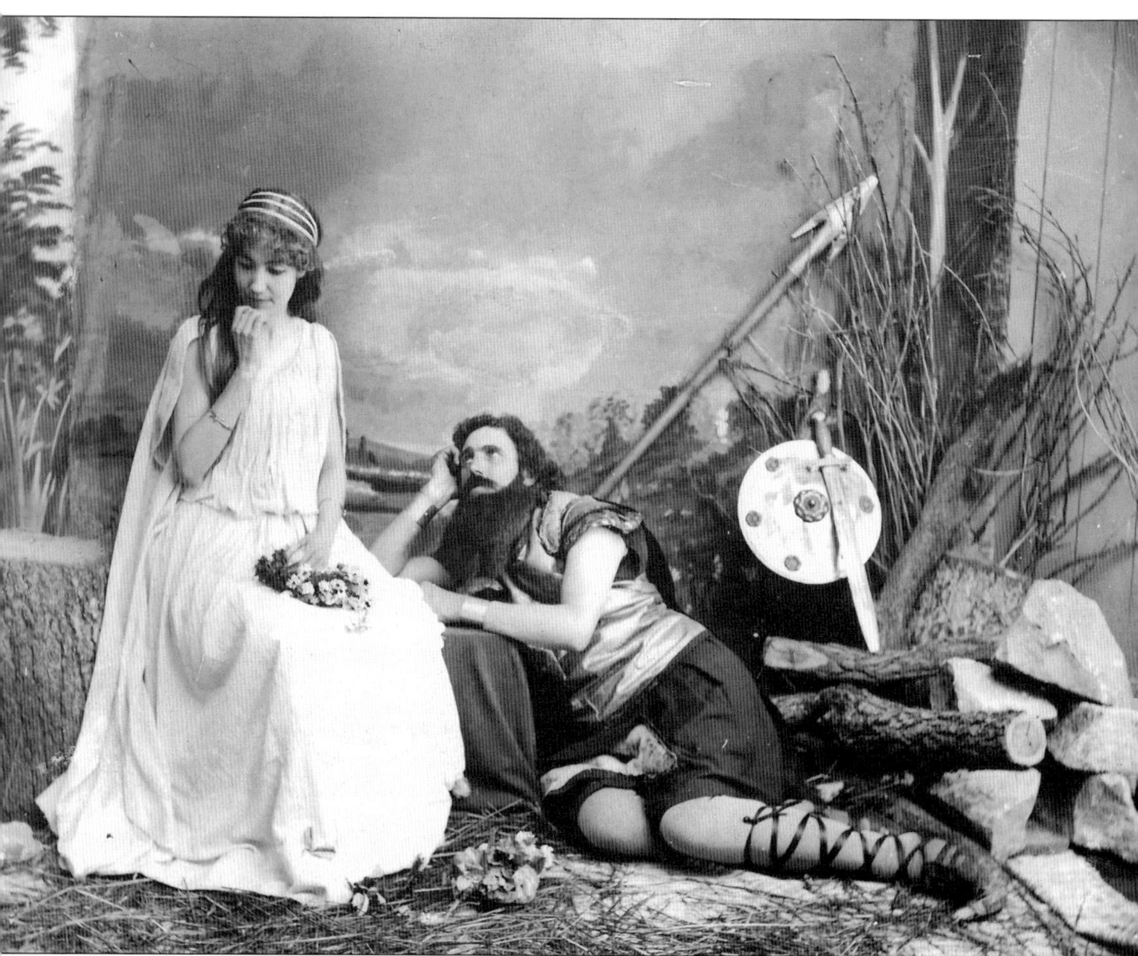

Actor John S. Lindsay. John S. Lindsay poses with an unidentified actress for a play scene around 1890. Lindsay was part of the Deseret Dramatic Association, which formed in 1850 and went around Utah acting out plays. The LDS prophet Brigham Young was devoted to theatrical entertainments and endorsed this type of leisure-time activity. In 1905, Lindsay wrote, "Salt Lake spends more money per capita in the theatre than any city in our country." (GEA photograph, courtesy of the Springville Historical Society.)

Sanford Children. From left to right are Frank J. Sanford, Arthur Velorus "Vee" Sanford Jr., and Alfred LaVell Sanford. All three boys were born in Hanksville, Wayne County, Utah Territory. Their parents, Ira Jr. and Susan Lucina Clark Sanford, were both 29 years old when they married and came to Utah with a traveling company, eventually settling in Springville. (Courtesy of the DUP.)

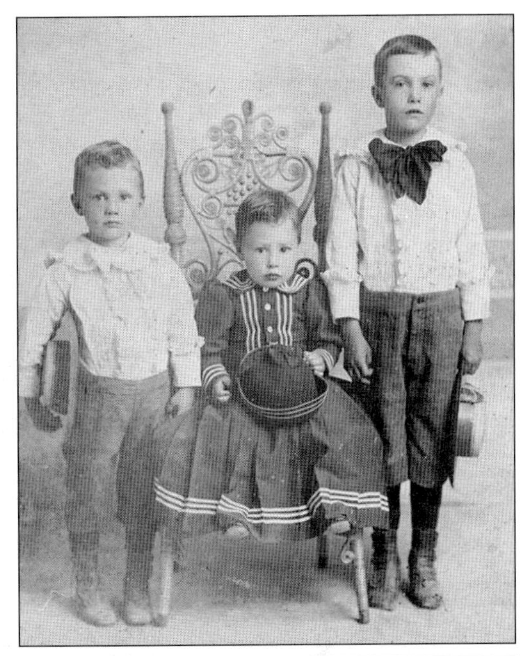

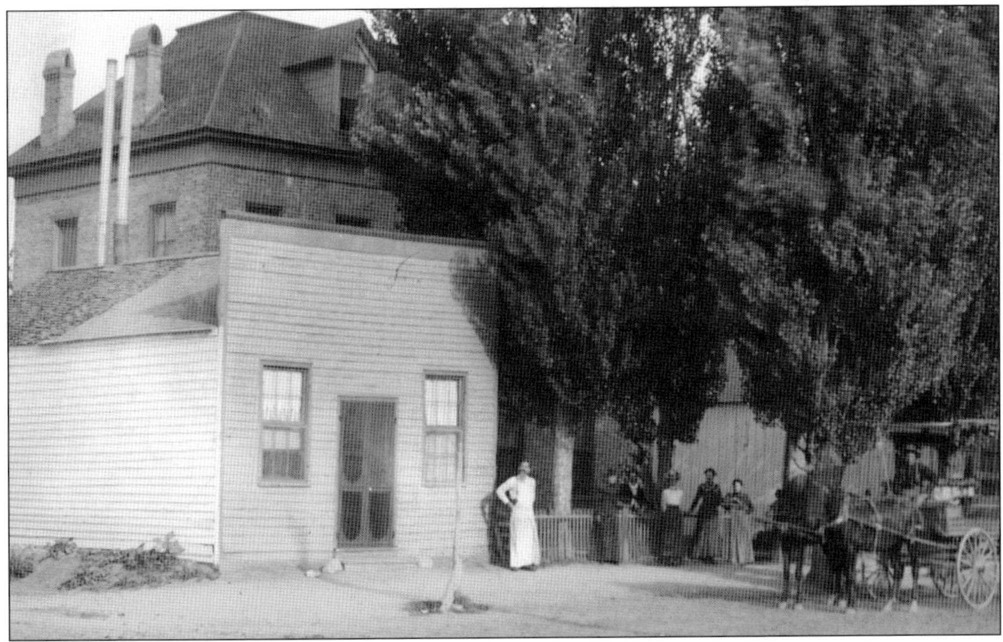

"Beefsteak" Harrison. The Harrison Hotel can be seen with "Beefsteak" George Harrison in front with the white apron. The small frame building on the left was a display area for salesmen. At 14, George fell ill with yellow fever while crossing the plains. He was left behind with a local Indian tribe in Wyoming in hopes that he would get better. After he recovered, he joined Johnston's Army as its cook since it was heading to Utah. He found his family in Springville and was allowed to leave the army in 1861. He earned his nickname for his one-pound steaks that were seared and baked. He built his three-story Harrison Hotel on Main Street between 200 and 300 South in 1880. Celebrated people visited the hotel, and Harrison's famous juicy steaks were known across the country. (Courtesy of the Springville Historical Society.)

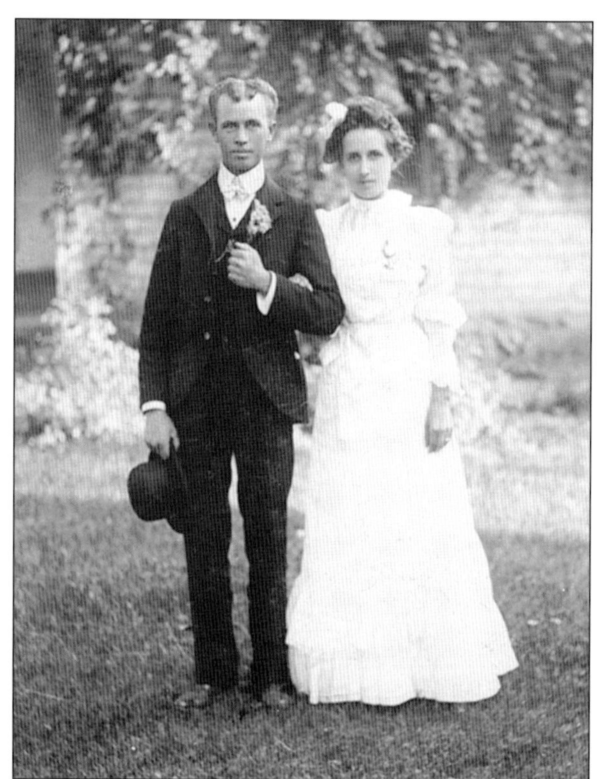

Allans. Charles and Elizabeth Allan's wedding picture was taken on July 24, 1869. They were married in the Salt Lake Endowment House, and at first lived in Springville. Later, they moved to Mapleton. They dug a well on their 120 acres and raised dry land grain. They were the parents of 12 children, and many of their descendants still live in the area. Elizabeth was thrown from a buggy on a trip and died from her injuries on August 16, 1911. Charles continued to live in the brick-adobe-lined home they built until his death on July 24, 1925. (Courtesy of the Springville Historical Society.)

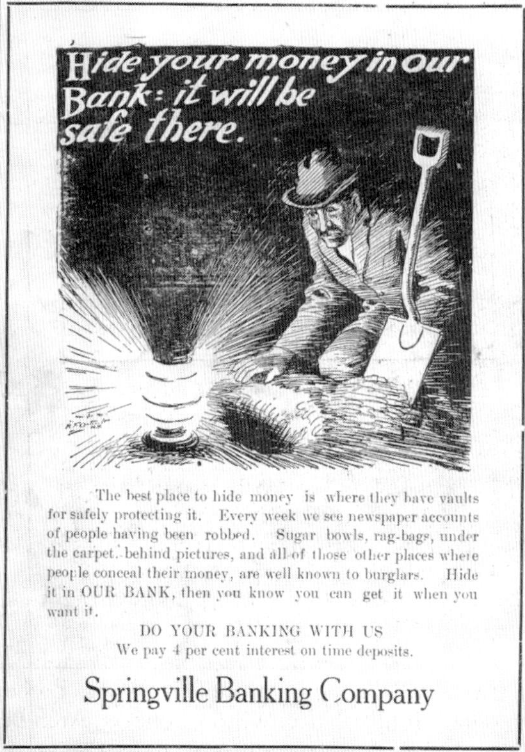

Bank Ad. A 1913 Springville Banking Company advertisement reads, "The best place to hide money is where they have vaults for safely protecting it. Every week we see newspaper accounts of people having been robbed. Sugar bowls, rag-bags, under the carpet, behind pictures, and all those other places where people conceal their money, are well known to burglars. Hide it in our bank, then you know you can get it when you want it. Do your banking with us. We pay 4 per cent interest on time deposits." (Courtesy of the Springville Historical Society.)

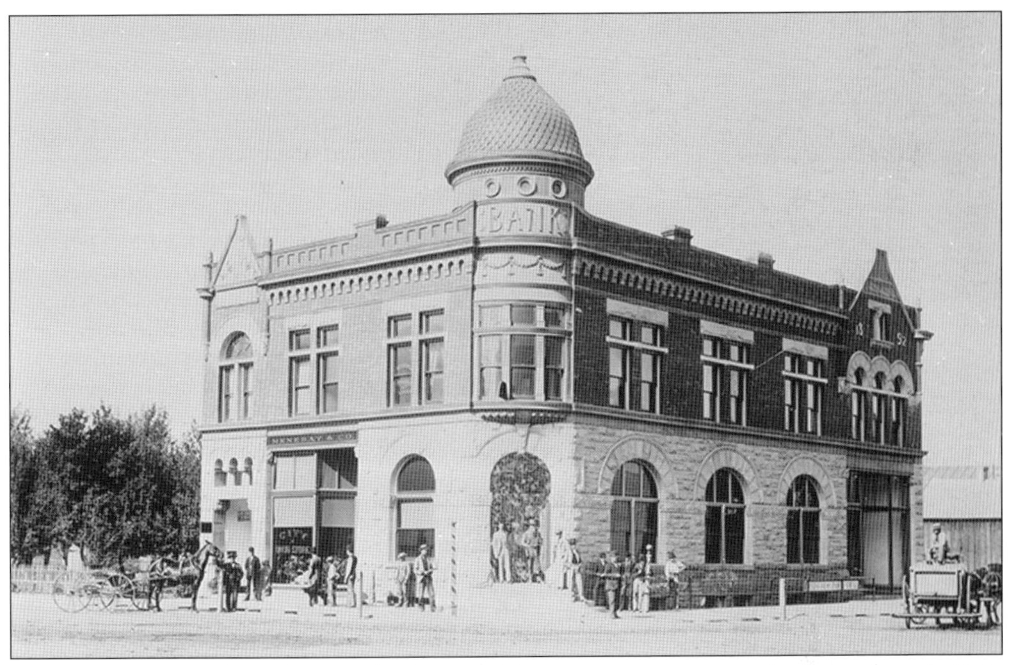

Springville Bank. The Springville Banking Company was established on October 17, 1891. For the first 40 years, Springville did not need a bank. Transactions were either in money or produce exchanged with locals. Up until 1890, spare gold was left in safes inside the few larger stores in town. This building, at Main and Second South Streets, was finished in 1892 and is still standing today, but was remodeled in 1942. (GEA photograph, courtesy of the Springville Historical Society.)

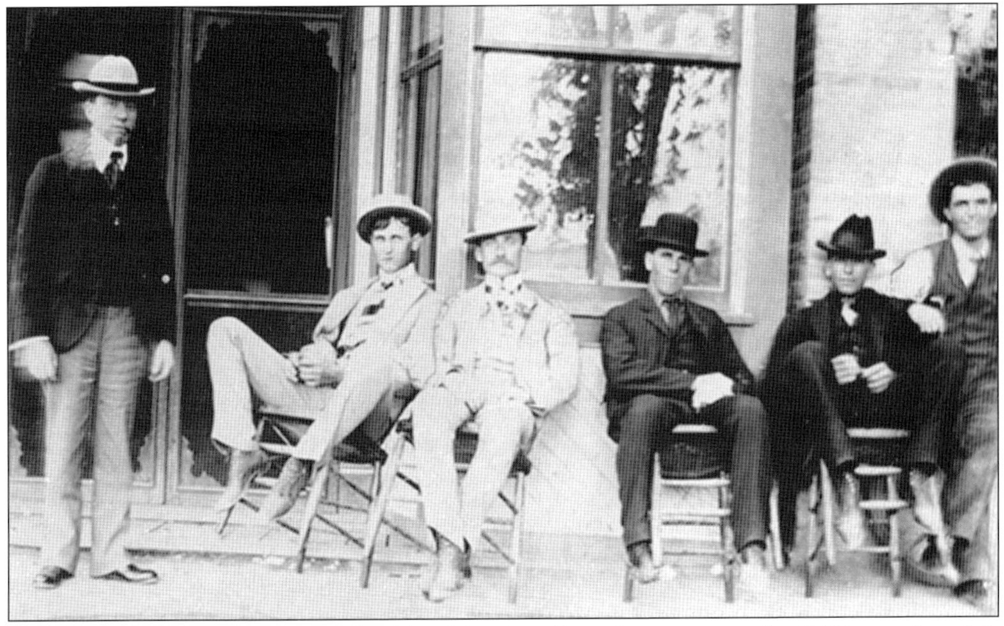

Relaxing. Relaxing in front of the Woods Barber Shop downtown in the 1890s are, from left to right, Mitt Roylance, Wilson Conover, Arch Bird, Frank Sumsion, John Blanchard, and Earl Haymond. This was a man's retreat, and was no place for women. (Courtesy of the DUP.)

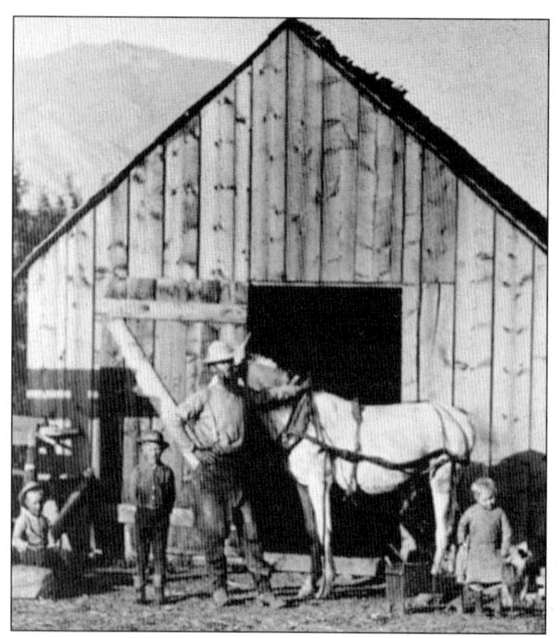

Joseph Allan and Barn. Joseph Allan is pictured in front of his barn with his children and horse. He had a blacksmith shop by his home and made all the shoes and nails for the oxen. He was also a noted hero of a bank robbery on May 28, 1898. Two men robbed the bank, and a posse led by Marshal Frank Gammel and Sheriff George Storrs went after the men, who tried to conceal themselves in the underbrush. One of the men obeyed the summons to give up, but the other retaliated with a bullet that struck Allan, piercing his leg. Shots were fired in return, and the other robber was brought out dead. Allan was taken to the hospital; his leg was amputated. The bank recovered $2,420 of the $3,020 stolen. (GEA photograph, courtesy of the Springville Historical Society.)

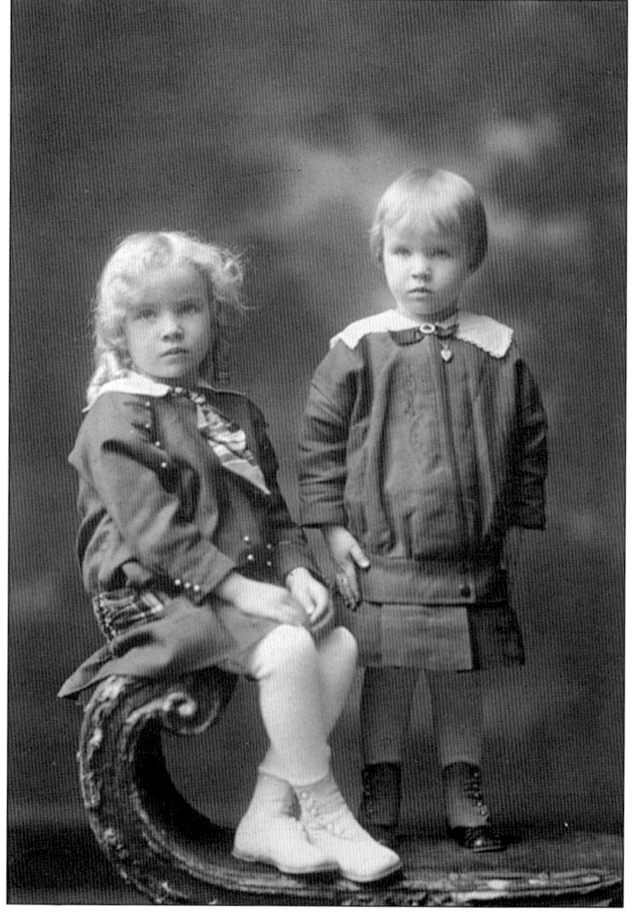

Allan Children. Pictured are siblings Harriet Maud Allan and Joseph William Allan (seen above). Their parents, Joseph William Allan and Fanny Kindred, were married on May 31, 1873, in Salt Lake City. Ira Allan, an extended family member, arrived within a few weeks of the first settlers in 1850, and his descendants helped make the two cities into what they are today. Ira Allan Park in Mapleton is named after the family. (Courtesy of the DUP.)

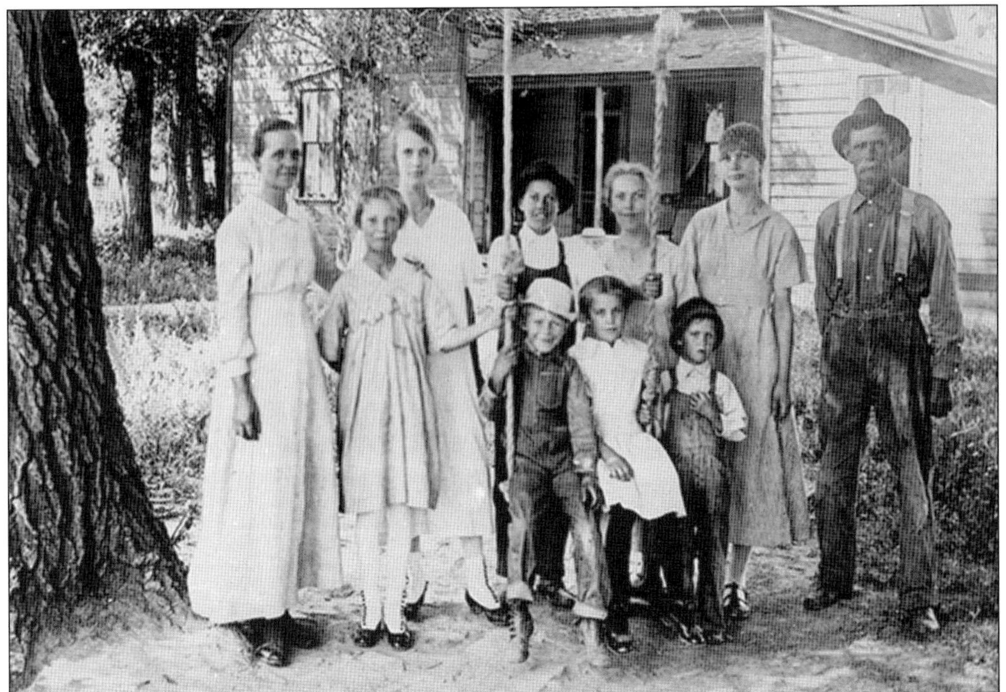

Dayleys. The Dayley family is pictured in front of their home around 1916. The large tree on the left had a swing in its branches. The children were Vyla, Emma, Thelma, Carrie, Nina, Arthur, Charles, and Delbert, and the parents were Carrie and Charles Dayley. Charles Sr. was gone much of the time during the winter working in the legislature in Boise. He also worked in the sugar factory. Carrie enjoyed raising flowers and crocheting. (Courtesy of the DUP.)

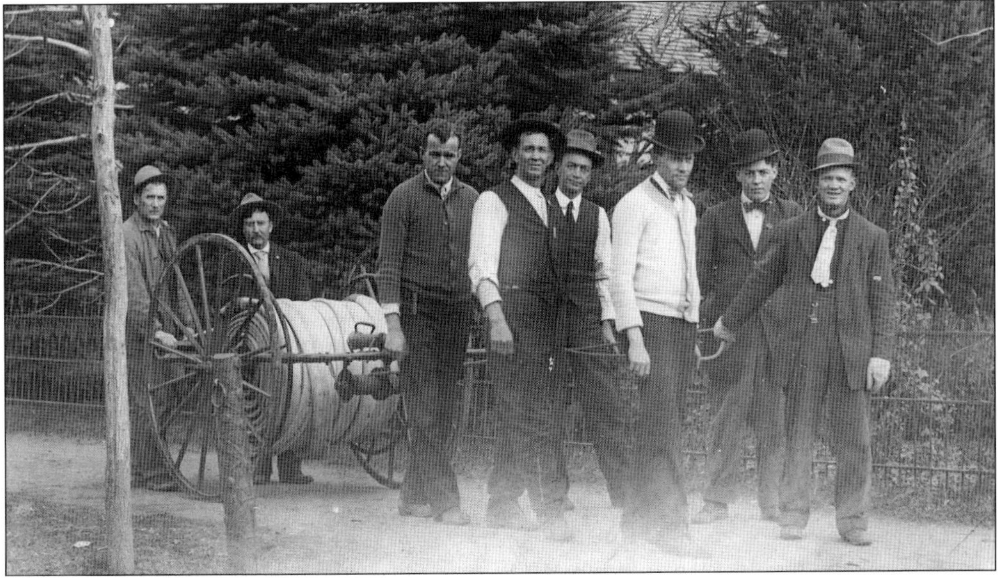

Firemen. Springville's early volunteer firemen are going on their first run with their brand-new fire-hose cart. From left to right are John Wiscombe, Elliott Jordan, Lyman Haymond, Isaac Brown, Amos Brown, Walter Graham, Piersol Brinton, and Zebe Huntington. The photograph was taken by J.D. Bagley at First South and Main Streets. (Courtesy of the Springville Historical Society.)

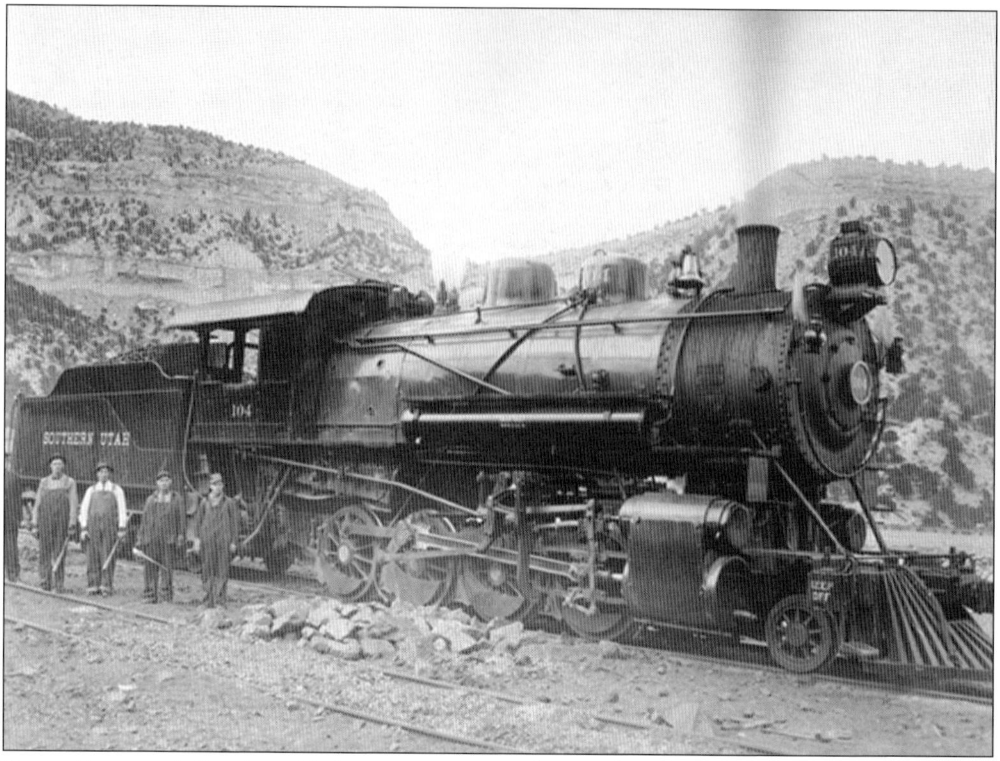

Train Engine. A Southern Utah engine is pictured around 1915. Maurice Johnson is at far left, and the rest are unidentified. Johnson was a railroad builder and helped to lay the Newhouse, Copper Gulch, and Sevier Lake tracks. (Courtesy of the DUP.)

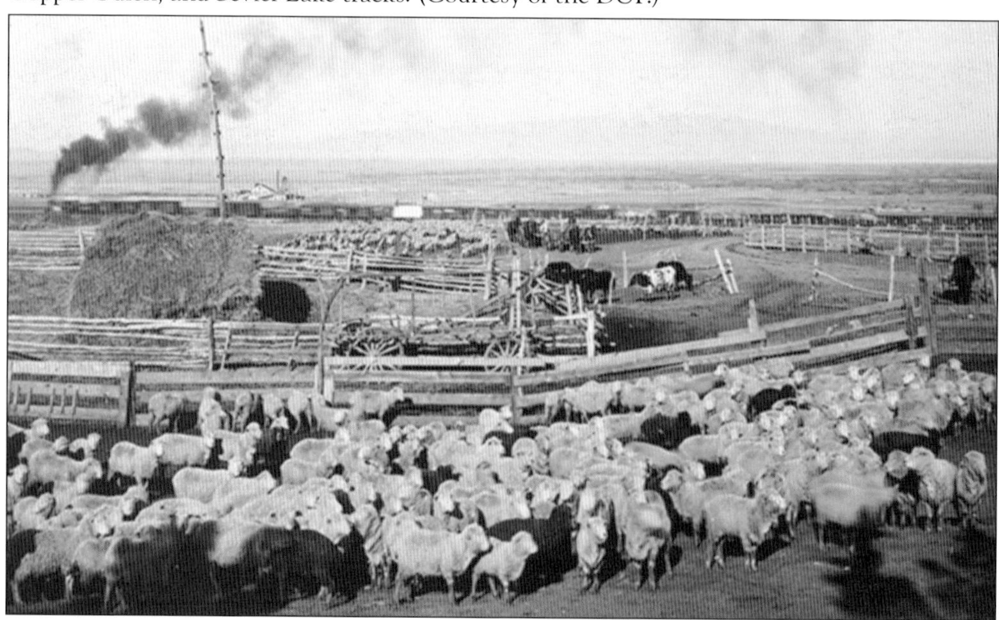

Sheep Ranch. The McFarland Sheep Ranch was in Mapleton. This picture was taken on March 19, 1905, by George Anderson. In the distance on the left, a train is going by. Currently, there are a few small operating sheep ranches in the area. (Courtesy of the Springville Historical Society.)

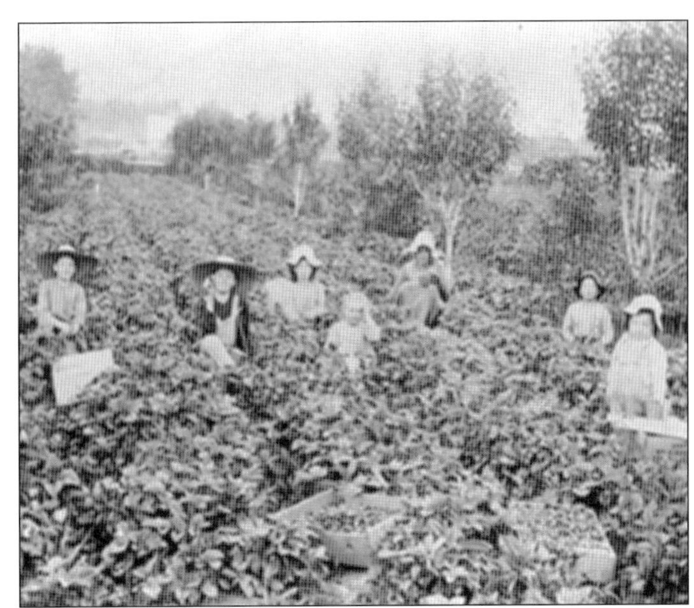

Fruit Bed. This fruit bed ran from Fourth West Street up to 250 West, behind the Boyer home. The picture was taken in 1904; the strawberries and raspberries supported John Selvoy Boyer while he was serving an LDS mission to England. From left to right are Catherine Boyer Buchanan, Margaret "Chole" Boyer Fox, Mahilda Boyer Wright, Mildred Boyer Jarvis, Susannah Bailey Jarrett Boyer (John's wife), Selvoy Jarrett Boyer, and Arthur Crandall Boyer. (Courtesy of the Springville Historical Society.)

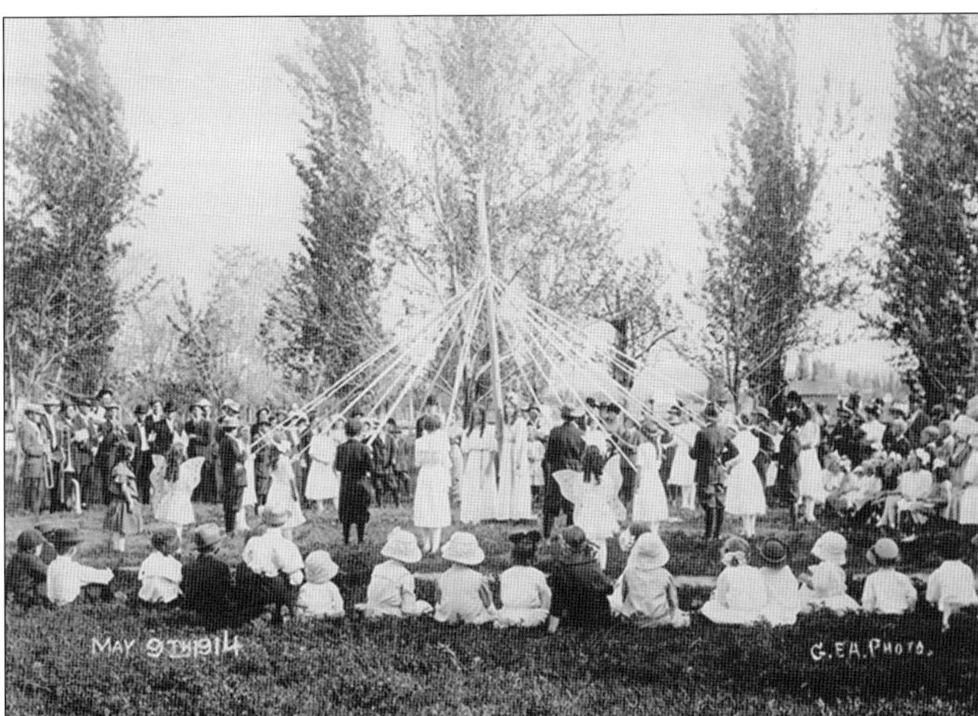

May Day. May Day is being celebrated on May 9, 1914. May Day is celebrated around May 1 and is a traditional spring holiday or festival. It is a ritual of rebirth and fertility. Children are pictured dancing around a Maypole with ribbons; other celebrations also take place on this day. (GEA photograph, courtesy of the Springville Historical Society.)

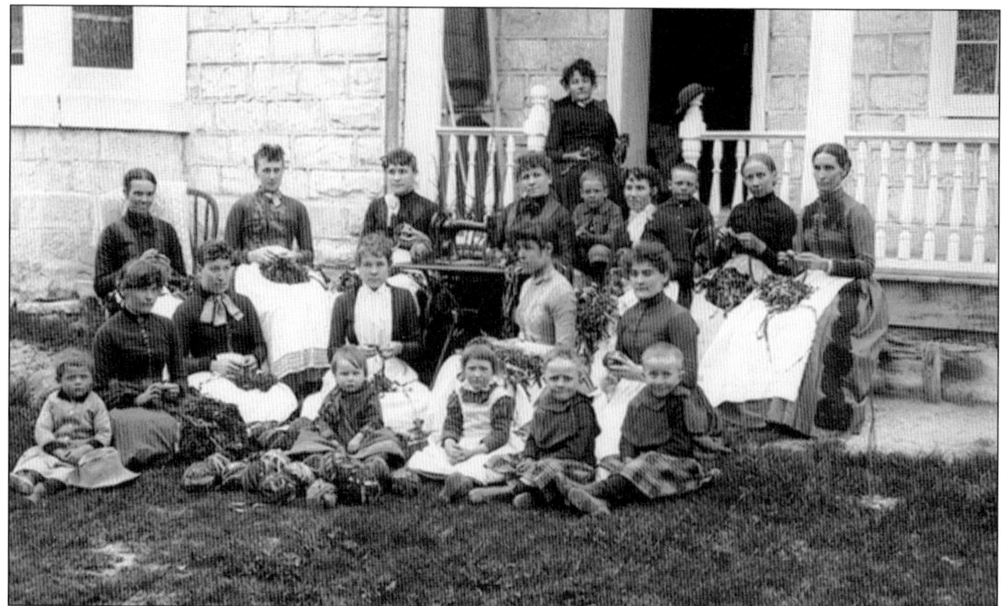

Rag Rug. A rag rug party is pictured at Mrs. Spicer's house. Rag rugs were made using odd scraps of fabric and other unusable material. The women and girls braided the items together to make a floor covering for inside the home. These rugs provided warmth and protection to the residents and their guests. (GEA photograph, courtesy of the Springville Historical Society.)

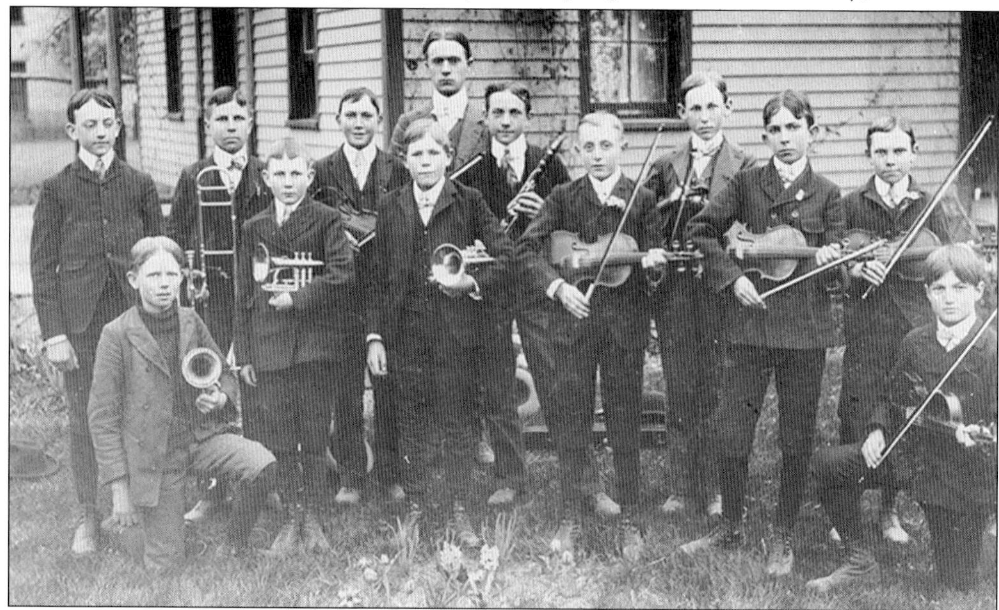

Band Students. Springville band students are shown around 1912. From left to right are (first row, kneeling) Zebina "Bine" Alleman and Paul Miner; (second row) Ernest Boyer, Reed Reynolds, William Singleton, and William Harrison; (third row) Ross Crandall, Arch Reynolds, Ruel Packard, Merrill Caffrey, Leon Harrison, and John Wiscombe. Instructor Moses Gudmundson stands in the back. He was a professor of violin and orchestra at Brigham Young University and was one of the founders of the Utah settlement of West Tintic. (GEA photograph, courtesy of the Springville Historical Society.)

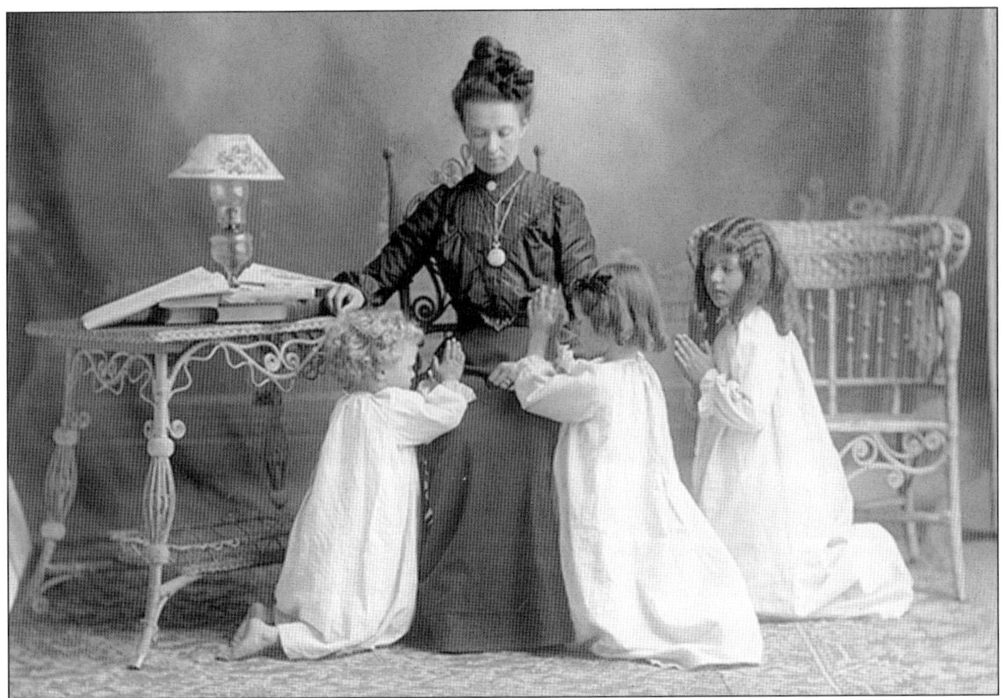

Mrs. Manwaring and Her Children. Bertha Charlette Perry Manwaring mailed a copy of this photograph to her husband, Albert, who was serving an LDS mission to England, around 1903. From left to right are Arvilla (who died at five), Ora Gardner, and Stella Brockbank. (GEA photograph, courtesy of the Springville Historical Society.)

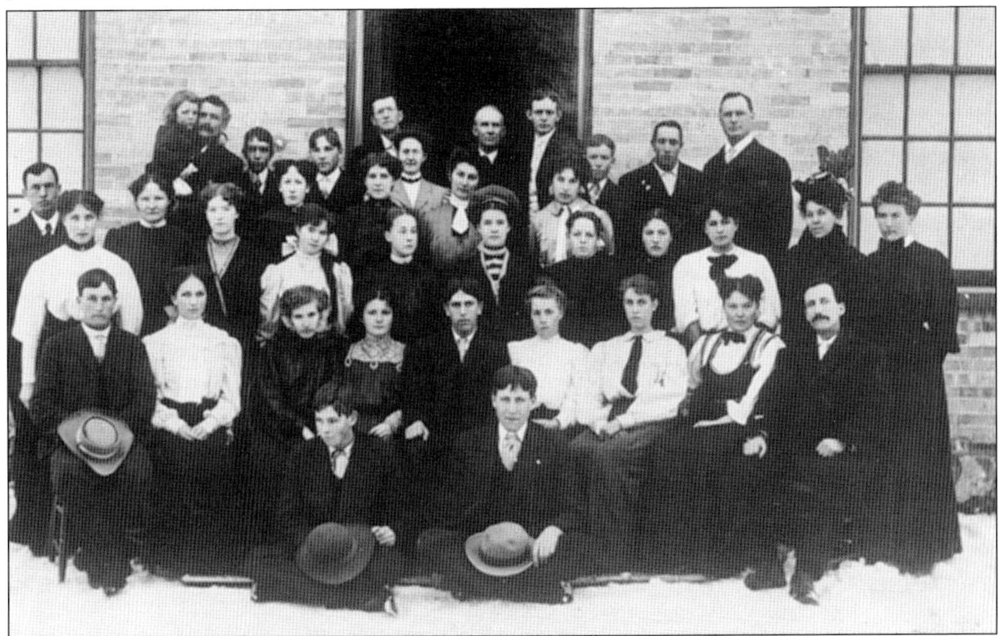

Sunday School Class. The LDS First Ward Sunday School class includes George Anderson, standing in the back on the left holding one of his children. Religious learning continues today, and Sunday school class is held every Sabbath in LDS congregations. (Courtesy of the DUP.)

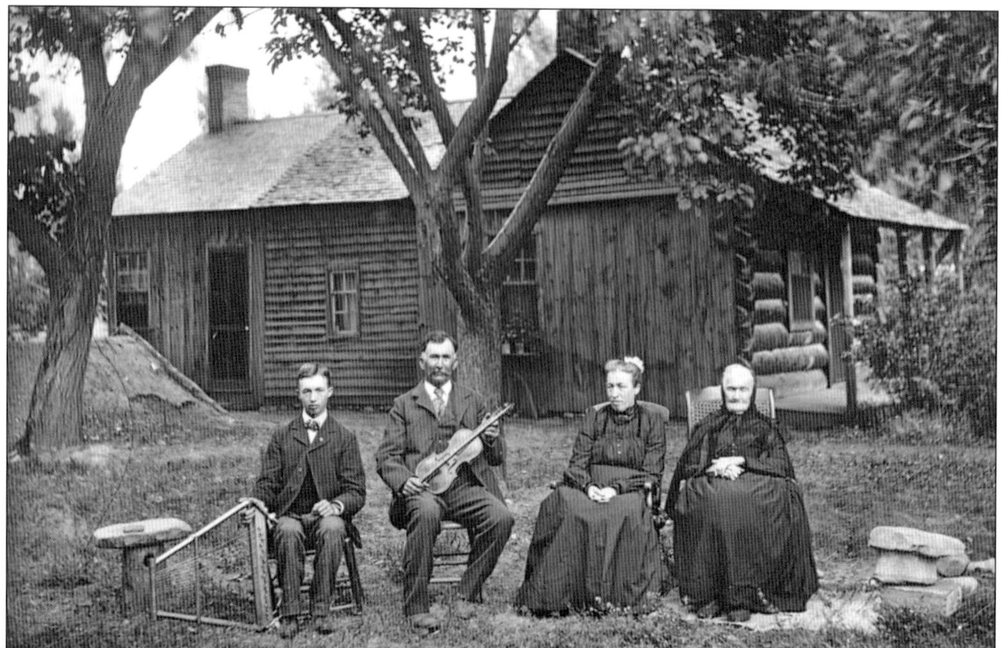

Blanchards. The Blanchard family, pictured around 1902, include, from left to right, Achilles "Chillis," Ether, Sylvia, and her mother, Margaret Goff, who lived to be 106. This home was on the corner of 900 South and 600 East. Chillis, like his father, was a violinist and wrote poetry and songs. He made his harp from an old bicycle frame. (GEA photograph, courtesy of M. Lee Taylor.)

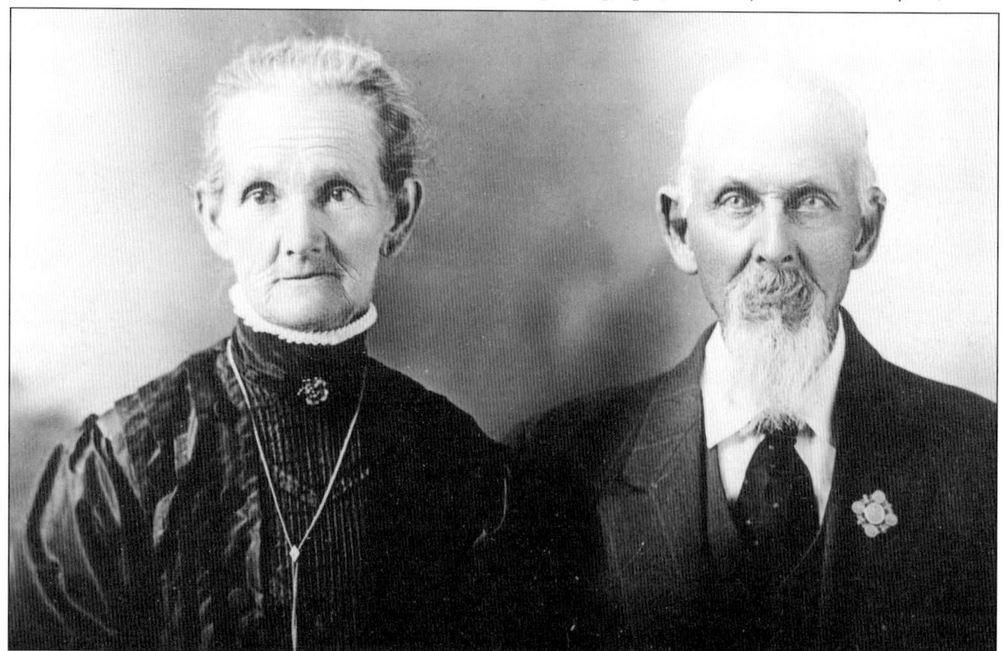

Oakleys. Fannie Palfreyman and James De Groot Oakley were married on July 19, 1869, in the Endowment House in Salt Lake City. James was a member of the Mormon Battalion, Company D. He took an active part in the Indian Wars and died on April 30, 1915. He had such a horror of debt that he never owed a dollar to anybody . (Courtesy of the DUP.)

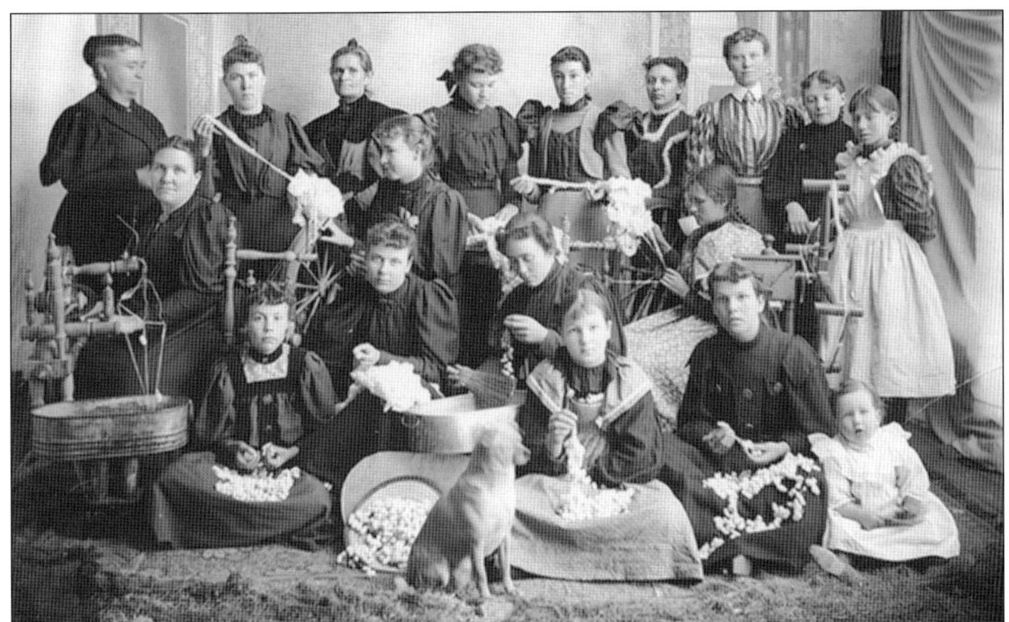

Silkworm Industry. In 1894, sponsored by the LDS Church, residents George Matson and Richard Mendenhall set aside land on their Mapleton farms to raise mulberry trees. Other residents in the two cities also planted trees. Many women and children gathered the leaves and fed them to silkworms. The Springville Bank donated one of its rooms for this work. The process was tedious, but the community kept it going for a while until the venture failed due to the climate. From left to right are (first row) Josephine Gammell, Minnie Hall, Maud Matthews, Patty Loveless, Destia Weight, and Maud Matthews's baby; (second row) Emma Dougall, Ruby Hall, and Mrs. Matthews; (third row) Mary V. Norley, Flora Blackett, Mary Catherine Streeper Dougall, Zella Brown, Lou Whitmore, Pearl Packard, "Piper" Phyfoher, Minnie Meneray, and Alta Bertha Haymond. (GEA photograph, courtesy of the DUP.)

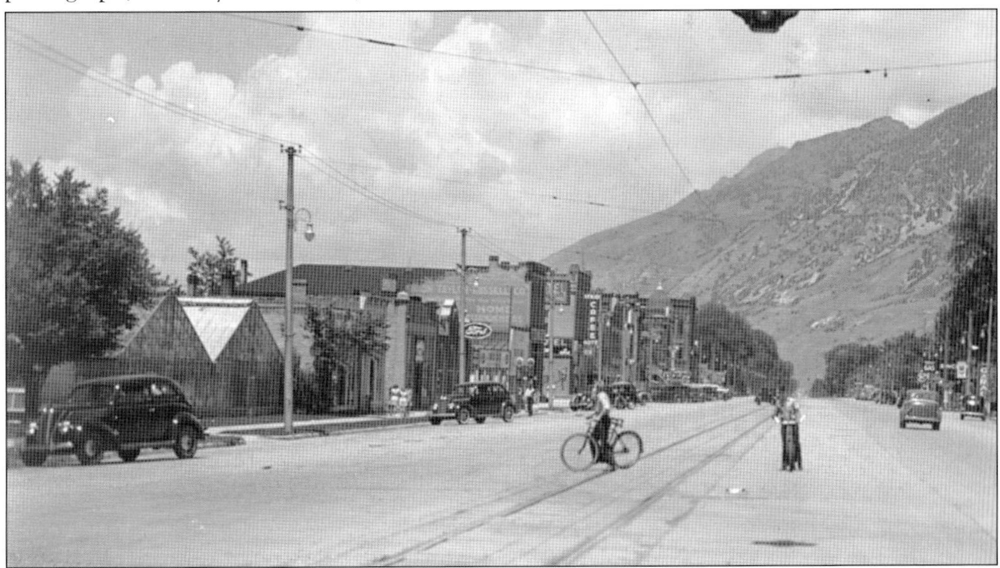

Main Street. The tracks of the Orem Interurban Railway are seen in the center of Main Street in 1940. (Courtesy of M. Lee Taylor.)

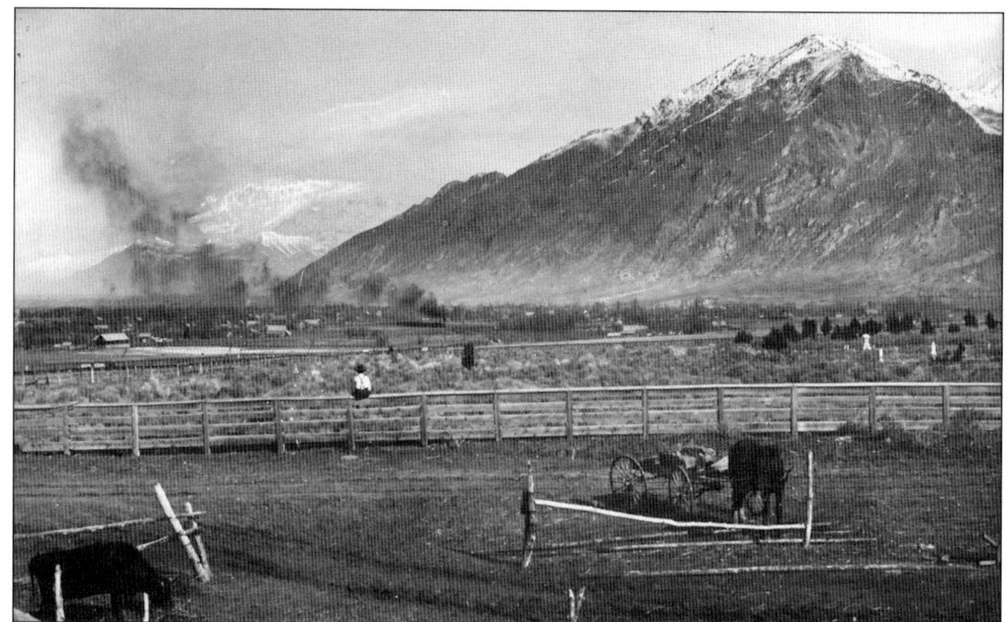

Cemetery View. A boy is sitting on the fence, and a train is going by. Cows are grazing, and the beginnings of the Evergreen Cemetery can be seen on the right. This beautiful image shows the countryside in the early days of the city, around the turn of the 20th century. Springville also has another graveyard, the historic Springville City Cemetery. (GEA photograph, courtesy of the Springville Historical Society.)

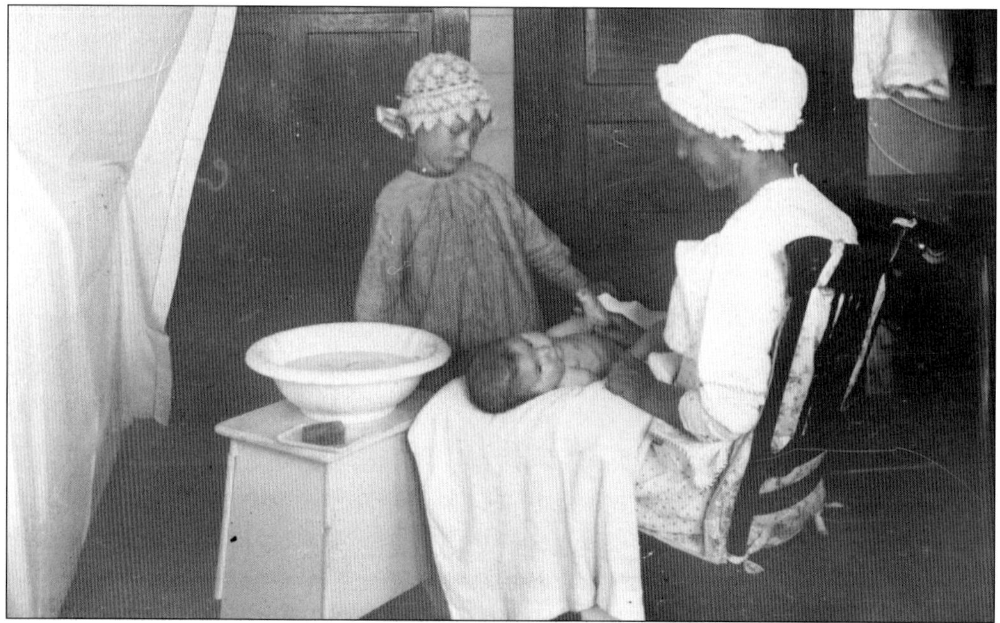

Bath Time. Lewis Jotham Whitney's wife is bathing her infant, and another child is helping her. Lewis's parents were Leonard Jotham Whitney and Tryphena Roseltha Perry. The Whitney and Perry families helped to establish Mapleton and Springville by cultivating the land, constructing buildings, and serving in community positions, and the families have living descendants in both cities today. (Courtesy of the DUP.)

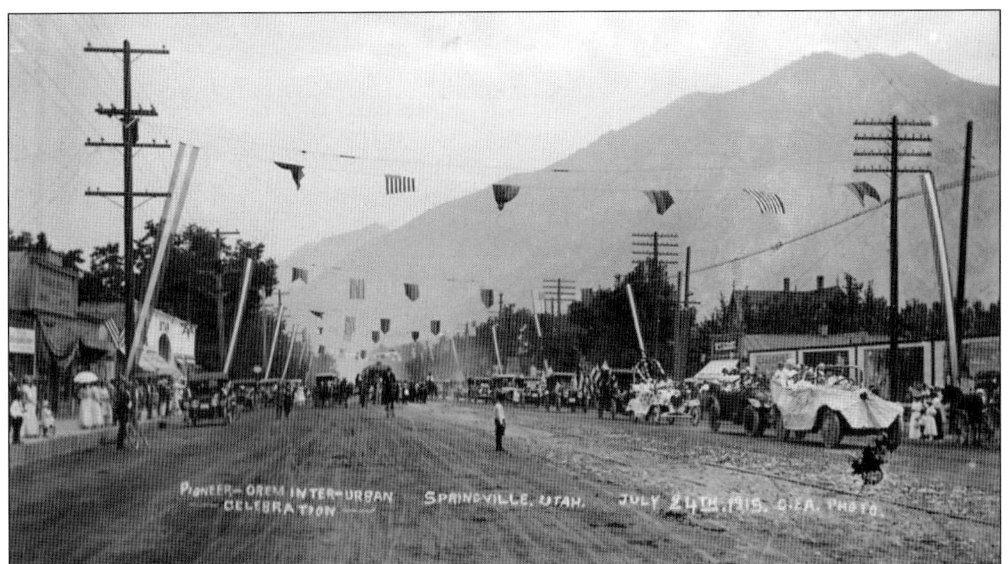

July 24, 1914. Springville is celebrating Pioneer Day and the Orem Interurban connection on July 24, 1914. This connection used an electric train instead of steam locomotives. The line ran from Salt Lake City to Payson, Utah. It ceased operating in March 1944, and the rails were taken up for the war effort. A bus service was instituted as its replacement. (GEA photograph, courtesy of the Springville Historical Society.)

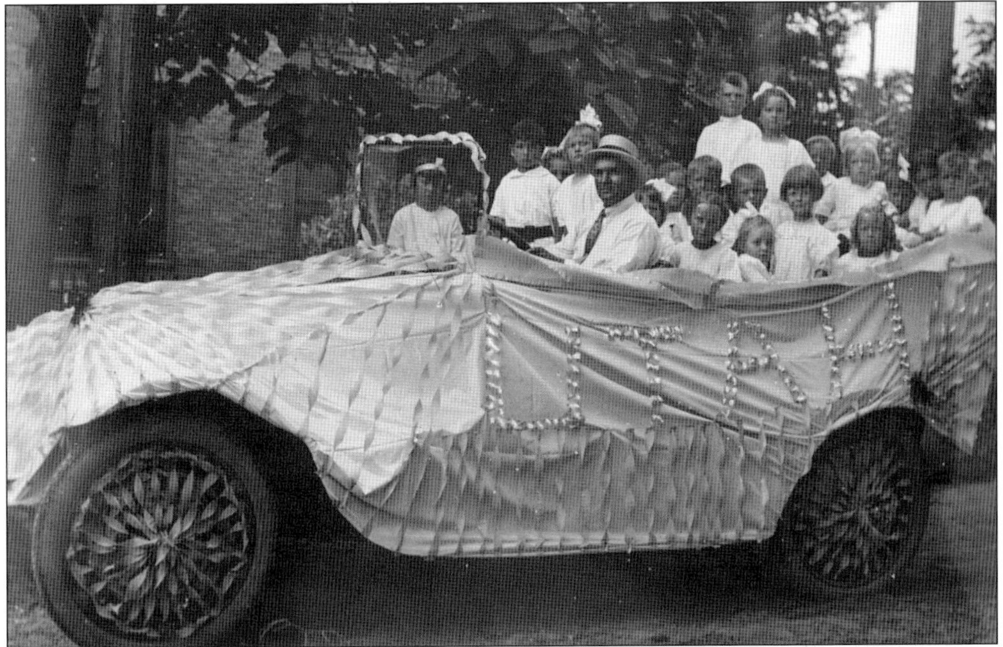

Studebaker. In 1914, one of the first automobiles came to town, a Studebaker owned by Amasa Bird. This car is visible on the right in the previous photograph. Driving the car is Vern Bird, Amasa's son, with a Sunday school class. Margaret Bird Conover is fourth from the right in the back row with a big bow in her hair. She was allowed a quarter to spend during the day's events and said, "I could get just about anything I wanted, with that amount." (GEA photograph, courtesy of the Springville Historical Society.)

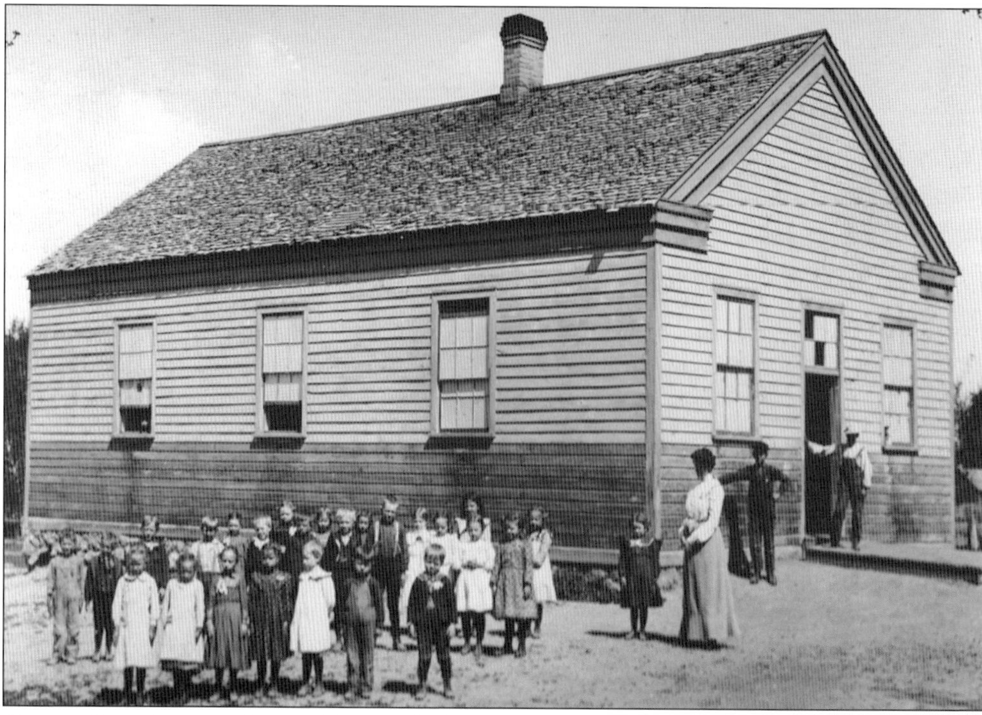

THIRD WARD SCHOOL HOUSE. Teacher Sadie Boyer is pictured with her students. LDS churches were being built in the area, and they functioned as schools during the week. Before the creation of the church school, daily instruction was held in people's homes, cabins, or other buildings in town or in the canyon. After a few years, larger schools were built, and the church school was discontinued. (GEA photograph, courtesy of the DUP.)

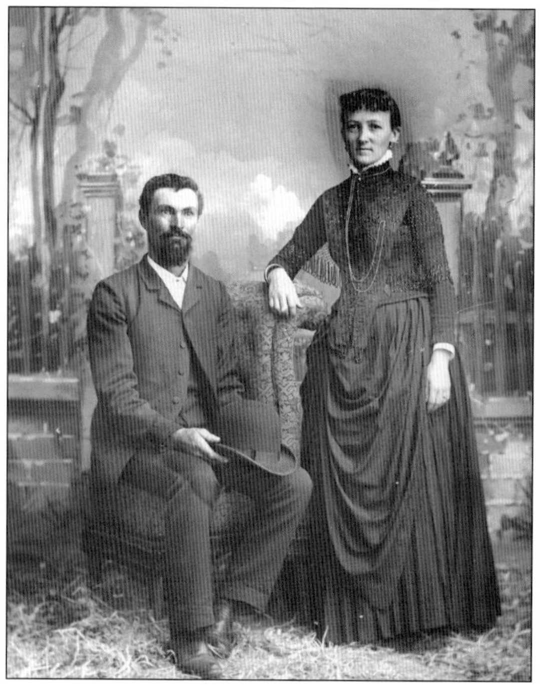

KELSEYS. William Henry and Selina Beddoes Kelsey were married in the Salt Lake Endowment House on August 23, 1883. William loved to hunt wild chickens and deer. He caught fish from the lake, and all this meat filled his cellar. He often won the local shooting matches, and the winning prize was a turkey. In Selina's biography, their daughter Effie shares that their evenings were mostly the same: mother would knit or sew, and father would read to her. The children would sit in the dining room studying. (GEA photograph, courtesy of the Springville Historical Society.)

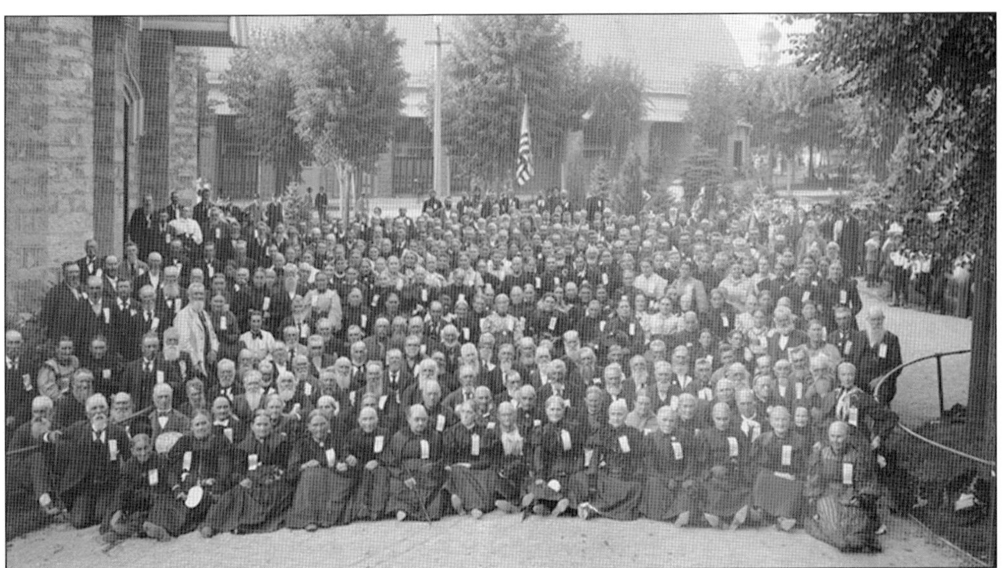

Pioneers and the Relief Society Gatherings. Pictured above is the Mormon Pioneer Jubilee celebration on July 24, 1897, in Salt Lake City. The Salt Lake Tabernacle is in the background. These individuals sacrificed and overcame incredible odds to make the journey westward and find their freedom of religion. George Anderson noted in his diary that he purposely tried to make the photograph show the individual faces of the pioneers. The Relief Society of the Second Ward for the Church of Jesus Christ of Latter-day Saints is pictured below on February 25, 1915, after a reorganization occurred within the ward. Many changes had taken place in the 32 years since it was formed. From left to right are (first row) Bishop Bringhurst, Ida Alleman, Willis Harmer, Ellen Harmer, Mrs. John Groesbeck, Ellen K. Wheeler, Sabina Alleman, Emily Crandall, Mahalia Bringhurst, Susie Boyer, Mrs. Burges Alleman, Mrs. John Sumsion, Jennie Hyde, and Mrs. Wiscombe; (second row) George Hyde, Olive Anderson, Mary Childs, Mrs. Shepherd, Ann Robinson, Caroline Bissell, Mrs. Clark, Lyda Crandall, Julia Friel Anthon, Mrs. Thomas Snelson, Mrs. Liss Curtis, Ada B. Harrison, Mrs. Wright, Ida Strong, Jane Dalton, Mrs. Balantyne, Mrs. Miner, Dora Crandall, Zina Crandall, Mrs. John Alleman, Mrs. Jonie Alleman, and Ray and Jennie Pierce. The building on the left in the background with the steeple was originally built as an Episcopalian church, but the congregation could not be sustained, and eventually the LDS Church acquired the building. It became known as the Elders Hall. (Above, GEA photograph, courtesy of the DUP; below, courtesy of the Springville Historical Society.)

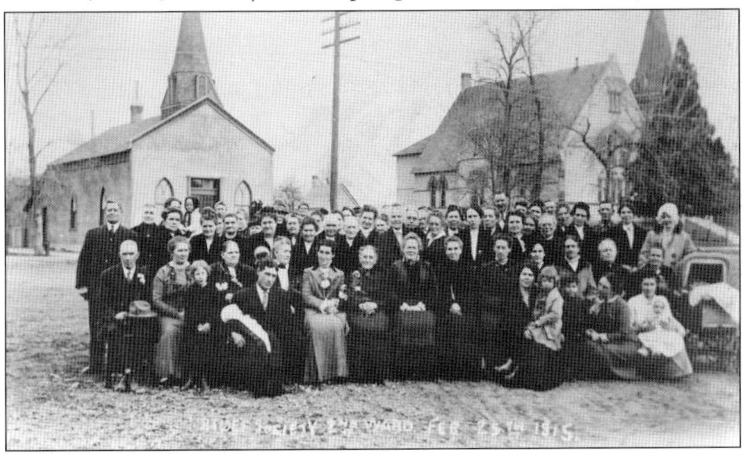

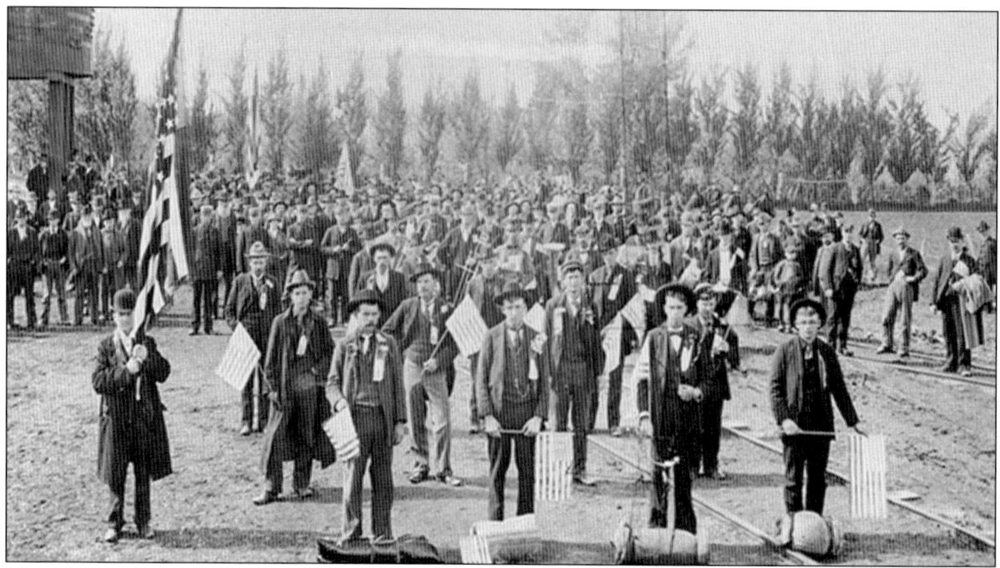

Off to War. Residents gather at the Denver & Rio Grande Western Depot to bid farewell to boys leaving to join the US Army to fight in the Spanish-American War in the Philippines on May 5, 1898. The Springville Band can be seen, along with the water tank by the train depot. Some of the young men in front are Sam Dallin, Ainer Humphrey, Ezra Oakley, Stanley Staton, Evans Chase, Anthony Ether, Frank Harmer, Elliott Jordan, and Will Tipton. Memorial Park is named after all the veterans from Springville who defended their nation. (GEA photograph, courtesy of the Springville Historical Society.)

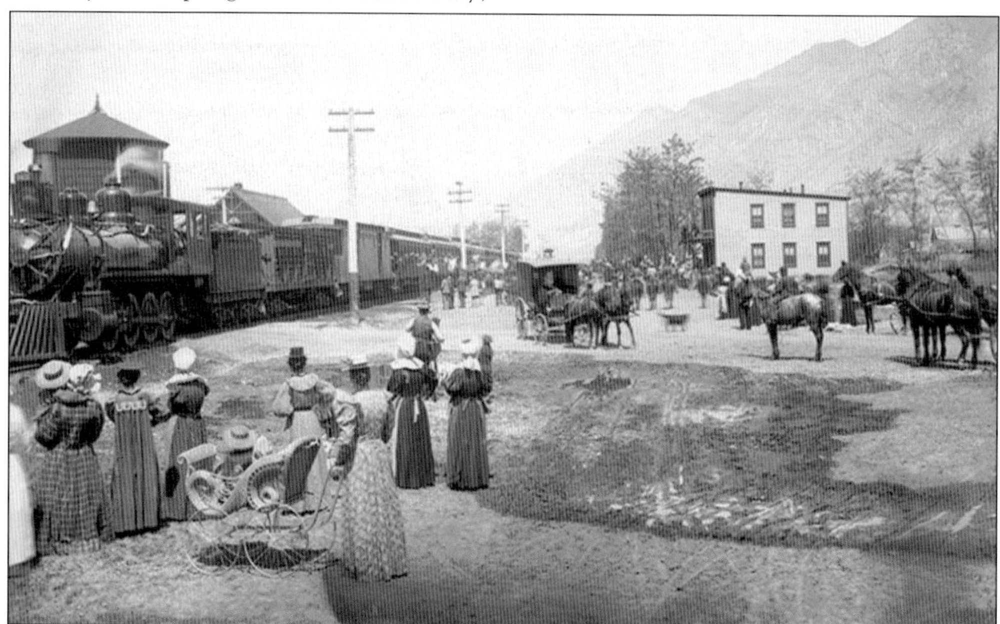

Train Station Welcome. Residents gather at 400 West and Second South Street in 1899 to welcome home the Spanish-American War veterans. The conflict between Spain and the United States lasted from April 25 to August 12, 1898. The Treaty of Paris ceded ownership of Puerto Rico, Guam, and the Philippine Islands to the United States. Spain also relinquished sovereignty over Cuba. (GEA photograph, courtesy of the Springville Historical Society.)

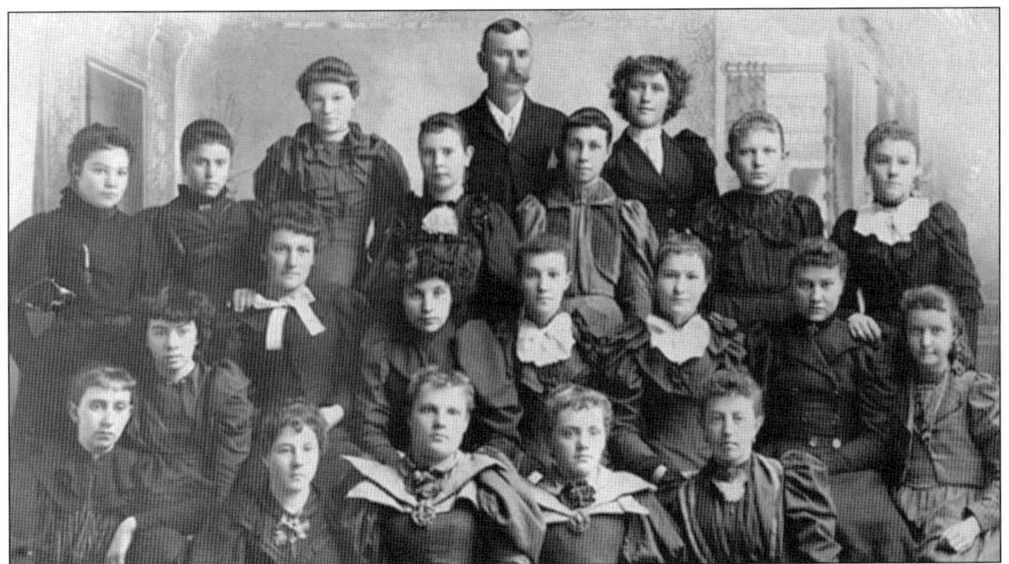

Sunday School Class. David Curtis's women's Sunday school class is pictured around January 1895. From left to right are (first row) May Lisonbee Packard, Rita Oakley Sumsion, Christie Sumsion Lee, and Nell Lisonbee; (second row) Mattie Caffrey Stone, Ella Storrs, Minnie C. Jensen, Ada Packard, Ida Rowland Weight, Amy Rowland Worthen, Myrtle Hall Harrison, and Emma Giles; (third row) Allie Averett Allen, Maud Curtis Roylance, Maggie Barnett Noakes, unidentified, David Curtis, Effie Kate Stevenson, Ms. Carlson, and Lottie Averett Hall. Sunday school classes meet once a week to discuss religious topics. (Courtesy of the DUP.)

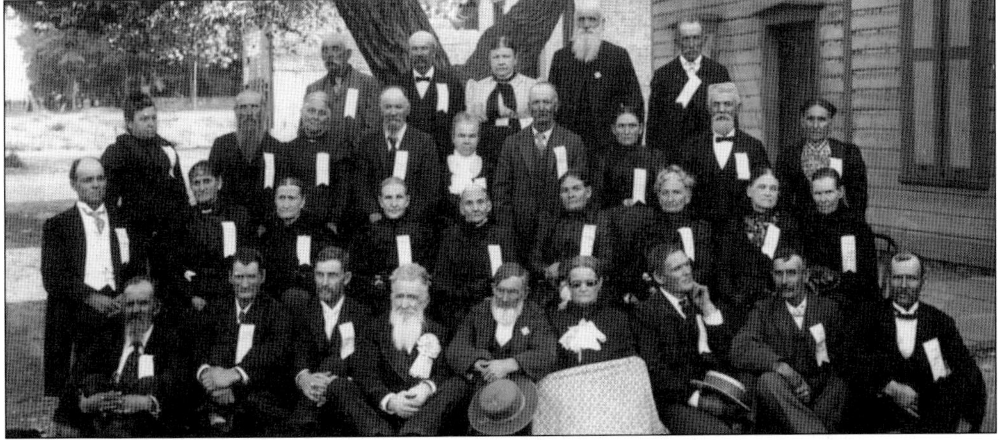

Pioneers' 50th Anniversary. September 18, 1900, commemorated the 50th anniversary of Springville and the surviving pioneers. Pictured at 75 North Main Street are, from left to right, (first row) Amos Warren, Cyrus Sanford Jr., Willis K. Johnson Jr., George Matson, Levi Kendall, Eliza Kendall, Aaron Johnson Jr., LeRoy Bird, and Myron Edgar Crandall; (second row) Don C. Johnson, Melissa Sanford Messenger, Sylvia Sanford, Laura C. Johnson Bird, Eliza Crandall Deal, Mary Deal Mendendhall, Mary Ann Johnson, Marilla Johnson Daniels Miller, and Julia Crandall Boyer; (third row) Tryphena Perry Whitney, William Smith, Polly Maria Perry Smith, Henry Roylance, Mary Francis Roylance Nelson, Alma Roylance, Emma Mendenhall Roylance, William Roylance, and Zebina Starr Alleman; (fourth row) Proctor Humphrey, Alma Spafford, Ann Bringhurst Houtz, LDS bishop George R. Hill, and Benjamin Blanchard. (GEA photograph, courtesy of the Springville Historical Society.)

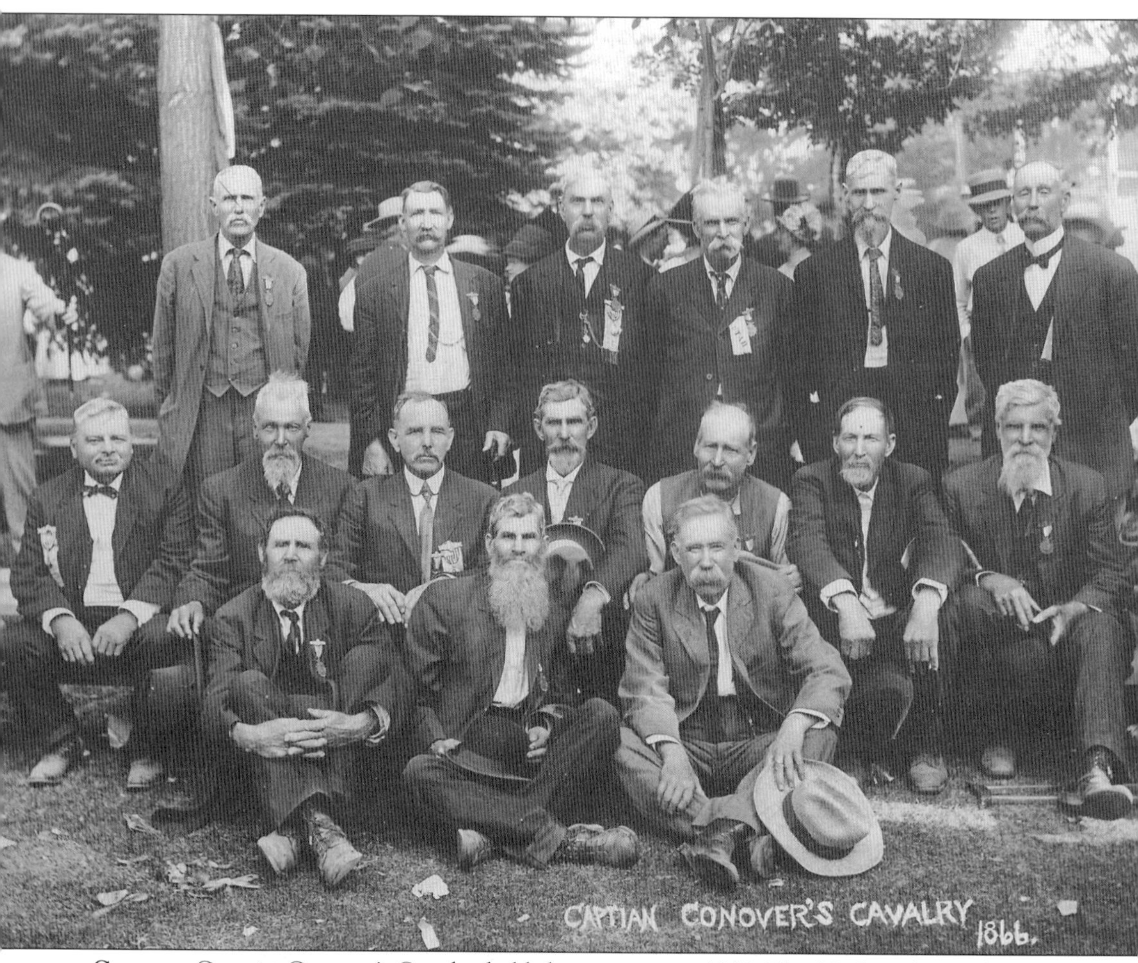

Cavalry. Captain Conover's Cavalry held this reunion in 1866. The Utah Militia volunteered during the Black Hawk Indian War. From left to right are (first row) John Henry Tanner, Edward Alma Bagley, and John Harvey Moore; (second row) unidentified, Mathew Henry Daley, three unidentified, Elijah Hancock, and William Loveless; (third row) Enoch Monk, John Staheli, and four unidentified. (Courtesy of the Springville Historical Society.)

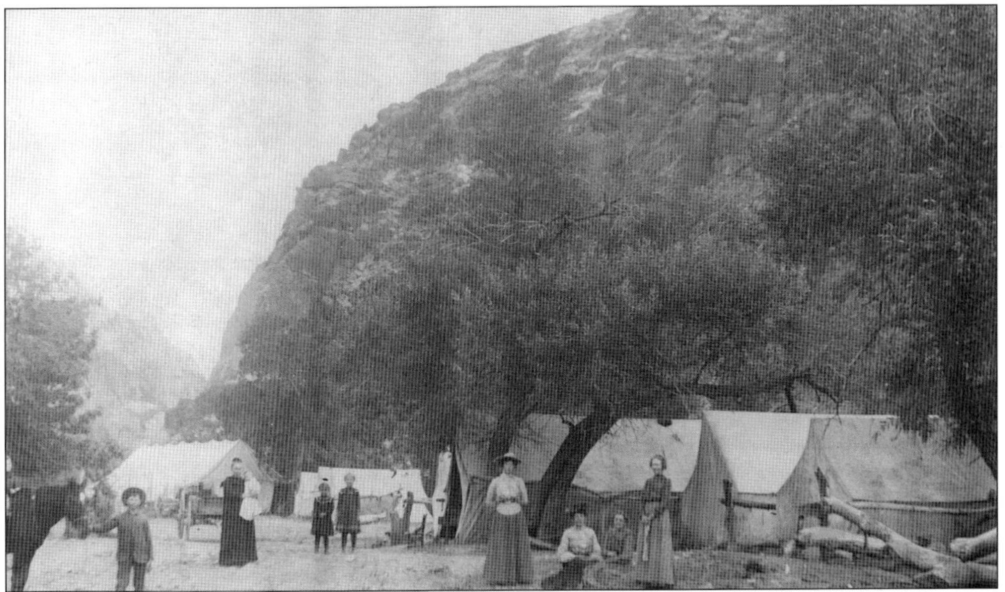

Diamond Fork. Camping in the Diamond Fork Canyon area, the Thorn family and friends are enjoying the countryside. The Thorns came to Springville in 1857 and shared a one-room house for a whole year with their friends the Chase family. The two families used their wagons for bedrooms until other arrangements could be made for the Chases. (Courtesy of the DUP.)

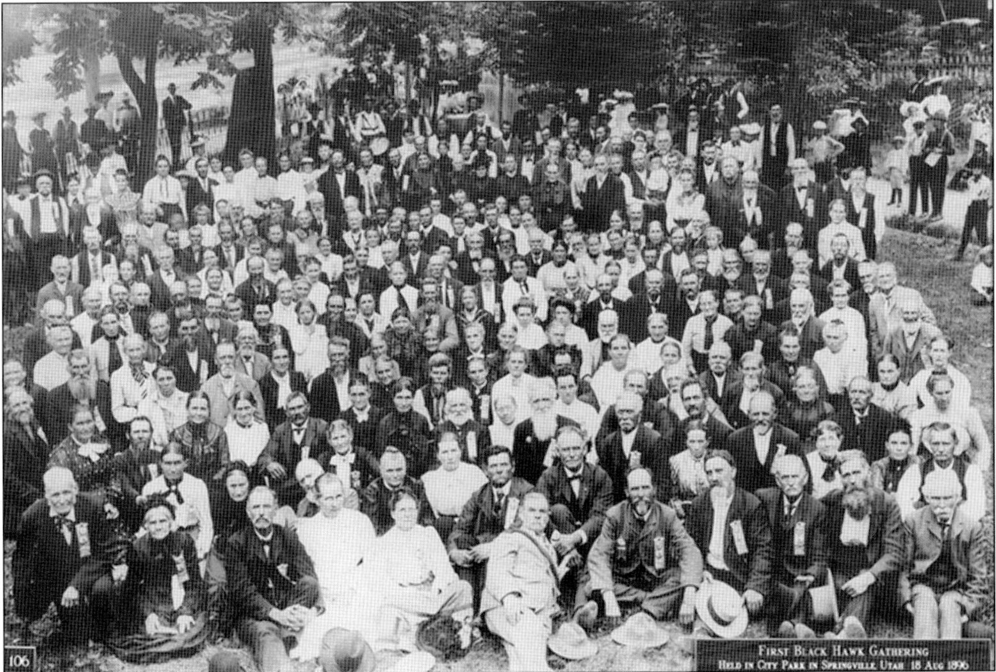

Black Hawk Gathering. Veterans of the first Black Hawk War (1865–1872) and family members gathered at the City Park in Springville on August 18, 1896. During the war, an estimated 150 battles, skirmishes, raids, and killings occurred between the Mormons and the Ute, Paiute, and Navajo tribes led by the Ute chief Antonga, or "Blackhawk." (GEA photograph, courtesy of the Springville Historical Society.)

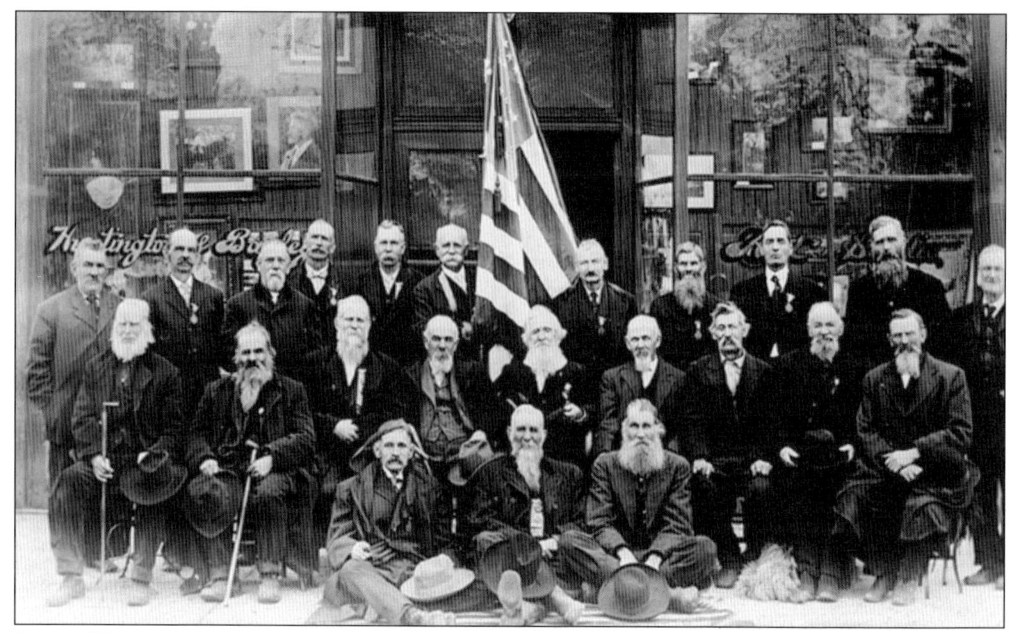

Black Hawk War Veterans Committee. From left to right are (first row) George McKenzie, Milan Packard, and J.H. Noakes; (second row) William Clyde, Amos Warren, Nephi Packard, John Lowery, George Matson, James Oakley, John Conover, Henry Roylance, and Moroni Miner; (third row) Moroni Fuller, Walter Wheeler, Frank Beardall, Don Huntington, Moses Devere Childs, Tom Brown, Hyrum Scoville, Elial Curtis, Samuel Buckley, Albert Harmer, and Edwin Lee. The Black Hawk War Veterans Committee petitioned the government to render services to the veterans. This is a Huntington Bagley photograph, and their studio building is in the background. (Courtesy of the Springville Historical Society.)

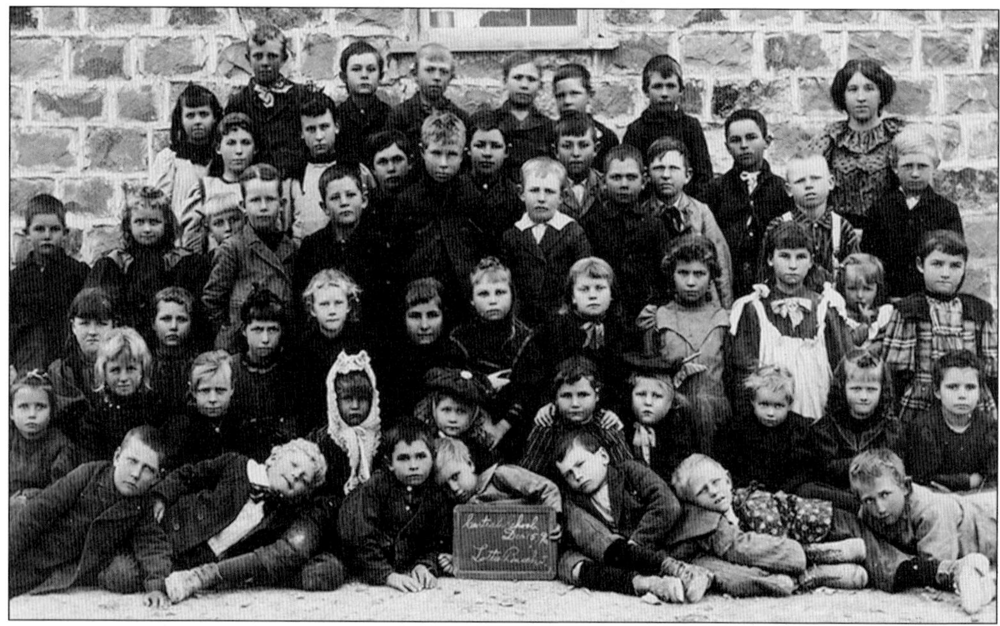

School Class Picture. Pictured is a class from the Central School taught by Lottie Busch on December 15, 1896. (Courtesy of the DUP.)

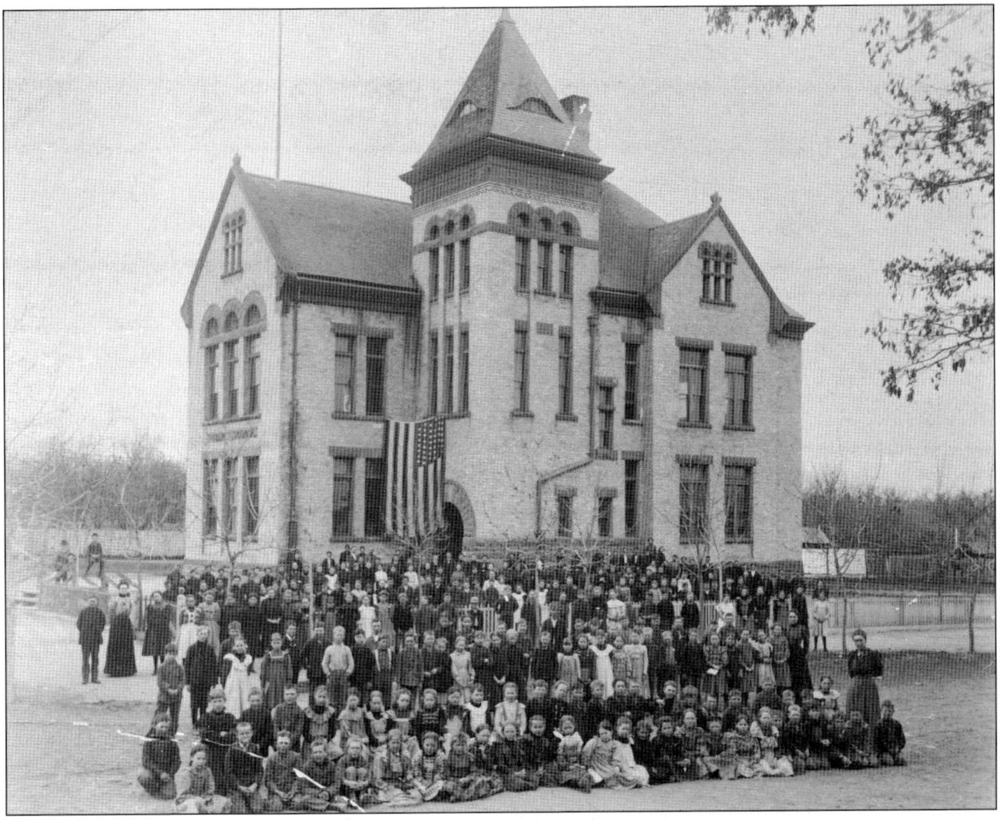

Washington School. Washington School was at first called the Central School and was at 300 South and 200 East. This school replaced the First District School. In 1937, the building materials from the demolished school were used in the construction of Springville High School's new gymnasium. (GEA photograph, courtesy of the Springville Historical Society.)

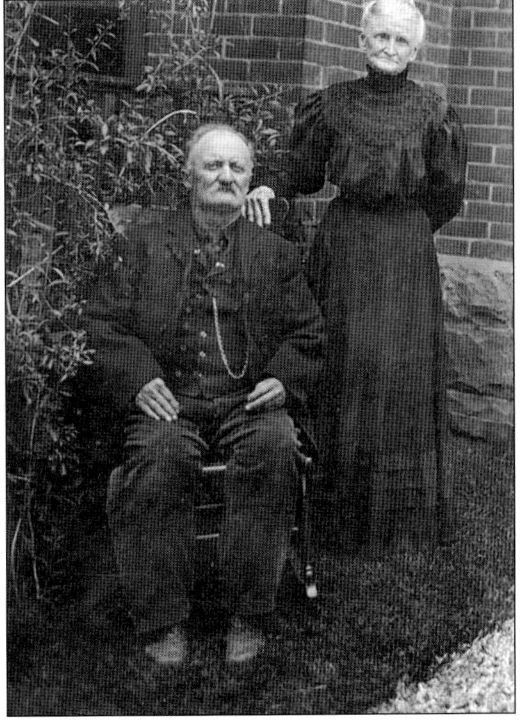

Siblings. Pictured are Cassius Glines, age 65, and his sister, Harriet Anna Glines Thorn, age 82. Harriet was visiting Cassius in Denver during the summer of 1908; they had not seen each other since they were very young. Harriet, her husband, Richard, and three of their children arrived in Springville in 1857. Glines was a Union soldier in the Civil War. (Courtesy of the DUP.)

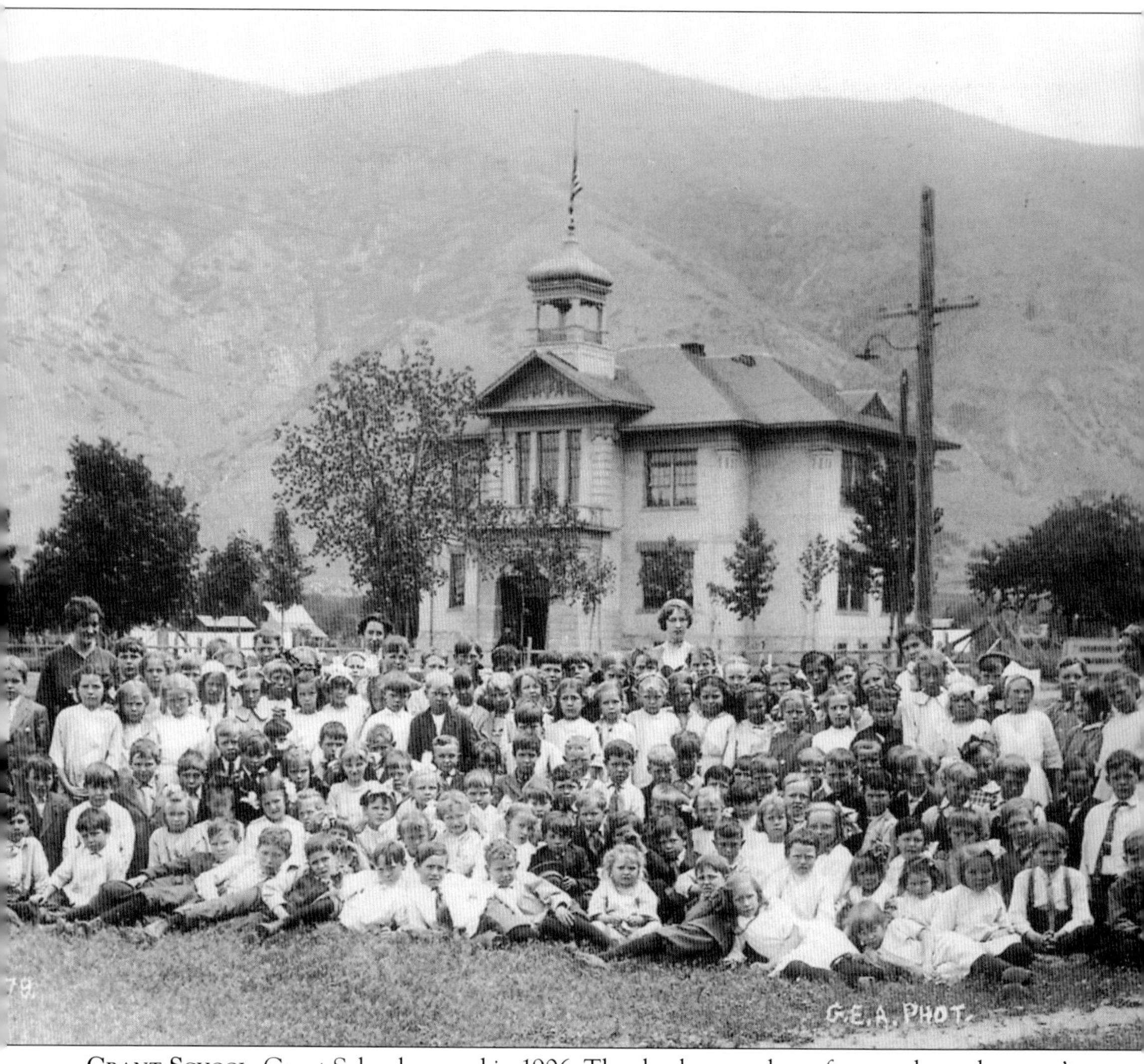

GRANT SCHOOL. Grant School opened in 1906. The shrubs served as a fence to keep the town's cows out of the yard, as they were herded past morning and night. The bell tower was removed in later years, and this school stood until the 1970s. A new Grant Elementary School was built in its place, and in 2006, the students were moved to another school. The building now houses special education offices and other district services, but no students. Springville boasts the first accredited public high school in Utah County. The city is also credited with the first junior high school in the state. (GEA photograph, courtesy of the Springville Historical Society.)

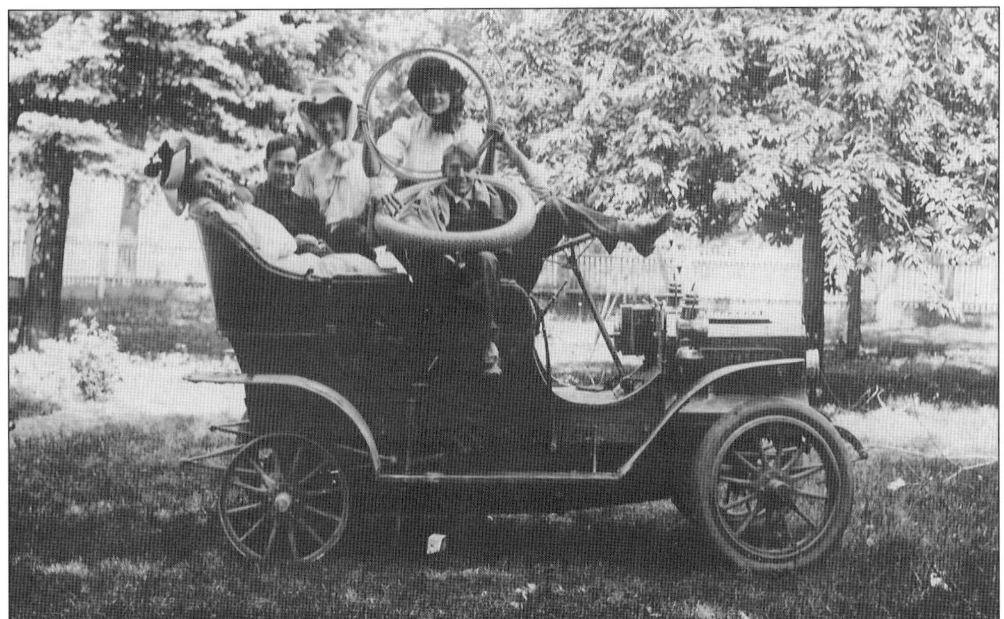

Electric Car. Here is Springville's first electric car, owned by Dr. Reynolds. He married Dora Brinton, and they were the parents of three children. From left to right are Floss, son Evan Reynolds, Zell, daughter Naomi Reynolds, and Mr. Farney. (Courtesy of the Springville Historical Society.)

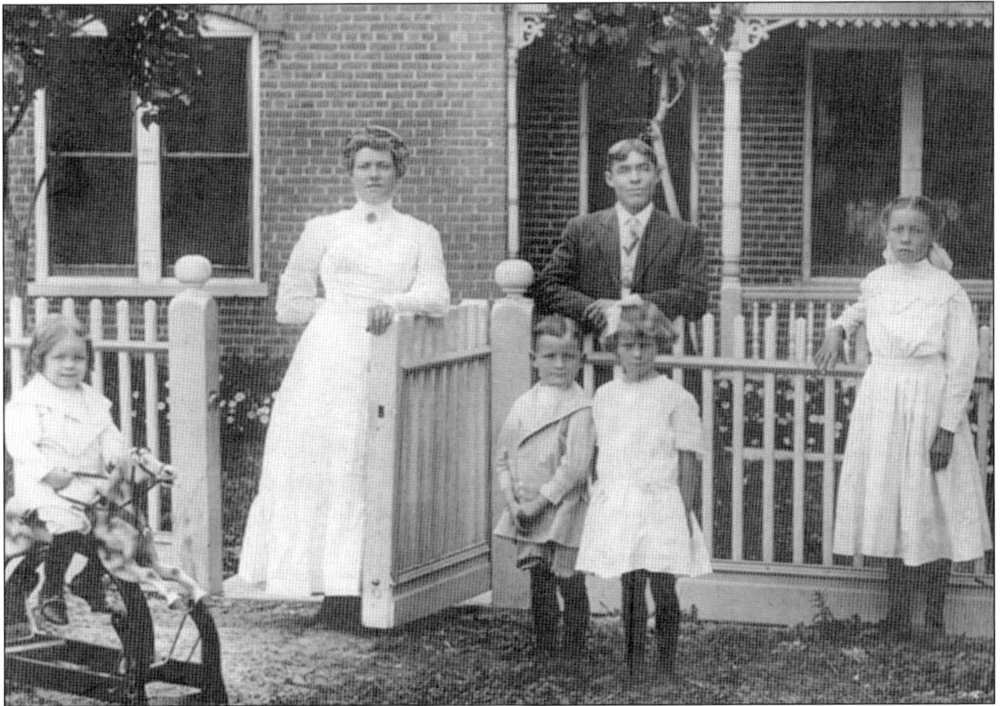

Family Picture. Bertha Alice Barnett Payne and Frederick John Payne are by the gate. In front of the fence are, from left to right, Jessie on the horse toy, Raymond, Lottie, and Edditha. Frederick was born on February 23, 1874, in Ontario, Canada, and all his children were born in Springville. (Courtesy of the DUP.)

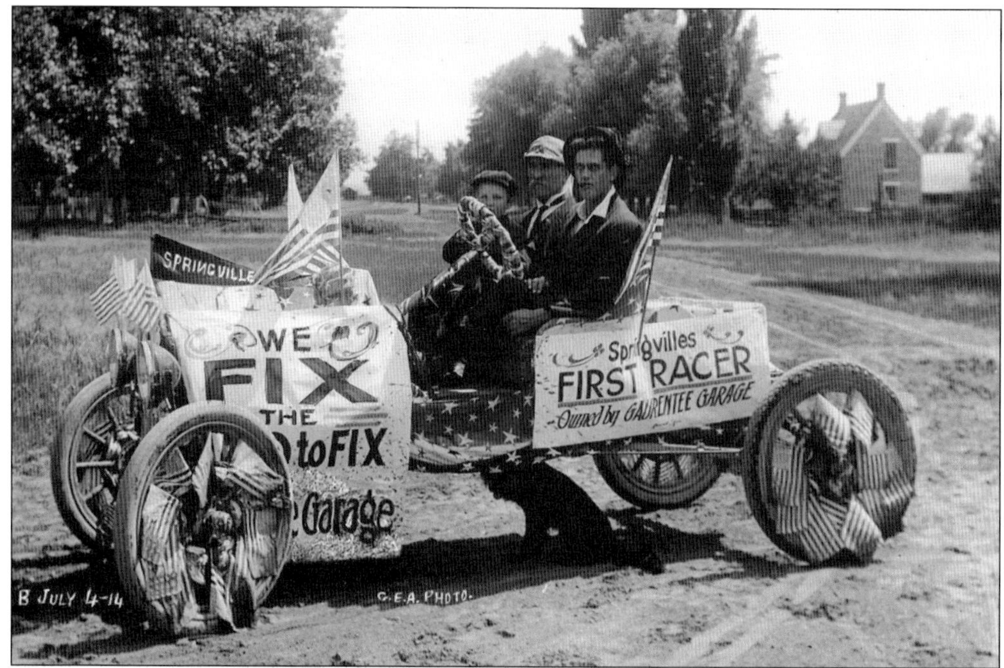

First Racer Car. Independence Day, 1914, is celebrated in Springville with its first racer car. Flags adorn the vehicle, and the men are poised to have a grand time in the parade, which would also feature horses, buggies, and dusty roads. Springville for many years celebrated two events in July, Independence Day on July 4 and Pioneer Day on July 24. (GEA photograph, courtesy of the Springville Historical Society.)

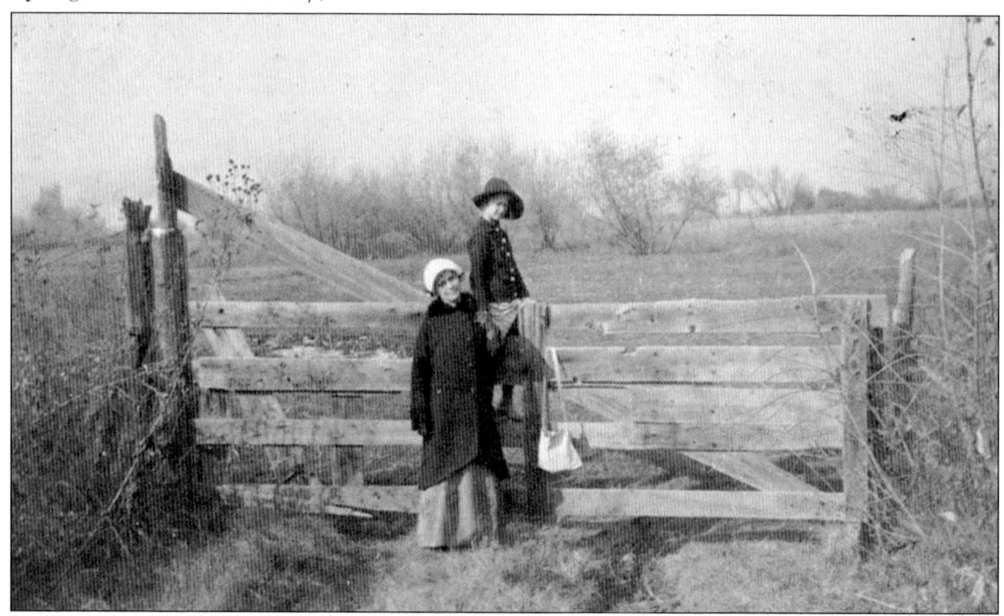

Children and Fence. Juanita Johnson Beck (left) and Helene Clark are on a school field trip. Helene's parents were James Monroe Clark and Drucilla Kast. James Clark, seen on the next page, was a carpenter who lived to be 75 years old. He was born in Iowa on August 26, 1861, and came to Springville in 1864. (Courtesy of the DUP.)

James Clark and Accordion. James Monroe Clark plays his accordion. Music was a blessed relief to many saints during the pioneer era; it was relaxing and joyful after a hard day's work. LDS prophet Brigham Young believed that "music can fill the air with harmony, comfort the hearts of men, and has a magical cheerful effect." This picture was taken in 1899. (Courtesy of the DUP.)

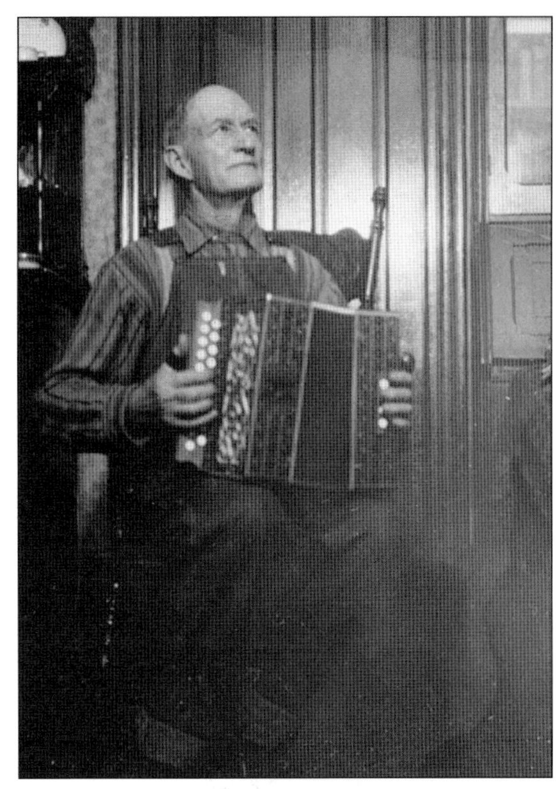

Cleanup Day. In this photograph of the annual cleanup day, everyone is taking a break. On the left, on the horse, are Lue Maycock and Jen Chase. From left to right are (first row) Ann Hutchins, Ella Condie, unidentified, Sarah White, Ella Deal, Maude Thorn, Lars E. Eggertson, and Clara Cherrington; (second row) Floyd Miner, Earl Crandall, Reed Bird, Tillie Wheeler, and Prudence Cherrington. (Courtesy of the DUP.)

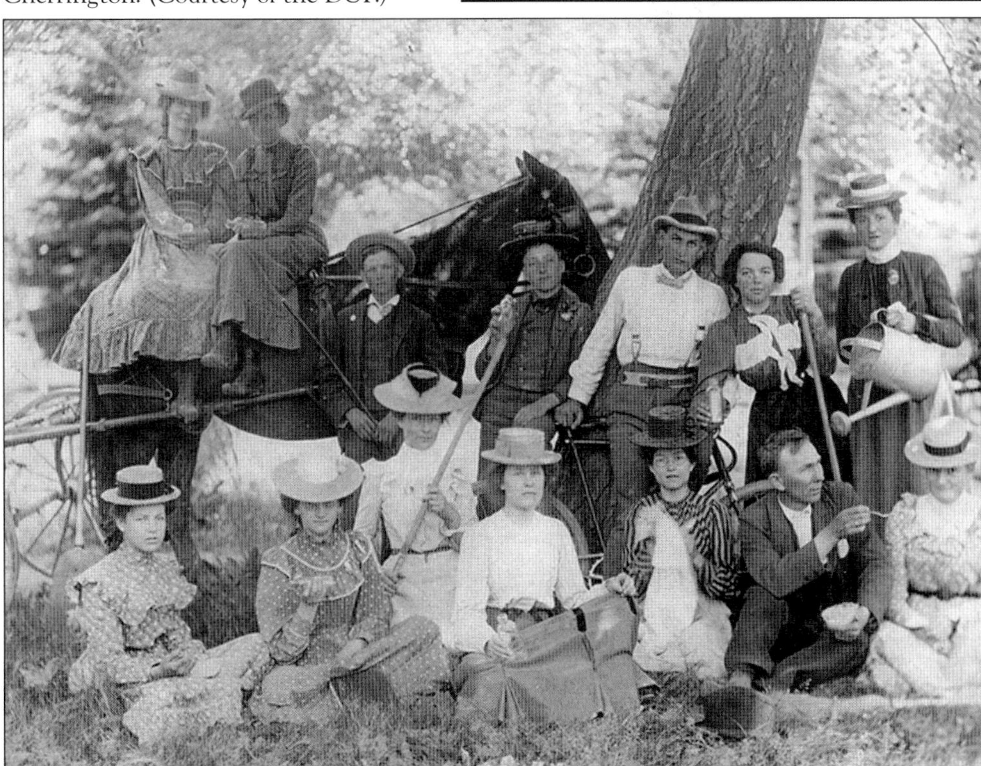

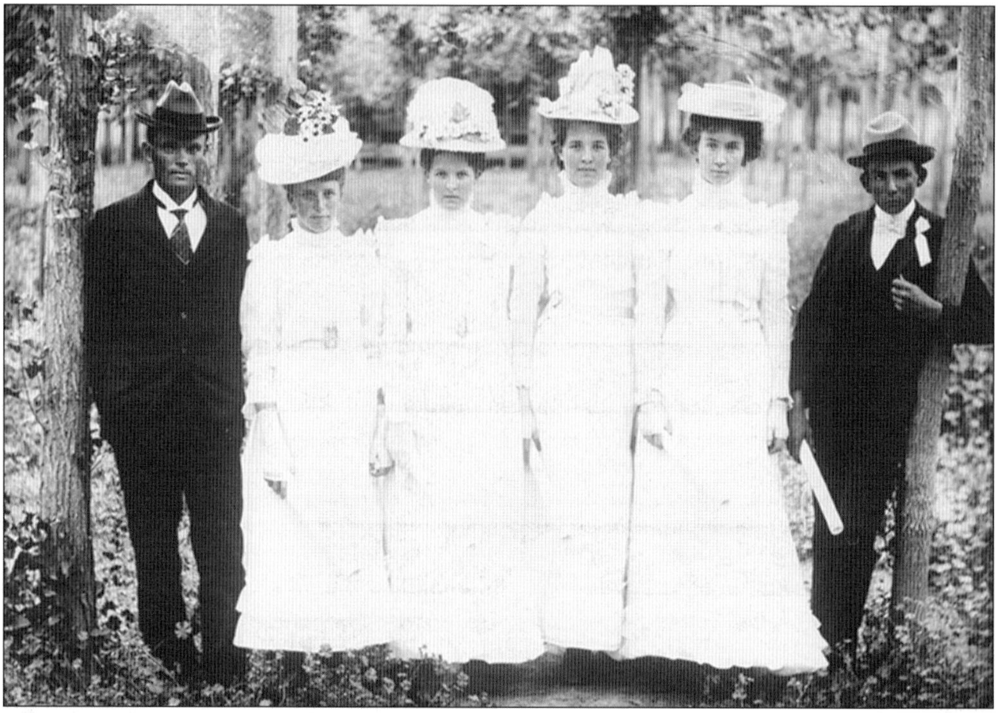

Mapleton Graduates. Mapleton does not have a high school, so students attend high school in one of the neighboring cities, divided up by school district boundaries. Charter and private schools are also available. Pictured with these graduating Mapleton students in the early 1900s is teacher Wayne Johnson. (GEA photograph, courtesy of the Springville Historical Society.)

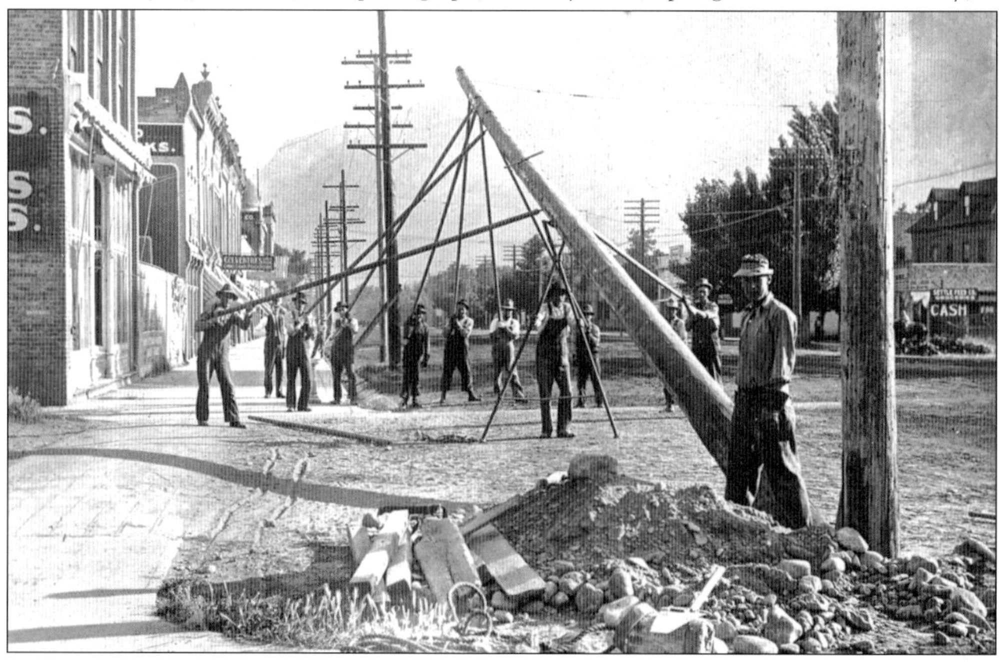

Power Poles. Workmen are erecting power poles at 300 South Main looking north in 1914. (Courtesy of M. Lee Taylor.)

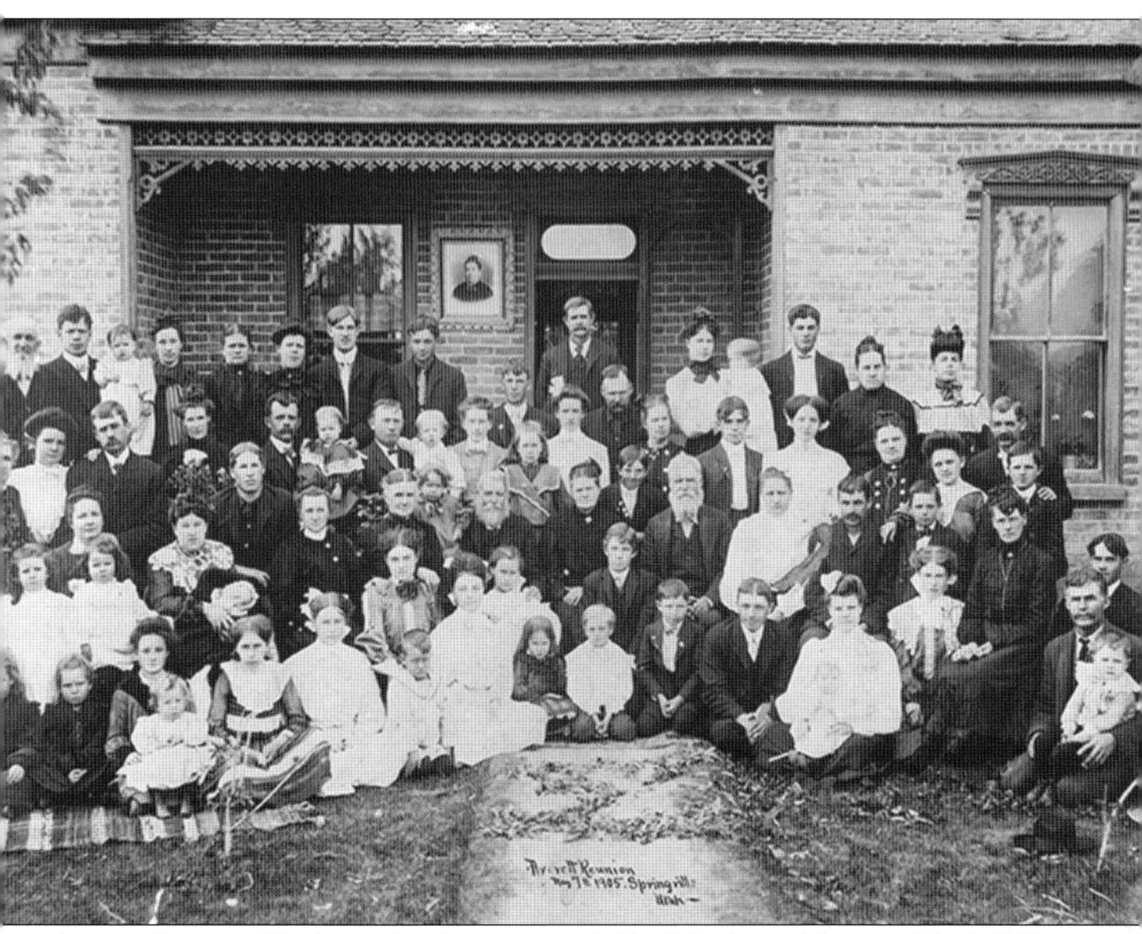

AVERETT REUNION. The Averett family reunion was held at Tobe Averett's house on May 4, 1905. From left to right are (first row) Zelma Averett (Barker Christiansen), Bessie Averett (Benson Gourley), Eva Averett (holding brother Edd), Flossie Johnson (Kates), Bertha Clyde (Fullmer), Leland Strong, McKenzie Johnson (behind Leland), Florence Johnson, Theo Strong (Thorpe), Grace Johnson, Bessie Strong (Averett, behind Grace), Elmo Allen (son of Will and Allie Averett Allen), Rufus Averett (behind Elmo), Lester Averett, Charlie Averett, Hilda Marshbanks Averett (with baby), Pearl Averett (Hall), Charlotte Weight Averett, John F. Averett (holding son), Fred Averett, and Ruel Averett (behind Fred); (second row) Minnie Averett (Barker), Mary Alice Mason Averett (holding Nora Averett), Joe Johnson (holding baby), Jim Hardy, Florence Clyde Johnson, Mary Farnworth Clyde, Sarah Spafford (with thumb wrapped), Jim Clyde, Jessie Spafford, Alice Farnworth Averett, Jay Averett, Jeduthun "Tobe" Hardy Averett, Lydia Ann Mason Averett, Johny Averett, and Norise Averett; (third row) Georgeanna Clark, Janie Averett Mason, George Edward Averett, Edna Hall Wheeler, Benny Wheeler (holding baby), Alma Spafford (holding his son Ray Spafford), Molly Clyde Spafford, Sol Clyde, Ida Clyde, Phillip Beard, Effie Averett Beard (Johnson), Jess Shepherd, Hazel Averett Shepherd, Lizy Perry Averett, Nellie Averett (Childs), Hardy Averett, and Tom Averett; (fourth row) John Davis Clark Sr., David Wheeler (holding baby), Zelda Lambson Wheeler, Jane Averett Wheeler, May Wheeler Jackson, Charlie Jackson, George Wheeler, John Davis Clark Jr. (in doorway), Jettie Averett Groesbeck, (holding her son Floyd), Frank Groesbeck, Olive Whiting Averett, and Myrtle Averett (Holt). Jane Singleton Farnworth Averett's picture is on the wall. The Averett family has a street named after them in Springville. (Courtesy of the Springville Historical Society.)

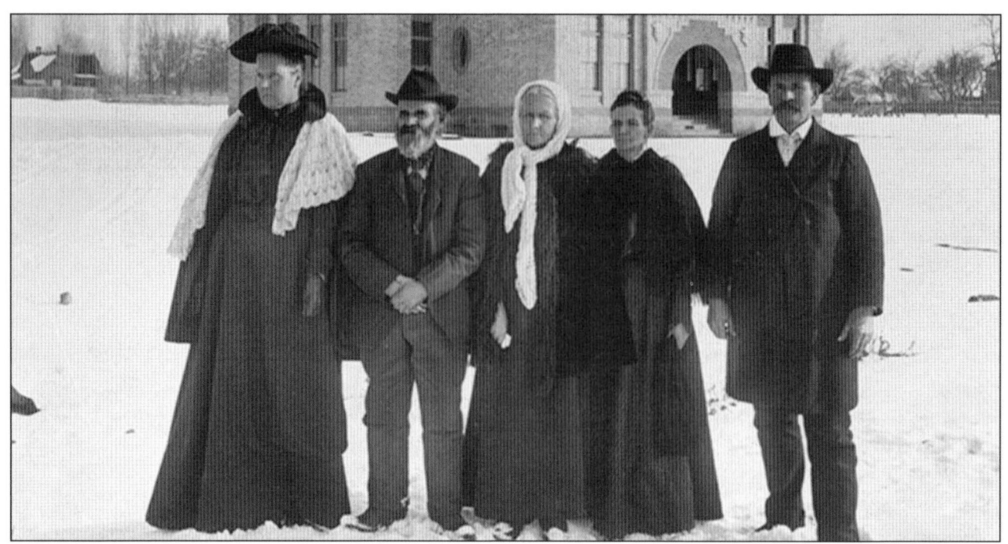

Golden Wedding Anniversary. From left to right are Sarah Jane Simmons, Amos Sweet Warren, Abigail Ardilla Childs Warren, Sarah Ardilla Warren Wordsworth, and Amos Benoni Warren (son of Amos and Abigail) at the same place where Amos and Abigail were married 50 years earlier. The picture was taken on January 1, 1903, and the Jefferson School was built on this spot in 1902. This school is still standing, now named the Jefferson Center. Amos kept a portion of his farm reserved as a campground for his Native American friends. He was well respected and knew many of the great chiefs of his day. They would visit for dinner, and his children had to wait to eat while the guests were fed. (Courtesy of the Springville Historical Society.)

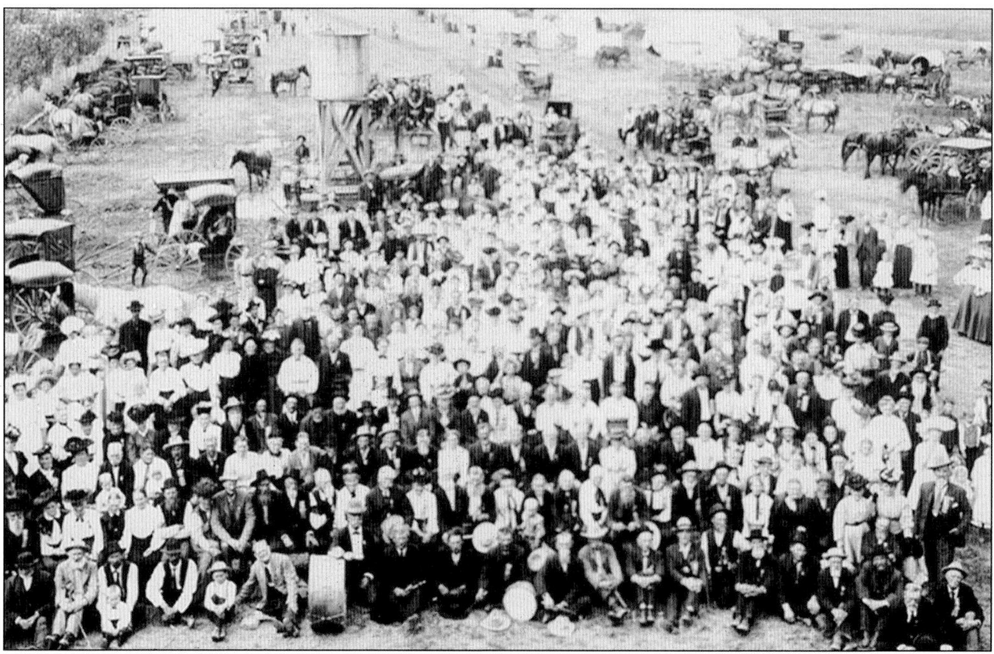

War Veterans Gathering. The Indian War veterans had annual gatherings to commemorate the wars and celebrate as families their freedoms in various venues around the area. This photograph was taken at the Provo Lake Shore Resort on August 30, 1906. (GEA photograph, courtesy of the Springville Historical Society.)

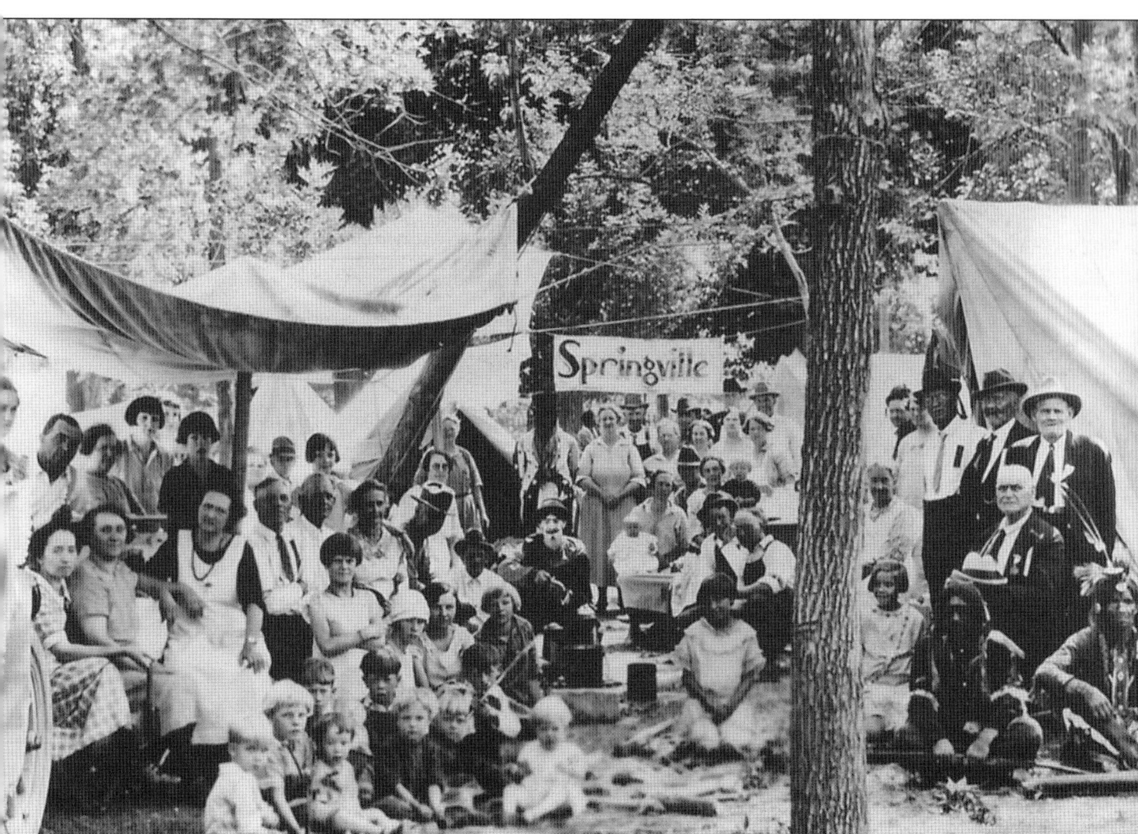

Black Hawk Days. The Springville Black Hawk Days gathering is pictured on August 14, 1923. In the picture are Ella Whiting, Dorothy Weller, Lise Parry Averett, Hardy Averett, Leona Averett Wilson, John Whiting, Bese Strong Averett, Tom Averett, Marie Alleman, Will Child, Nille Averett Child, Von Averett, Alma Fuller, Wills Strong, John Barney, two Native Americans who were passing by, Maureen Fullmer, Herald Averett, Verl Child, and Wilda Fullmer Ridgy. (Courtesy of the Springville Historical Society.)

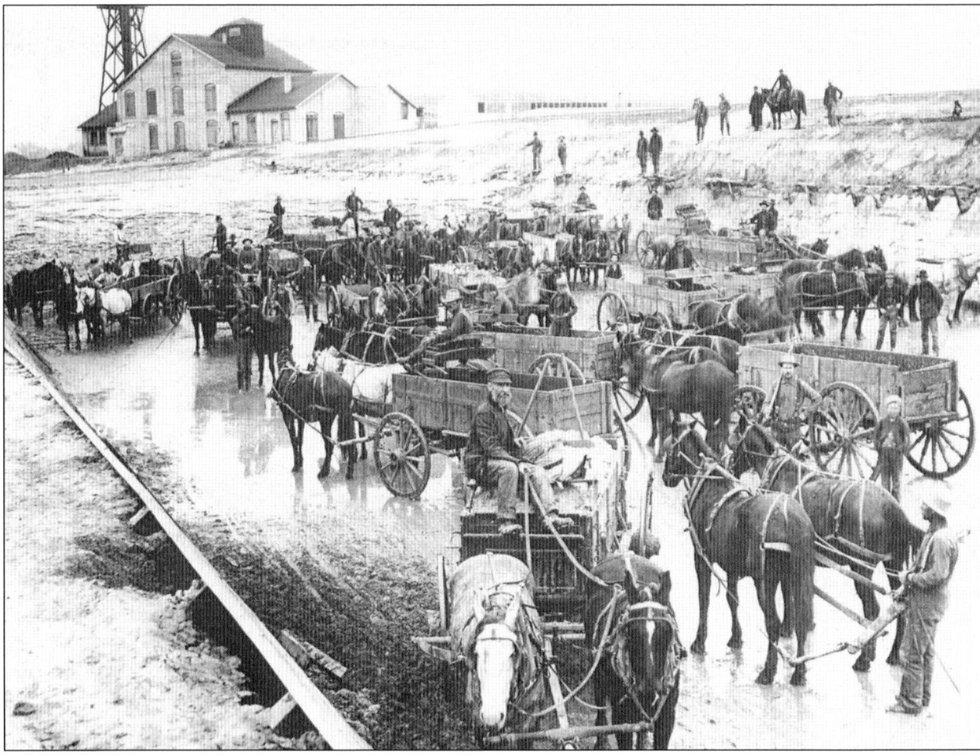

SUGAR BEET FACTORY. Springville's sugar beet factory and silage pit are shown here. Utah became one of the first states to successfully manufacture refined sugar from sugar beet crops. Above, around 1900, is the pulp or silage, a by-product of the refining process; it was loaded from the pit and fed to livestock. Below, the inside of the plant is pictured on December 8, 1925. (Both, GEA photographs, courtesy of the Springville Historical Society.)

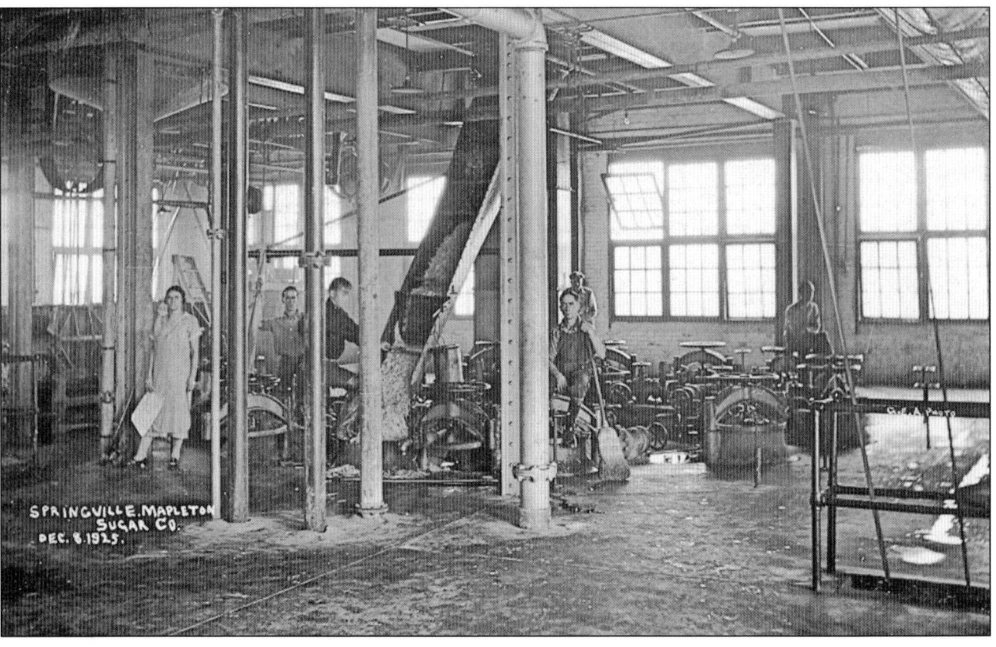

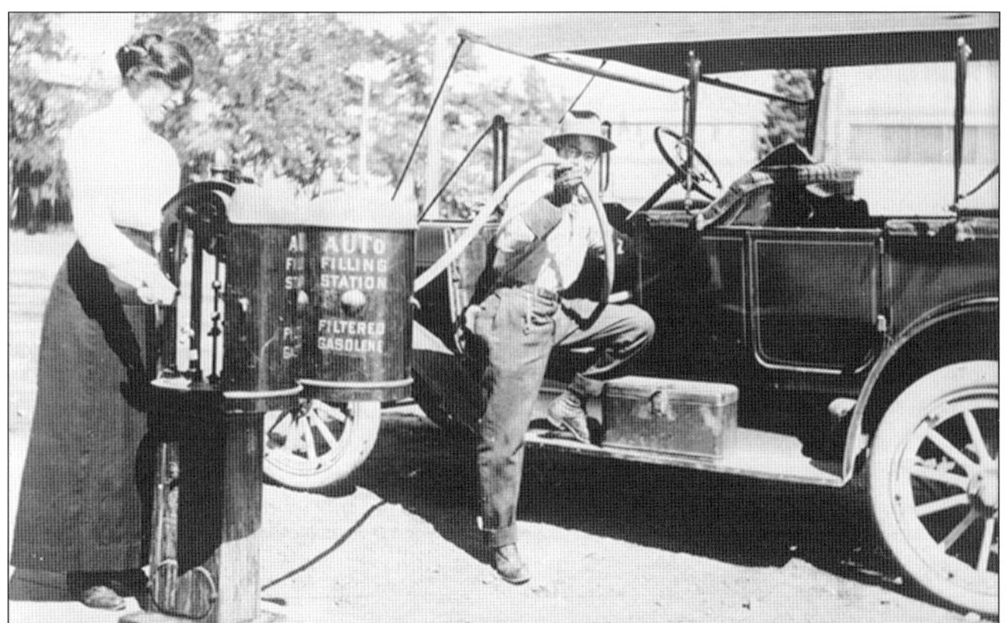

Filling Station. This filling station was at the rear of the SOS Drug Store. Clara Benson was on hand to help the man fill up his automobile with gas. The SOS Drug Store is still in business in the downtown area. (Courtesy of the DUP.)

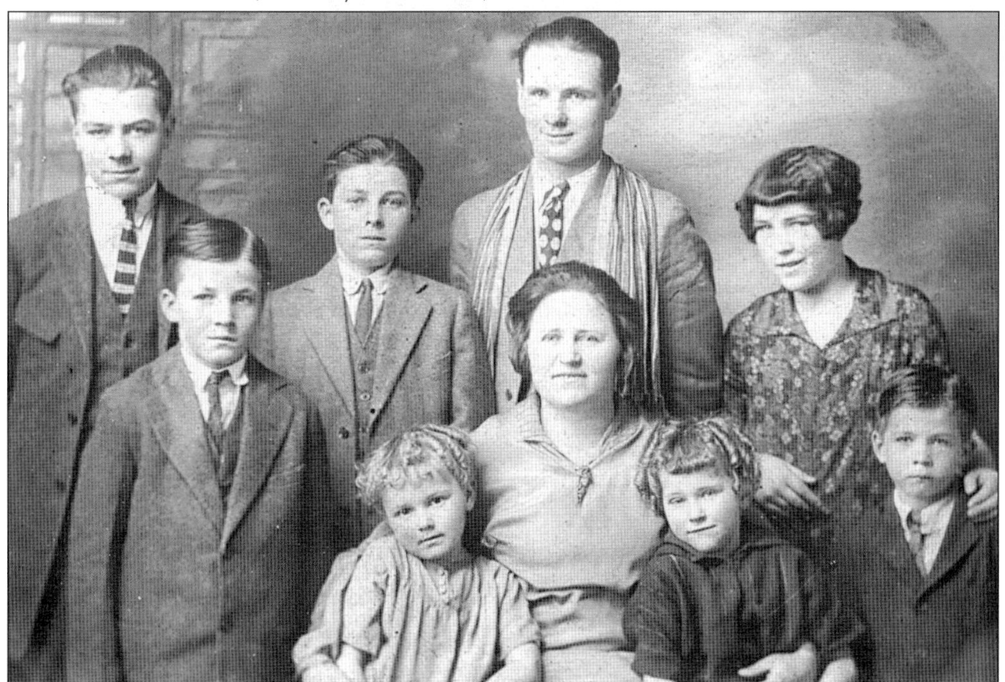

Childs. From left to right around 1927 are (first row) Thelma Moselle Childs Mayne Bair and Ada Childs Taylor, M. Lee Taylor's mother; (second row) Robert Acil Roundy, Cassie D. Fullmer Roundy Childs (sitting), and Edmund H. Roundy; (third row) Edmund Eugene Roundy, Samuel Alonzo Roundy, Parley Elias Fullmer (brother of Cassie), and Myrle Roundy Fowler. (Courtesy of M. Lee Taylor.)

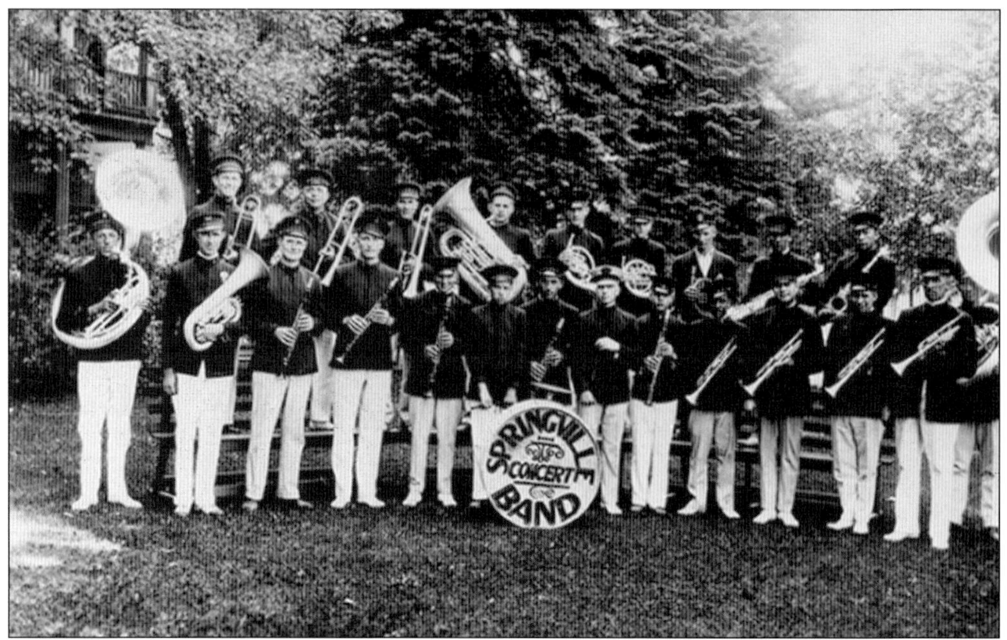

Band. Springville High School's concert band is pictured in the 1920s. The school was established in 1902. There are two high schools currently in Springville. (Courtesy of the DUP.)

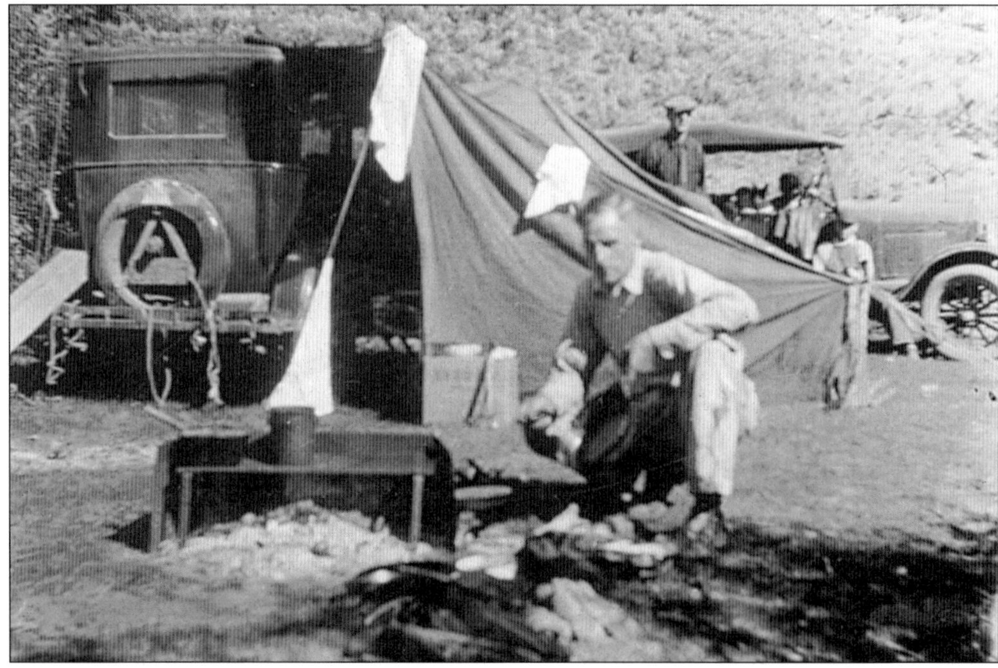

Car Tent Camping. John Jansen is next to the fire pit. They are car tent camping at the Springville Crossing by Diamond Fork, which is a side canyon of Spanish Fork Canyon. In the 1920s, car camping using lean-tos and makeshift shelters was widely popular. When the price of cars dropped, the average worker could afford to own one. Thousands of families could take to the road, using their cars as mobile extensions of their homes. (Courtesy of the Springville Historical Society.)

Three

Springville's Treasures

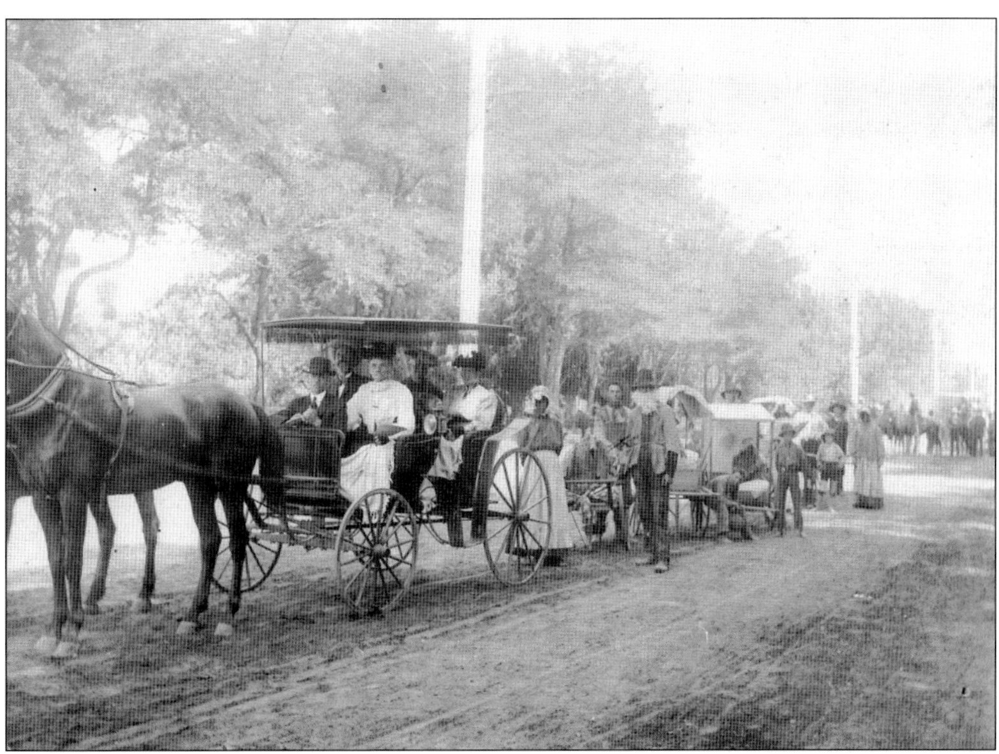

Pioneer Day. These townspeople are dressed up for the annual Pioneer Day celebration. Pioneers arrived in Utah on July 24, 1847. Currently, Mapleton celebrates this holiday, and Springville residents attend. The lady in white in the buggy is Mrs. Alleman. The man next to her on the left is "Beefsteak" George Harrison. The two men immediately behind the buggy are William "Billy" Wiscombe (left) and Loren H. Harmer (with the fake white beard). (Courtesy of the DUP.)

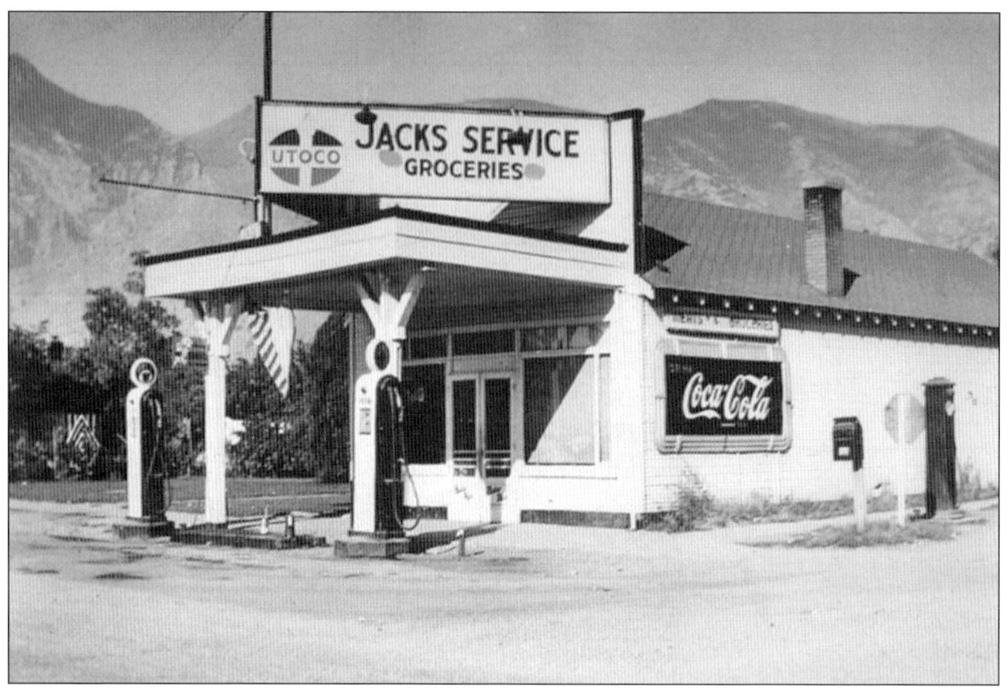

Jacks Service. Jacks Service, owned by Jack Fletcher, is pictured in the mid-1930s. The building is still in use as a barbershop; the pumps have been removed, and the building, at the corner of 700 South and Main Street, has been remodeled. (Courtesy of M. Lee Taylor.)

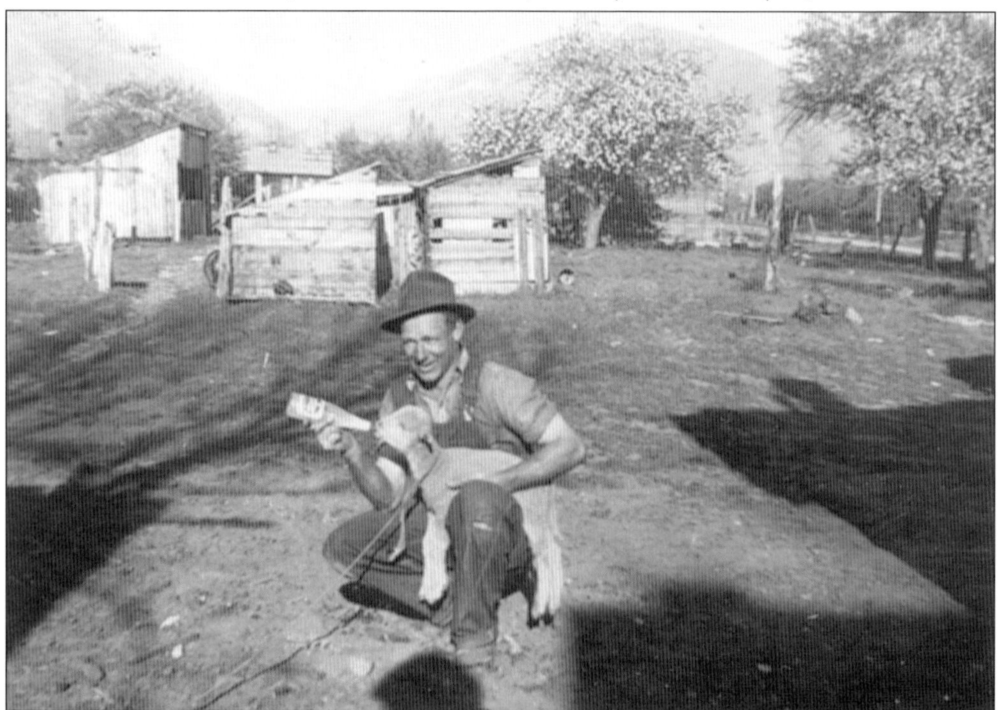

Lamb Feeding. Morris Taylor is feeding this orphaned lamb around 1942. Taylor nursed it back to health and raised it at the family home. (Courtesy of M. Lee Taylor.)

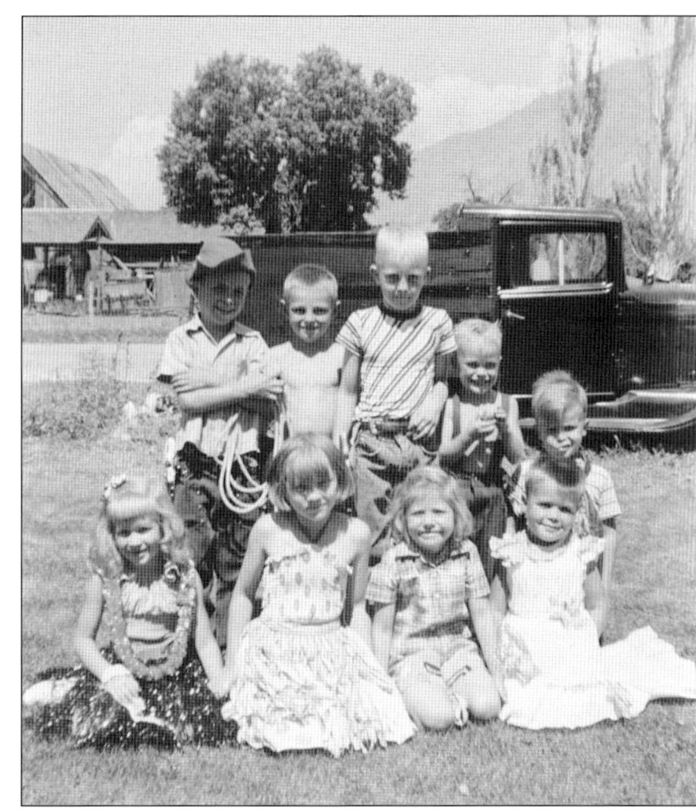

Neighbor Kids. In this 1953 photograph taken by Morris Taylor, neighborhood children have gathered for a parade. The parade was staged annually by some of the older girls of the area. It went around one block, bound by 500–600 East and 900–1000 South. The old Lewis Childs barn and shed are in the background. This photograph was taken at 450 East and 1000 South. The truck in the background belonged to Glade Tuttle. From left to right are (first row) Sandra Tuttle, Evelyn Taylor, Nina Roundy, and Steven Tuttle; (second row) Lynn Roundy, Roger Reid, Lanny Daybell, Jack Daybell, and Kay Tuttle. (Courtesy of M. Lee Taylor.)

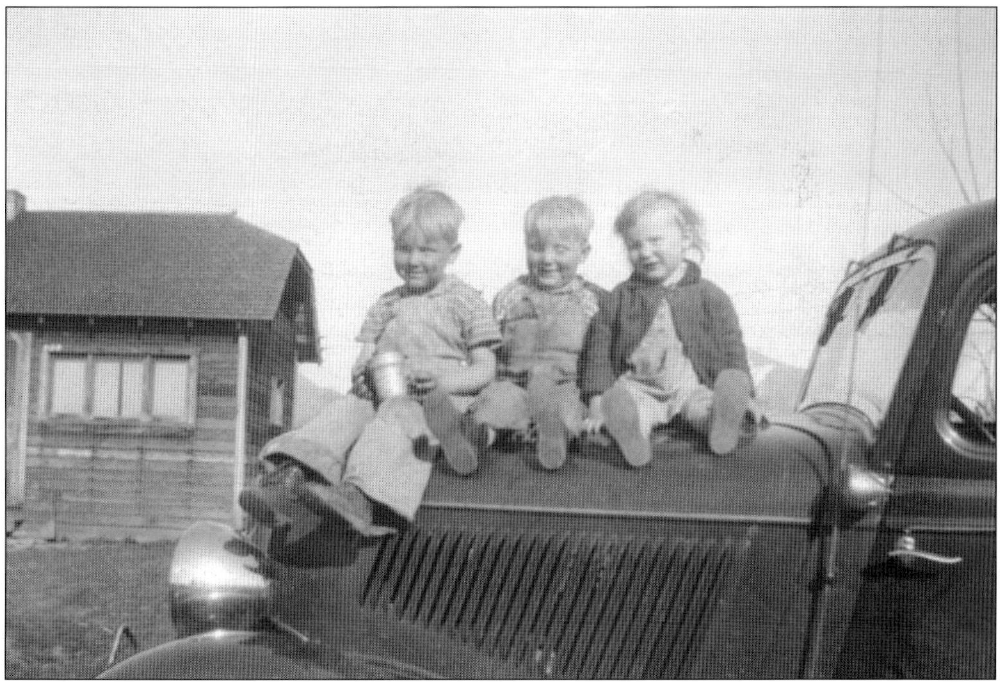

Kids on a Car. These cousins are enjoying sitting on top of a 1934 sedan. From left to right are Bob Mayne, Gerald Mayne, and Marlene Taylor Bott White. (Courtesy of M. Lee Taylor.)

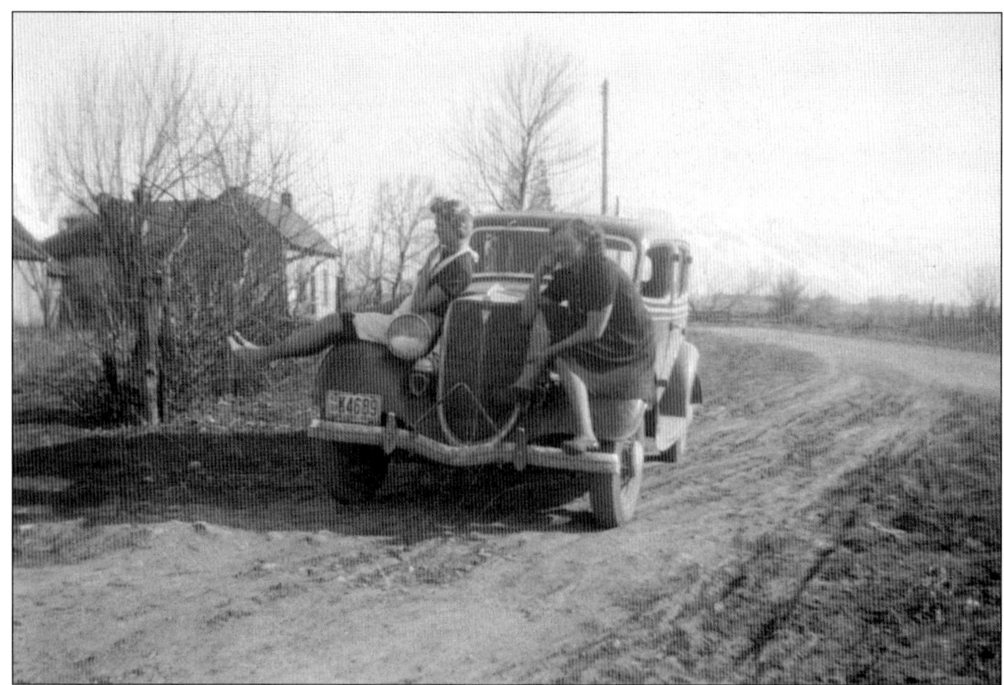

Relaxing on a Car. Thelma Childs Mayne (left) and Ada Childs Taylor sit on a car around 1942. The home in the background is where M. Lee Taylor was born, on the corner of 500 East and 1000 South. (Courtesy of M. Lee Taylor.)

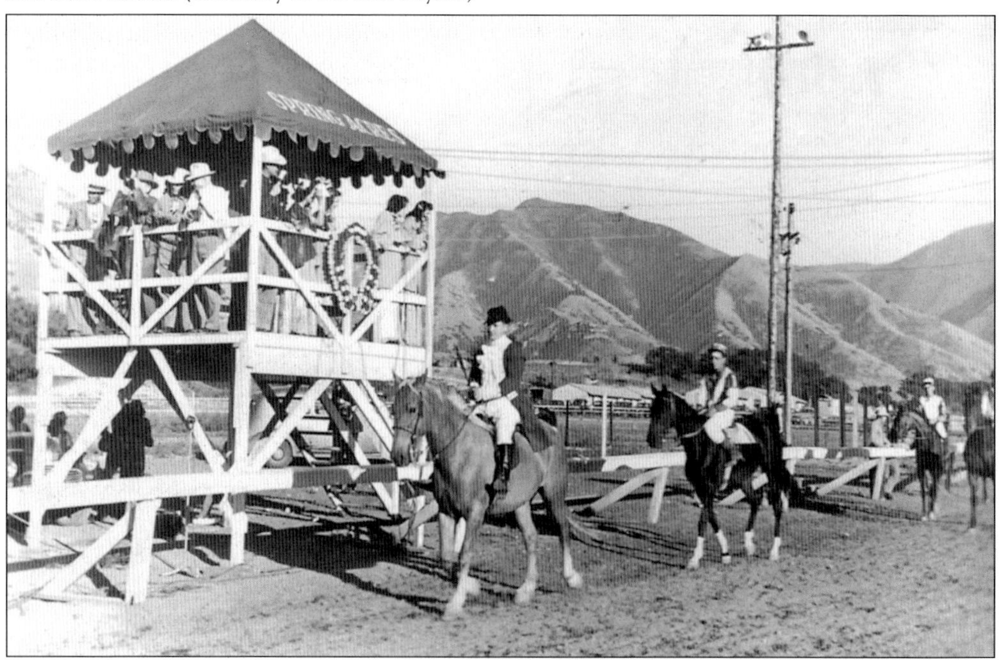

Racetrack. Spring Acres racetrack is pictured in May 1954. Pete Morgan, in front, rides Poney Boy. The horse track operated from 1947 to 1963. The Spring Acres Arts Park, at 700 South and 1300 East, is named in honor of the track. This new park hosts special events throughout the year, like movies in the park, concerts, and festivals. (Courtesy of the Springville Historical Society.)

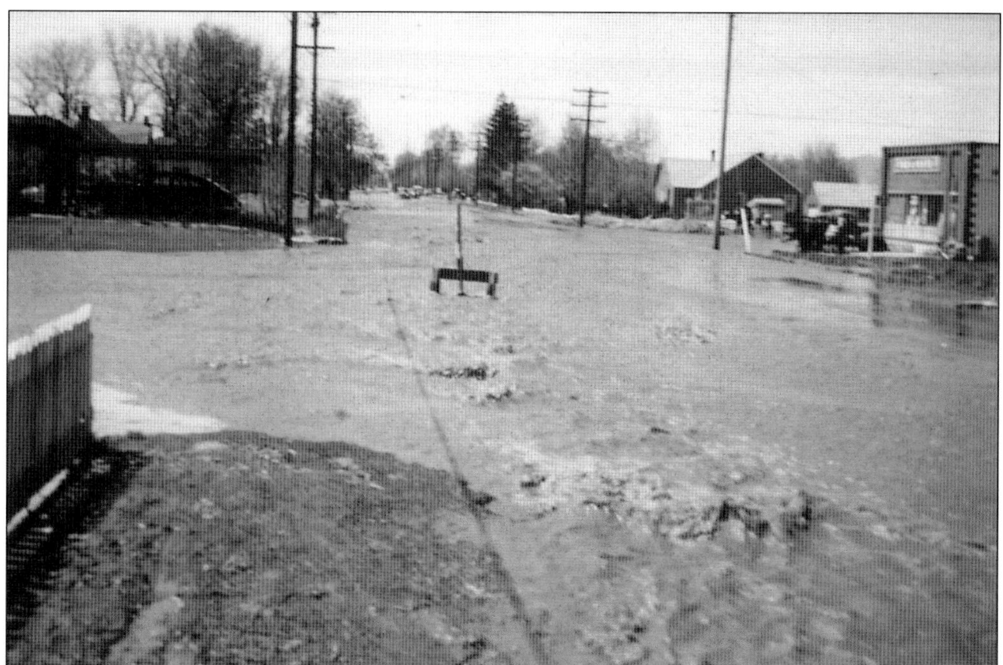

Flood of 1952. Above is a westward view of 400 South with water coming out of Brookside Drive during the big flood of 1952. Brookside Market is on the right. Below, a person on the left needs to get rescued near the area of 600 South and 600 East in the same flood. Sand bagging crews were on hand to try to divert the water onto the streets, which filled up fast and covered the sidewalks. Given the proximity to water that Springville enjoys, heavy snowfall in the winter and a rainy spring meant that water overreached its normal boundaries. (Both, courtesy of the Springville Historical Society.)

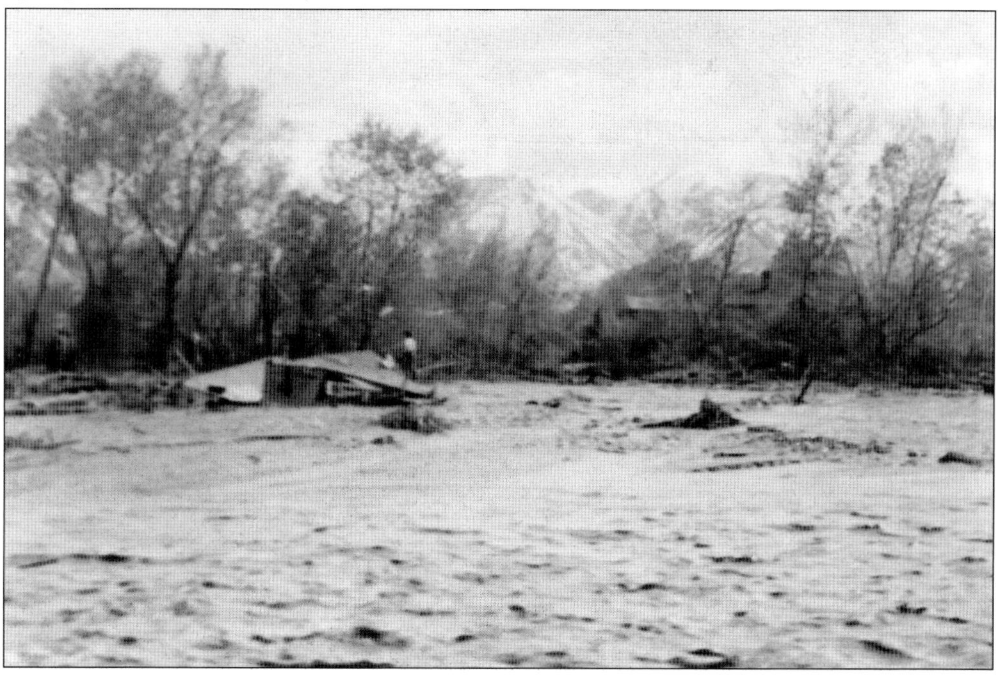

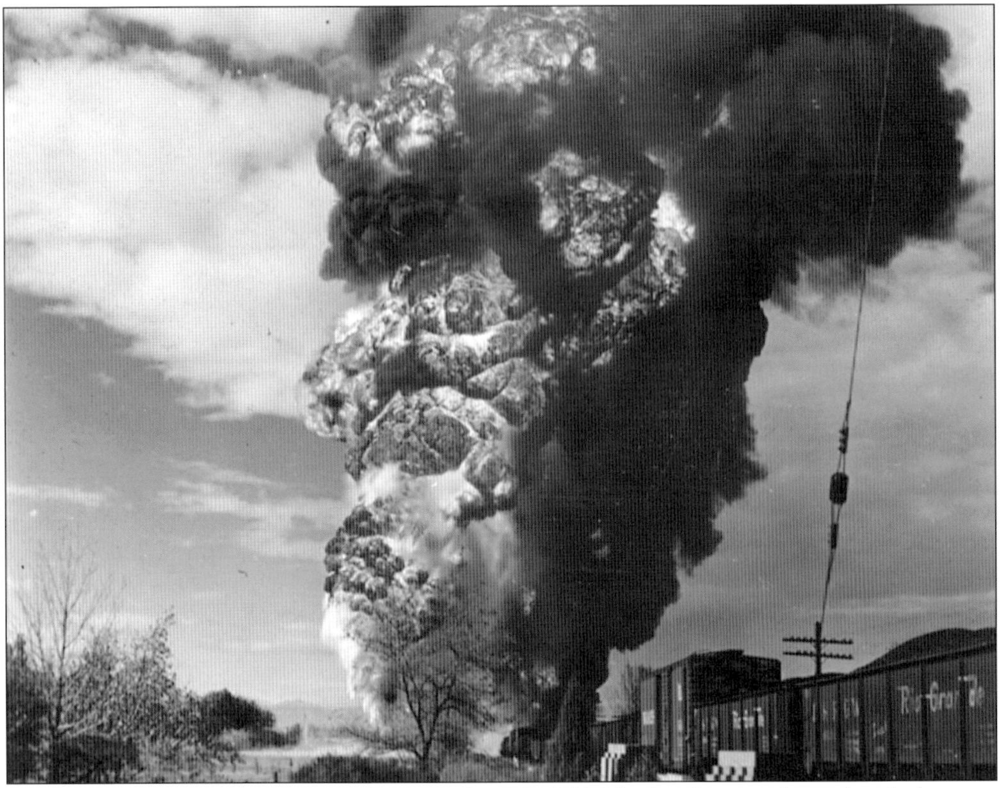

TRAIN FIRE. This accident occurred on October 30, 1956. The hot box overheated and a bearing went out, causing a partial derailment. Coal and oil cars were in the train, and the fire burned for some time. (Above, courtesy of M. Lee Taylor; below, courtesy of Mack Boyack.)

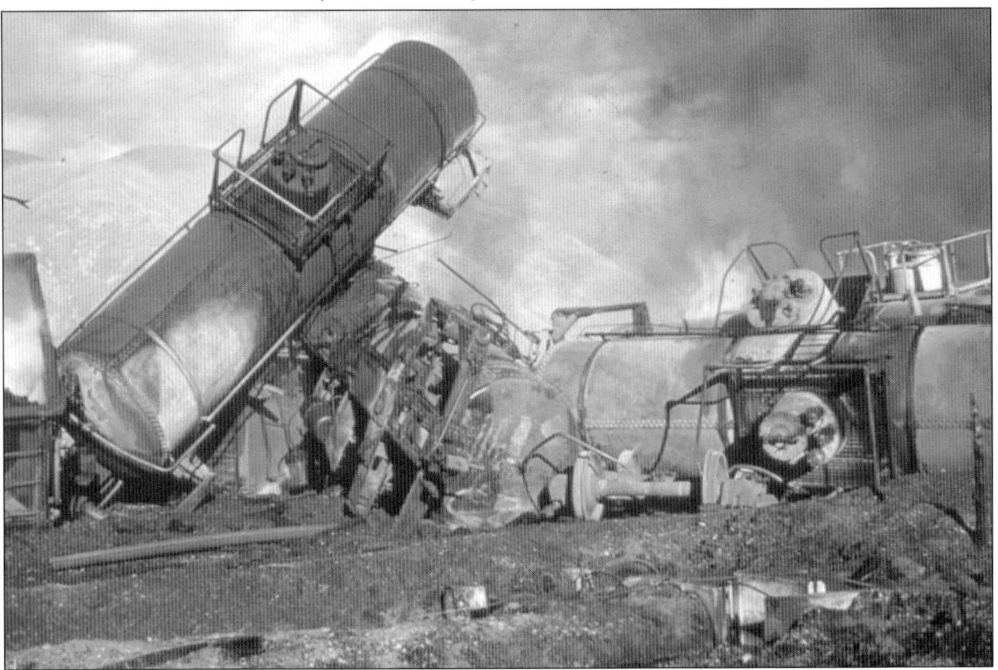

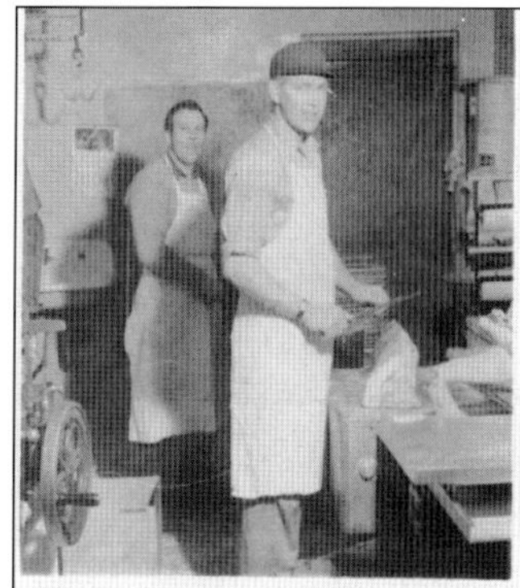

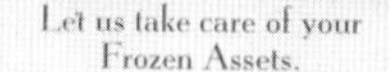

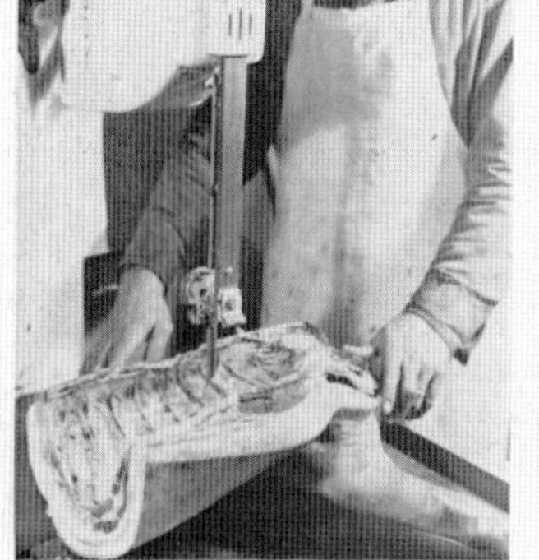

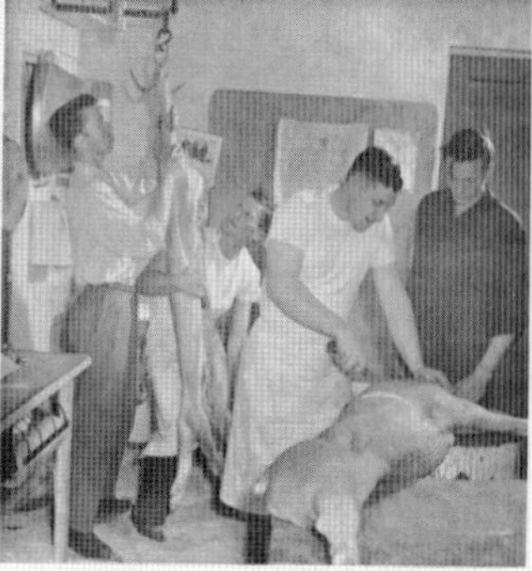

MEAT LOCKER AND THREE ADS. Springville meat locker's advertising includes, from left to right, a c. 1948 Joe Hudson photograph, Bill King, and Keith Weight. King's advertisement was published in 1950 and Weight's in 1951. The Springville Meat Company was owned by Morris Anderson; in the 1940s, it was bought by James Cope and his two sons, Ray and James. Ray and his two sons are the current owners. The facility at 268 South 100 West focuses on custom meat processing for local customers. (All, courtesy of the Springville Historical Society.)

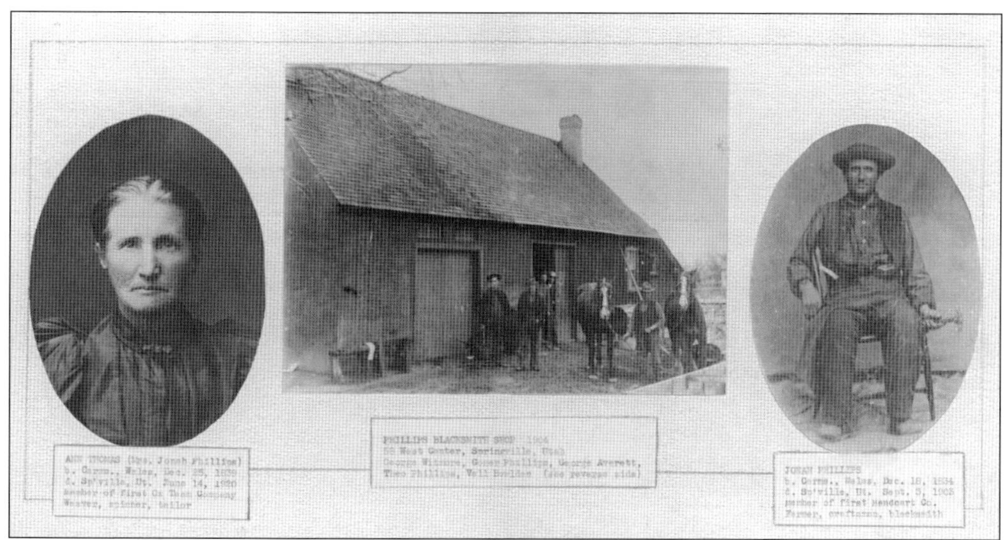

PHILLIPS. Ann Thomas Phillips and Jonah Phillips are pictured with their blacksmith shop in 1904. Ann arrived in America by boat in 1860 and then crossed the plains. Jonah came to Utah with a handcart company in 1856. They married on October 26, 1861, in Springville and later married again in the Salt Lake City Endowment House. In the photograph of the blacksmith shop on the banks of Hobble Creek are, from left to right, George "Tex" Whitmore, Gomer Phillips, Theo A. Phillips, George E. Everett, and Val Boroldew. Some of Jonah's blacksmithing items are displayed at the DUP museum. (Courtesy of the DUP.)

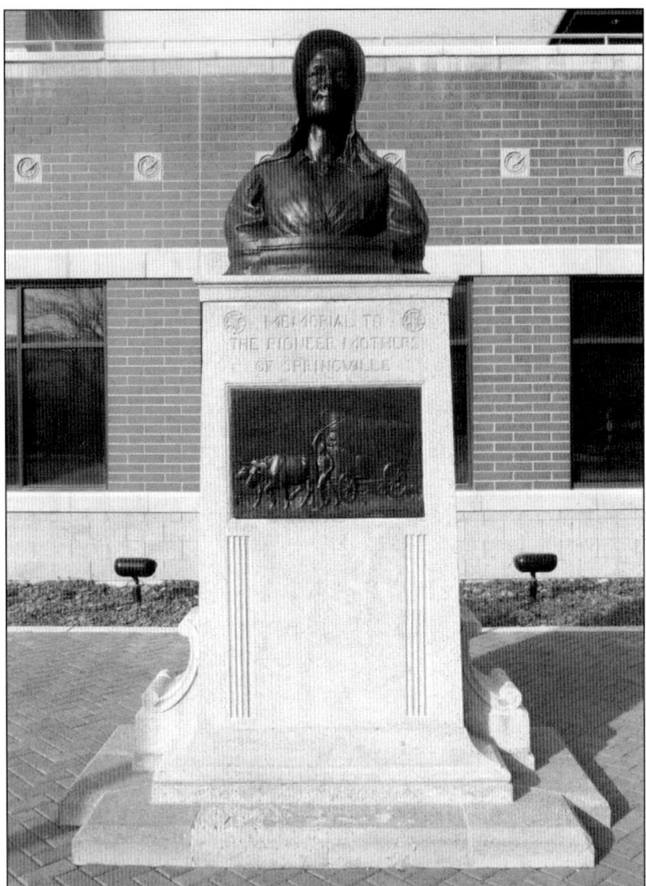

OLD CITY MONUMENT. The old city hall was built in 1860 and torn down in 1964. The Pioneer Mother Monument is pictured in front of the new city hall. Cyrus E. Dallin, a noted Boston sculptor and a native son of Springville, was asked to erect a monument to the pioneer mothers. The unveiling took place on July 25, 1932. Quite a few monuments adorn Springville. This photograph was taken in the spring of 1952. (Courtesy of M. Lee Taylor.)

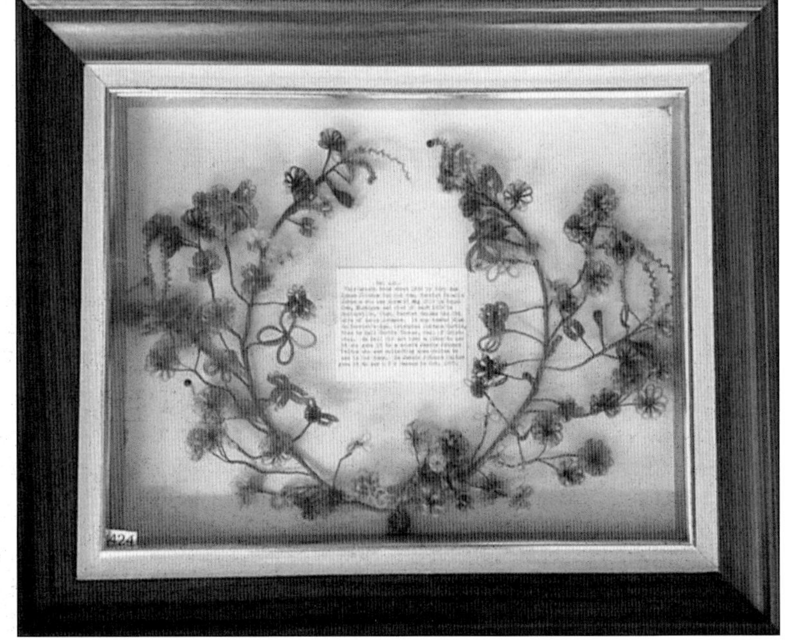

WREATH. This human hair wreath is on display at the DUP museum. It was made in 1850 by Mary Ann Lyman Johnson for her daughter, Harriet Fedelia Johnson. The wreath was donated to the museum in October 1970. (April Clawson photograph, courtesy of the DUP.)

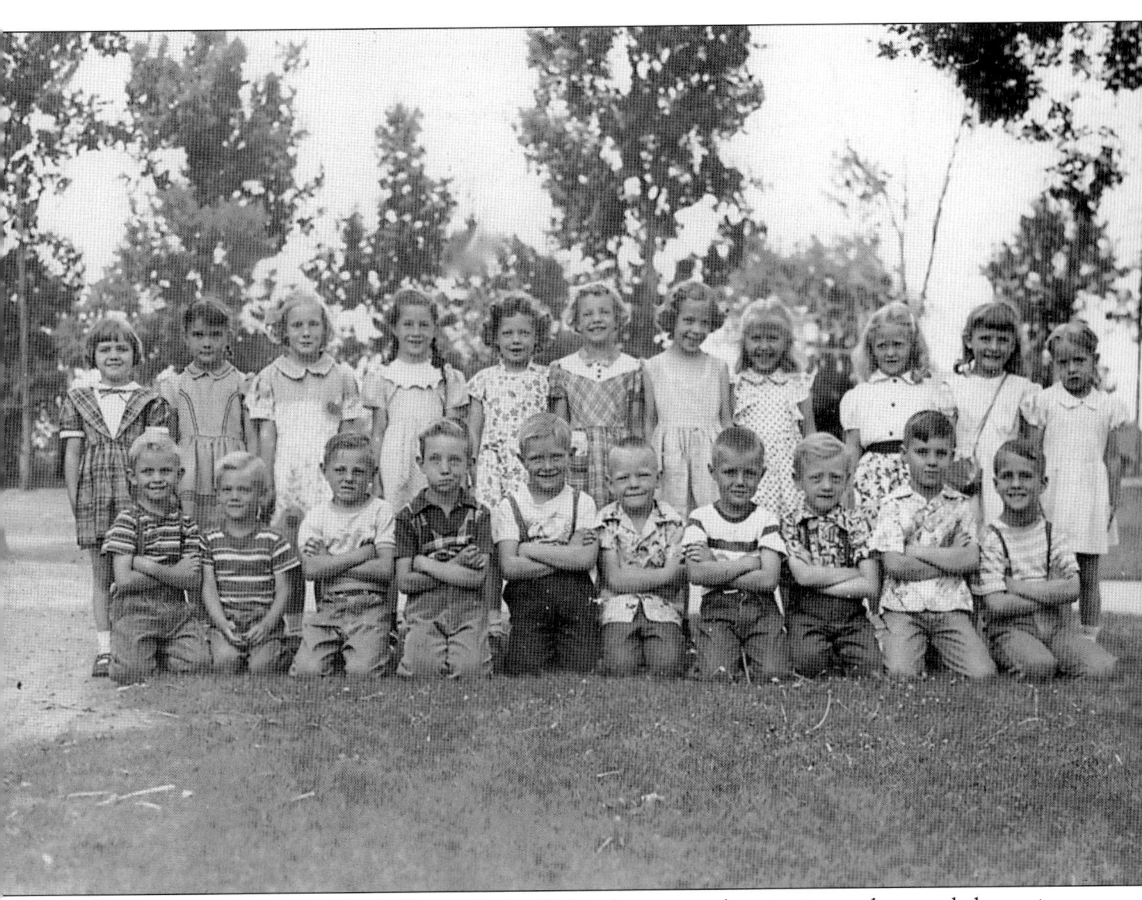

Kindergarten Class. The Jefferson School's kindergarten class is pictured around the spring of 1952. From left to right are (first row) Cyril Crandall, Gordon Peterson, Roger Reid, Richard Ollerton, M. Lee Taylor, Jud Harward, Glenn Deeben, Wayne Shurtleff, Maylon Fackrell, and unidentified; (second row) Pat Stewart, Anita Blanchard, Janet Paulson, Marie Q., unidentified, Leeta Boyer, Jeanine Boyack, Nancy Robinson, Sharon Chadwick, Diane Bartholomew, and Jane Newman. The teacher is Irene Moon. (Courtesy of M. Lee Taylor.)

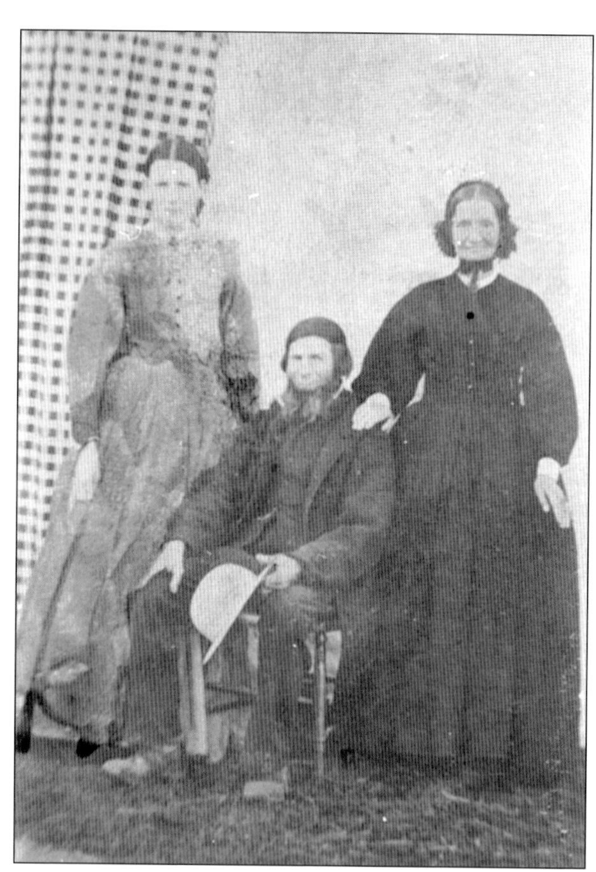

EDWARDS AND HEADSTONE. At left is the Edwards family, with Joshua John Edwards seated and his wife on the right. Their daughter is on the left. An image of Joshua John Edwards's headstone is on display at the DUP museum. (Below, April Clawson photograph; both, courtesy of the DUP.)

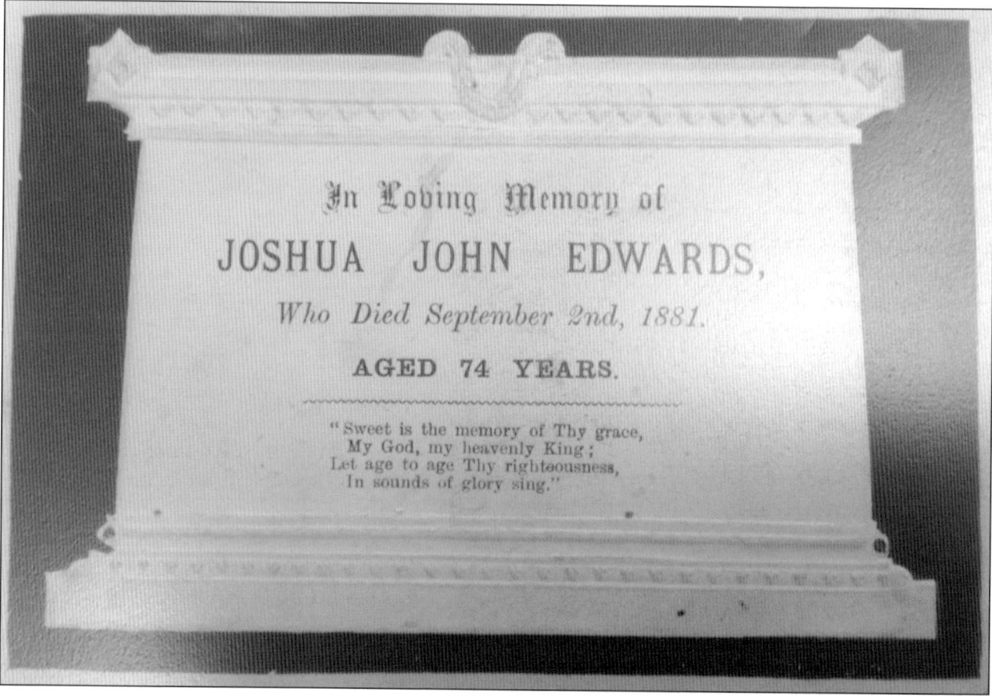

Levi Kendall. Levi Kendall was one of the original pioneers of 1847. The Kendall cabin is on display at the Mapleton City Park, just a short distance from its original site. Kendall helped with the construction of canyon roads and irrigation canals in the towns. He had two wives, who were sisters, and they each had 12 children with him. At first, he lived with Elizabeth, but that marriage ended in divorce; the practice of plural marriage had been stopped by the LDS Church. Kendall finally repaired his relationship with Eliza, and they lived in Mapleton until his death on March 10, 1903. Eliza died on January 2, 1915, in Springville. Elizabeth died on February 1, 1924, in Idaho. (Courtesy of the DUP.)

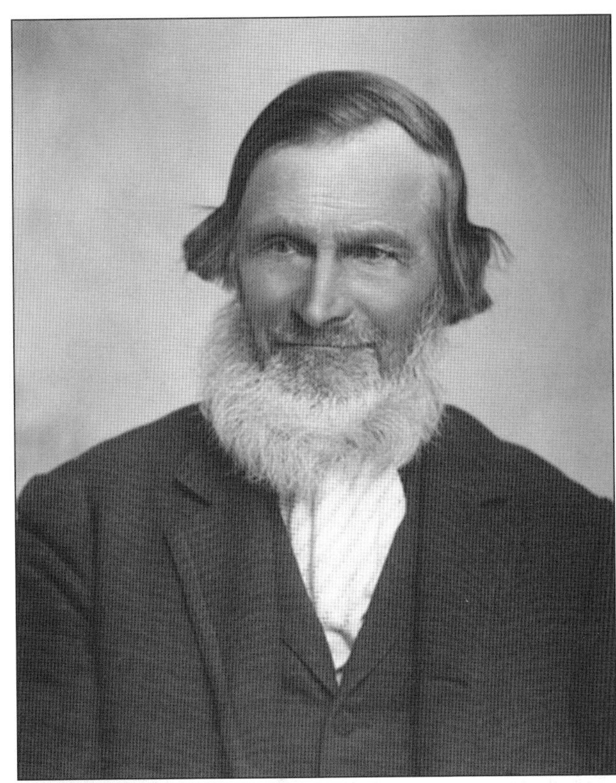

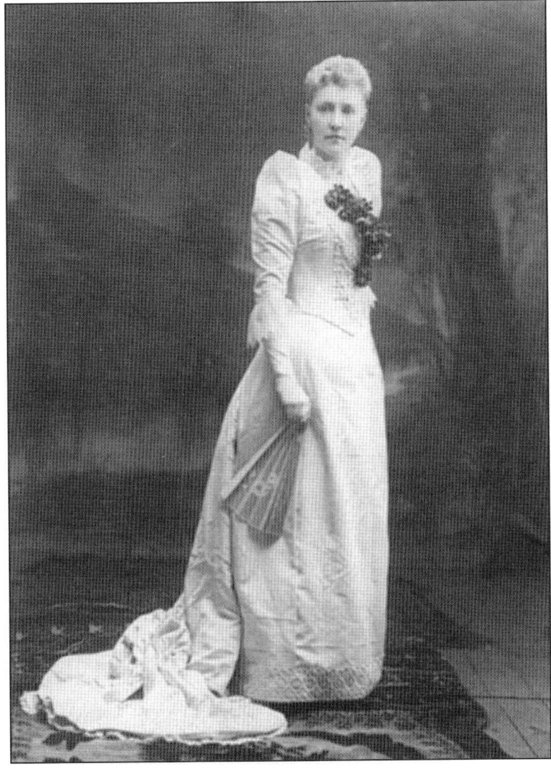

Exquisite Dress. Rhoda Rebecca Groesbeck Dougall wears an exquisite dress in a photograph taken by Anderson & Crandall around 1891. The silverware set of Rhoda's mother, Mary Hannah Rhoda Sanderson Groesbeck, and her dress (pictured) are on display at the DUP museum. (Courtesy of the DUP.)

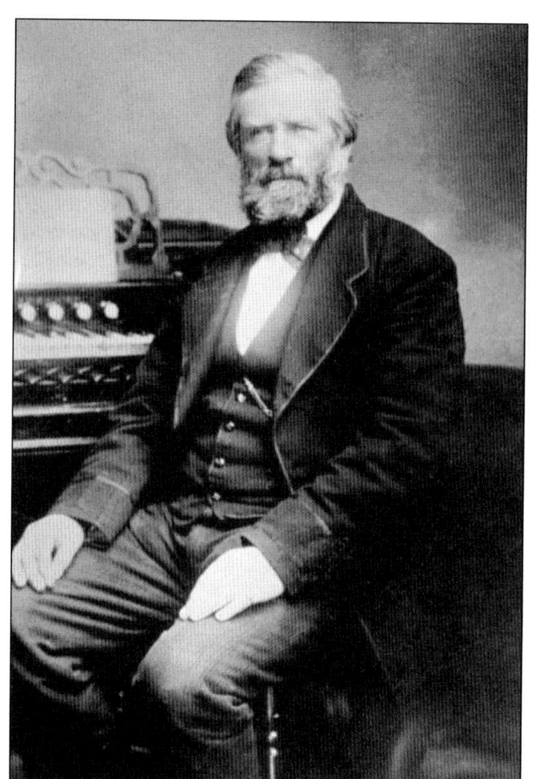

Fredrick Weight. Fredrick Weight was born on June 18, 1828 in Stroud, Gloucestershire, England. He had a rare gift for singing notes on true pitch. He wrote in his diary that he "Walked, carrying my cello four miles to and from my music lessons, after I had worked ten hours in the Iron Factory." He arrived in Springville in 1856 and during his career made three organs, four violins, a guitar and case, a bass, a cello, and two dulcimers. He also made furniture. He was the organist and choir leader for over 45 years. A few of his handmade instruments are on display at the DUP museum. (Courtesy of the DUP.)

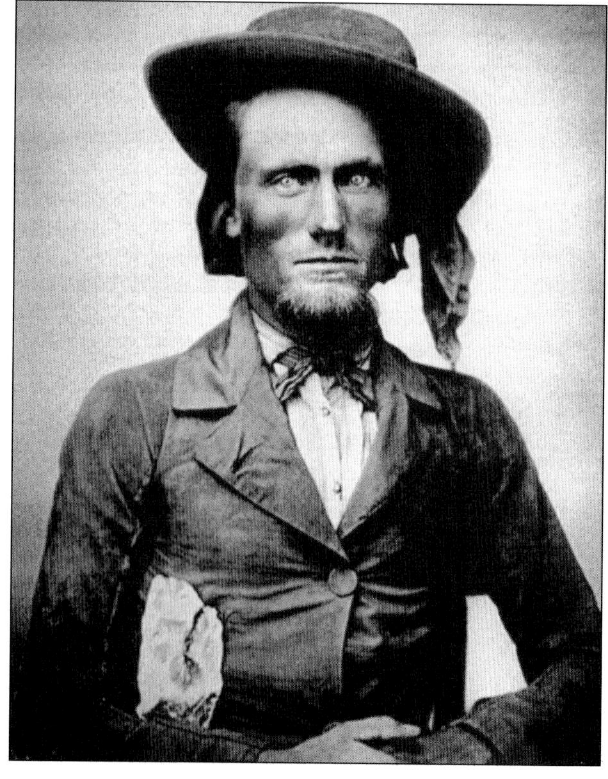

Levi Metcalf. Metcalf guided a freighter to New Mexico and was paid in gold upon arrival. He hired two fellow travelers to accompany him to Fort Laramie, to pick up the Mormon Trail and return to Utah. Somewhere along the trail in Colorado, he was robbed and murdered. Mark Blanchard wrote *Going to my Grave* about Levi Metcalf's life. (Courtesy of the DUP.)

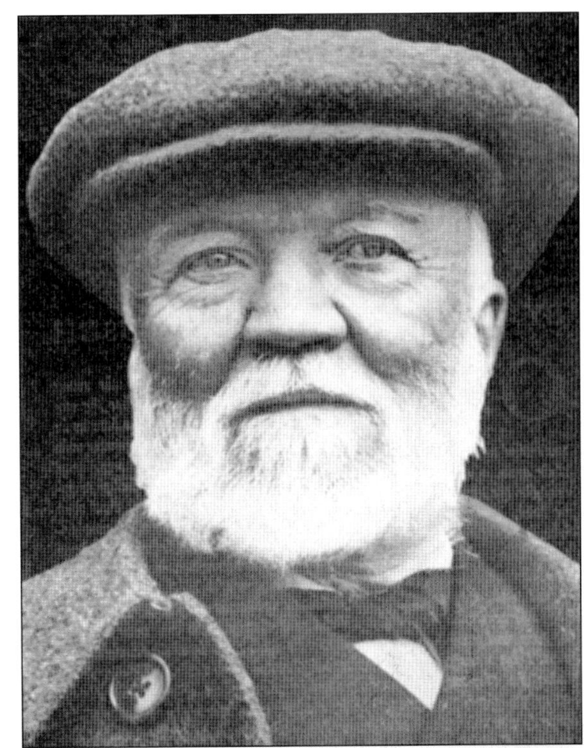

ANDREW CARNEGIE AND LIBRARY BUILDING. The Prairie-style Carnegie Building was formerly Springville's library. It opened in January 1922 and is now the home of the DUP museum and the historical society. Andrew Carnegie (right) was at one time the richest man in the world. He gave money to fund 1,689 public libraries across the country. Springville's new library is just a block away from the old one (below). (Right, courtesy of the DUP; below, courtesy of Lois Bartholomew.)

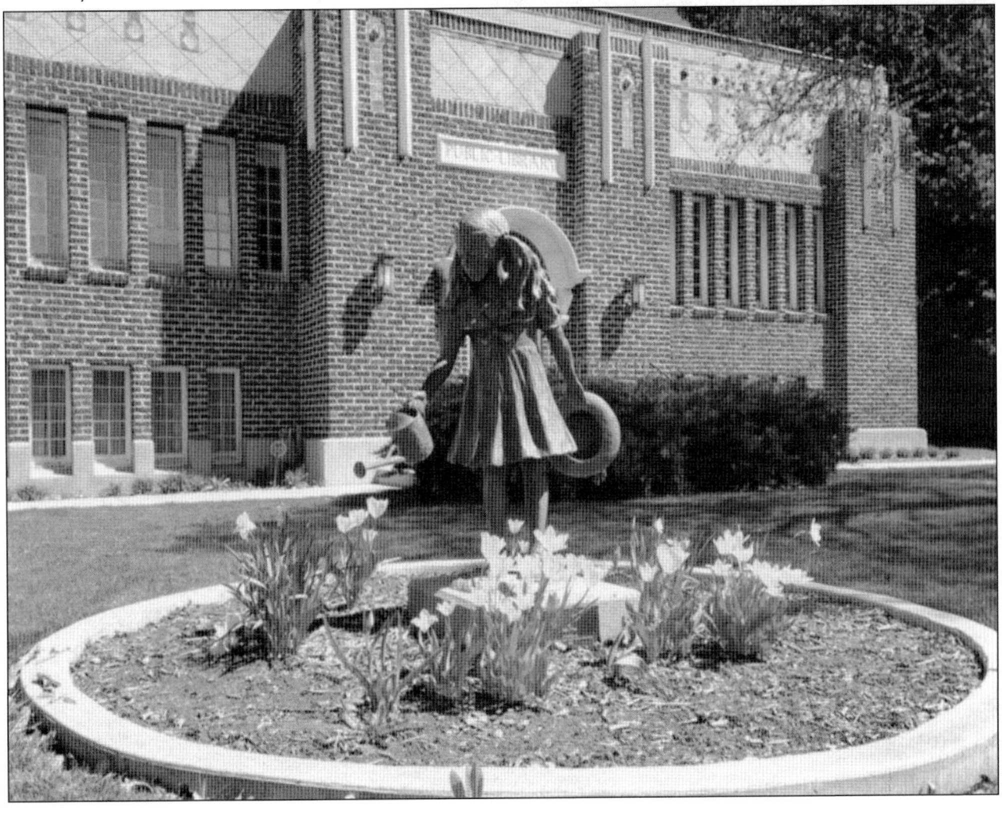

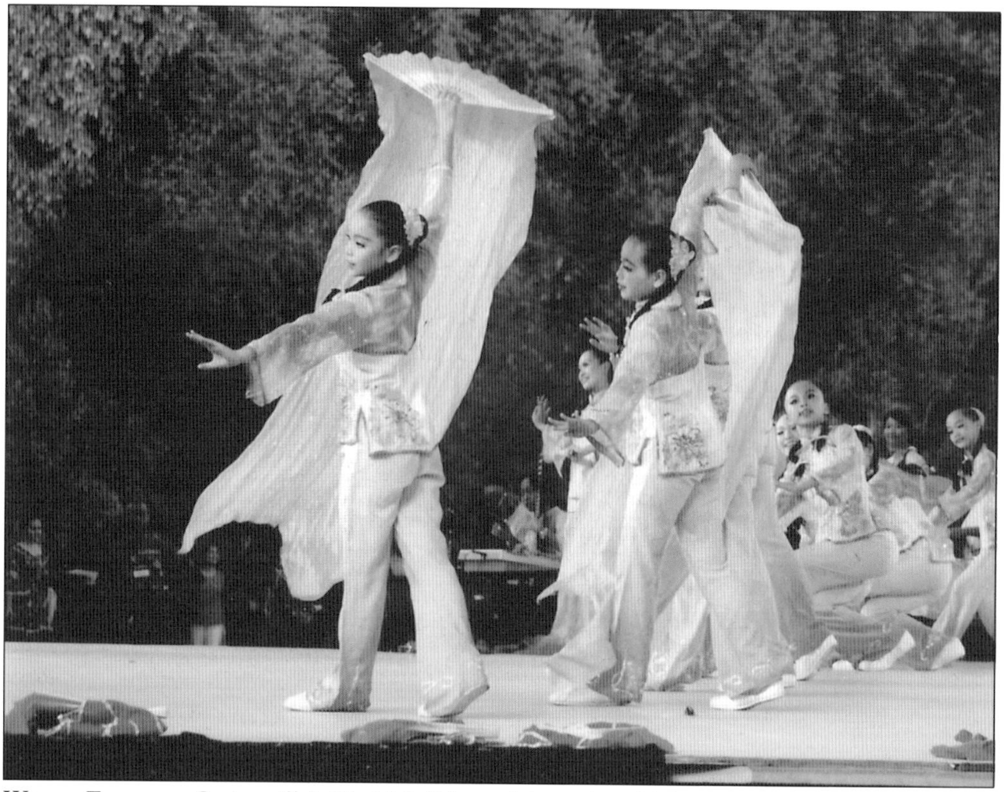

World Folkfest. Springville's World Folkfest celebrated its 30th anniversary in 2016. Chinese dancers are pictured at the weeklong event in 2013. This celebration features folk dancers and musicians from around the globe. The event has become one of the largest festivals of folk dance and music in the United States. Annually, 250 performers dressed in native costumes come together and share their talents with the community. (Courtesy of World Folkfest.)

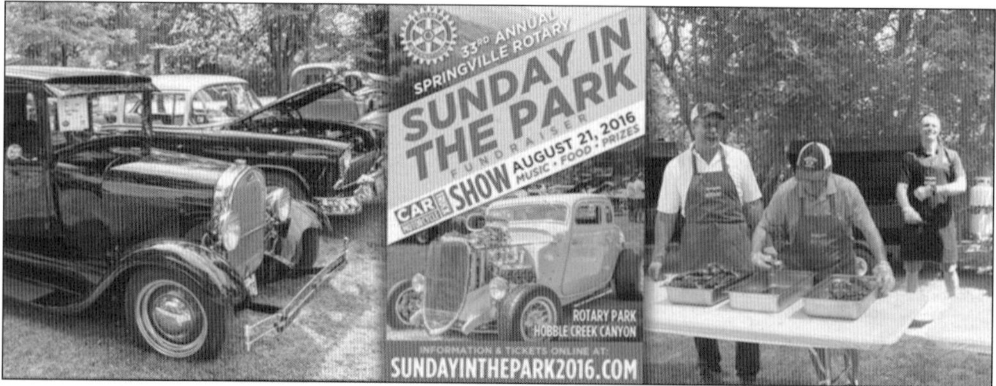

Springville Rotary Club. The Springville Rotary Club hosts the annual Sunday in the Park with a car show. The club was established in 1964, and Sunday in the Park was in its 33rd year in 2016. The club participates in local and national projects. (Courtesy of Springville Rotary Club.)

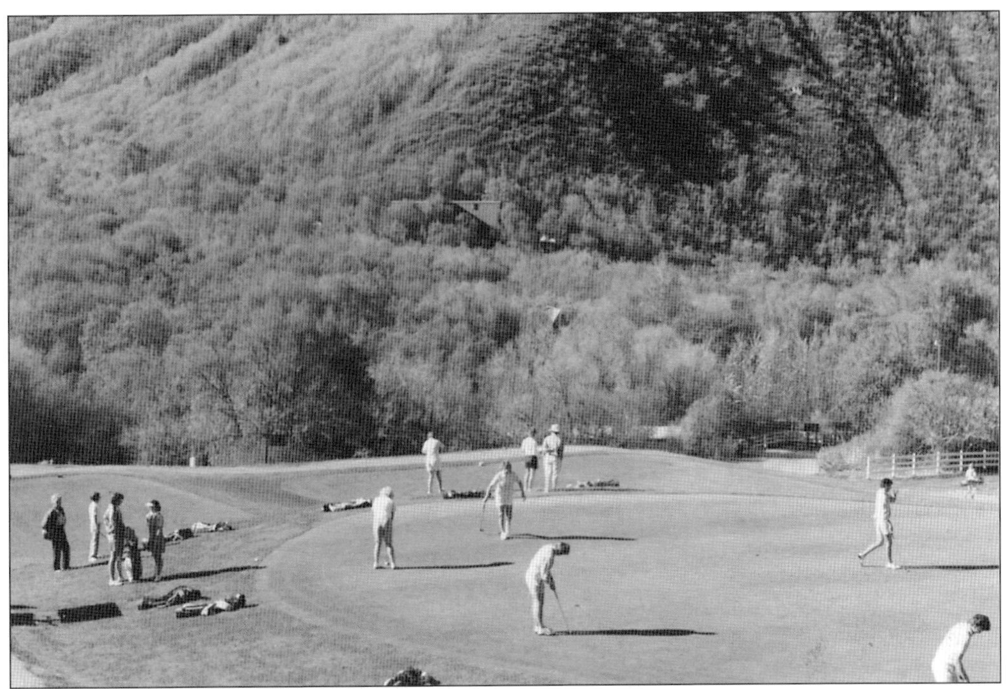

Golf Course. The Hobble Creek Golf Course opened in 1967. Above, people take golf lessons in 1986. Below, a father and son play a round. The 18-hole championship course has all the latest amenities and has been critically acclaimed by *Golf Digest* magazine. The natural beauty that surrounds the course has welcomed several great players to its greens. It is known as one of the most beautiful golf courses in the state of Utah. (Both, courtesy of Hobble Creek Golf Course.)

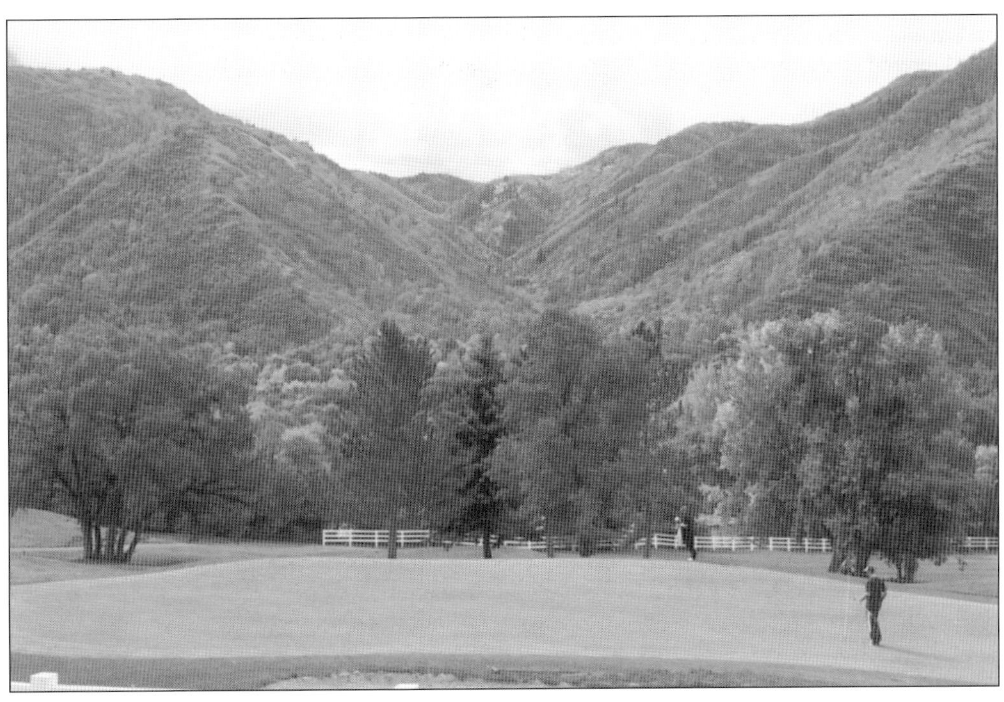

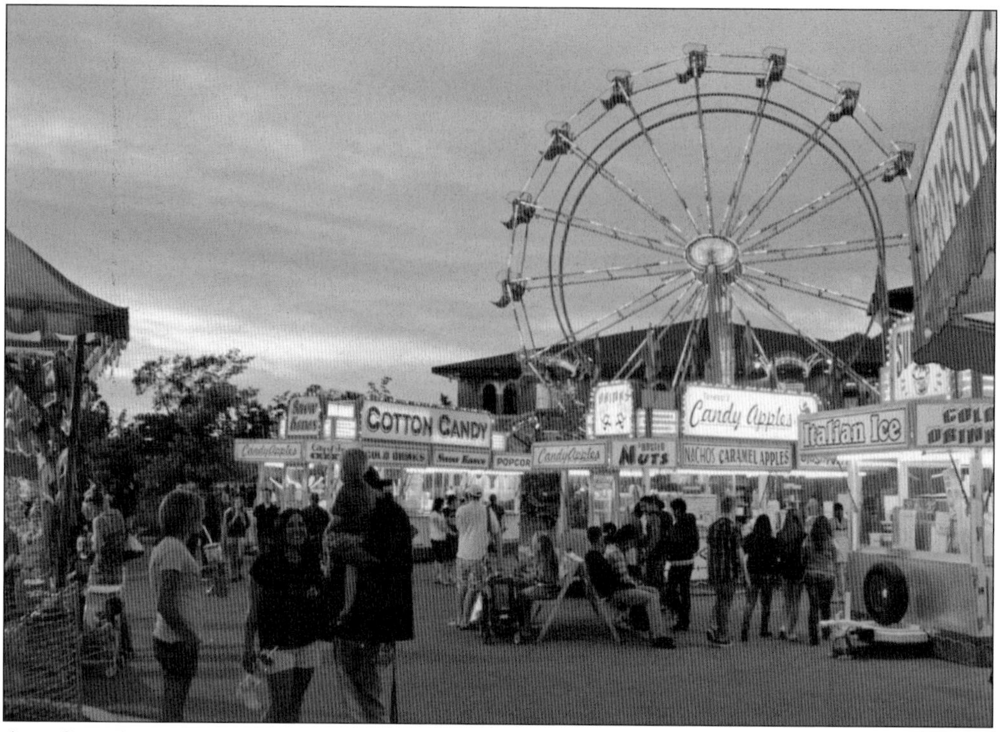

ART CITY DAYS. Art City Days celebrated 51 years in 2016. It attracts people from all over the state. The weeklong community event features activities, a carnival, a parade, and lots more. Springville is nicknamed "the Art City." This commemoration celebrates the arts and brings traditional and fun things for the whole family to enjoy. (Both, courtesy of Dennis Robertson.)

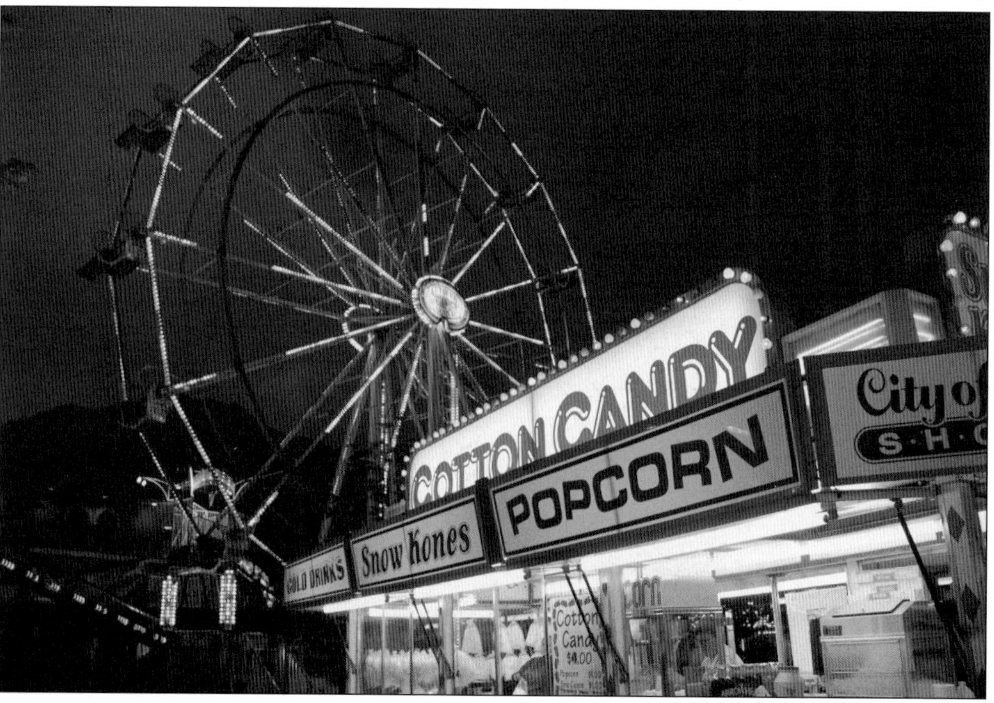

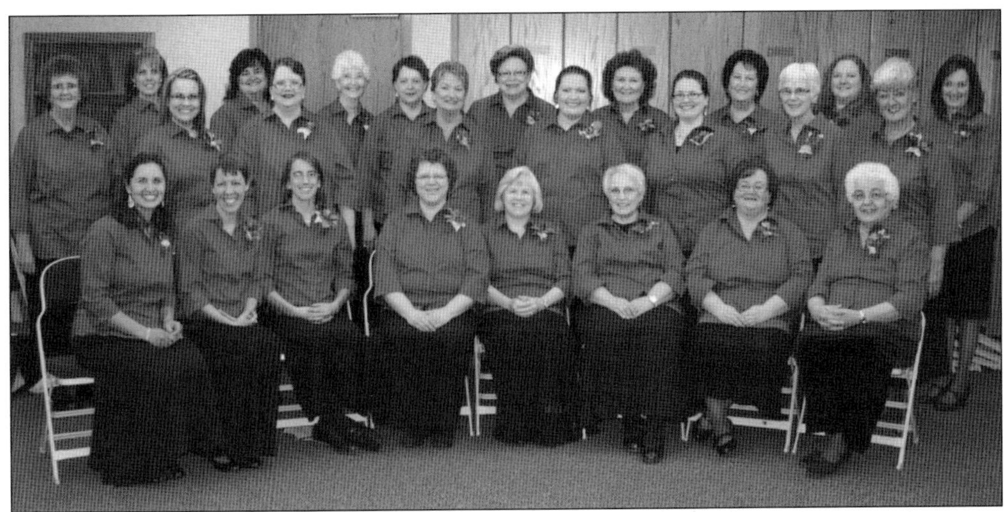

Musettes. Musettes is a local choral group that began in 1950. From left to right on December 13, 2013, are (first row) Candice Poole, Lela Allmendinger, Sara Baker, Angie Lofthouse, Susan Crawford, Mary Gray, Debbie Parker, and Vonnie Clark; (second row) Shirley Smith, Renee Palfreyman, Marsha Clark, Mary Jo Taylor, Tina Yeagley, Maureen Clark, Jane Harris-Hagner, Lynda Golding, Carol Curtis, Erin Willson, Arlene McGregor, Danielle DeGriselles, Carolyn Paxton, Janet Parker, Camille Segeberg, Linda Cluff, and accompanist Jackie Snelson. (Courtesy of Linda Cluff.)

Springville Playhouse. The Springville Playhouse was organized in 1947 and is the largest continuously running theater group in the state of Utah. One of the most unique aspects about this community group is that no one is paid for their efforts. This nonprofit organization presents theater and musical performances on a regular basis. (Courtesy of Springville Playhouse.)

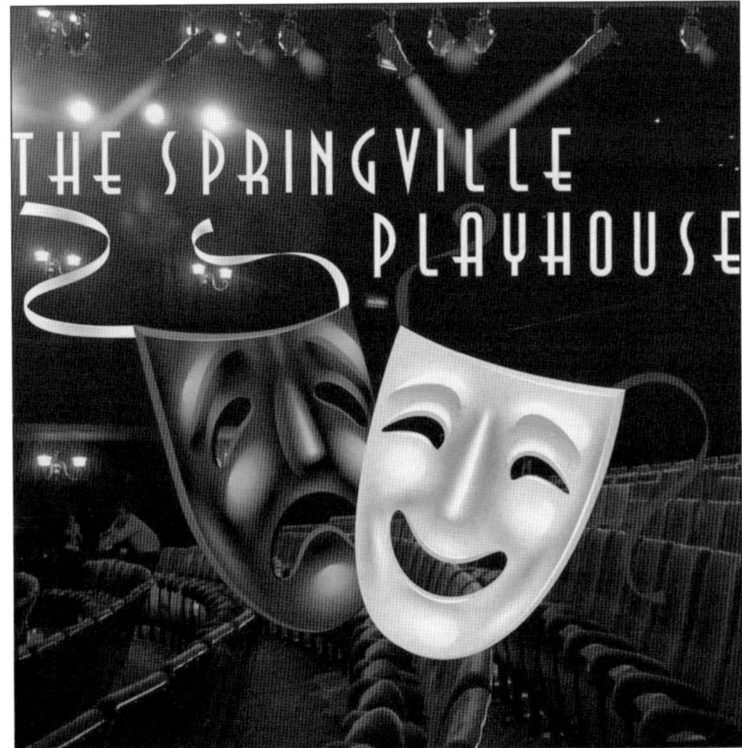

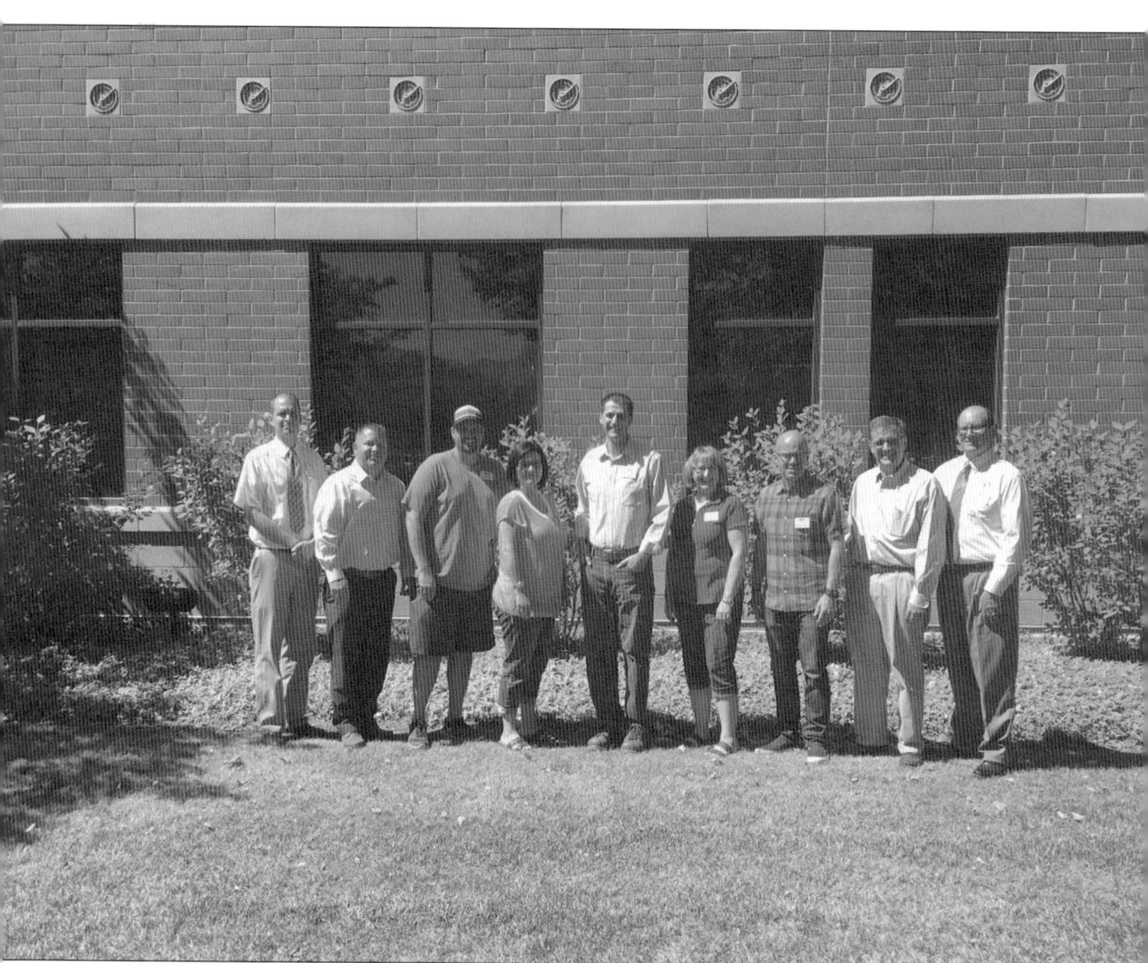

Chamber of Commerce. The Springville Chamber of Commerce was organized on May 17, 1939. Now called the Springville-Mapleton Chamber of Commerce, its mission statement is "To Create a Business Climate that is as Dynamic as our Citizens!" The current chamber board is, from left to right, Jason Packard (Central Bank), Erik Busath (Holt and Associates CPA), Luis Muzquiz (president, LaCasita), Amberly Brimhall (Reams), Brad Gassaway (Namify), Shirlene Jordon (chamber director), Brian Johnson (Sunroc), Craig Conover (council representative), and Rod Oldroyd (Springville City Corporation). (Courtesy of Jared Clawson.)

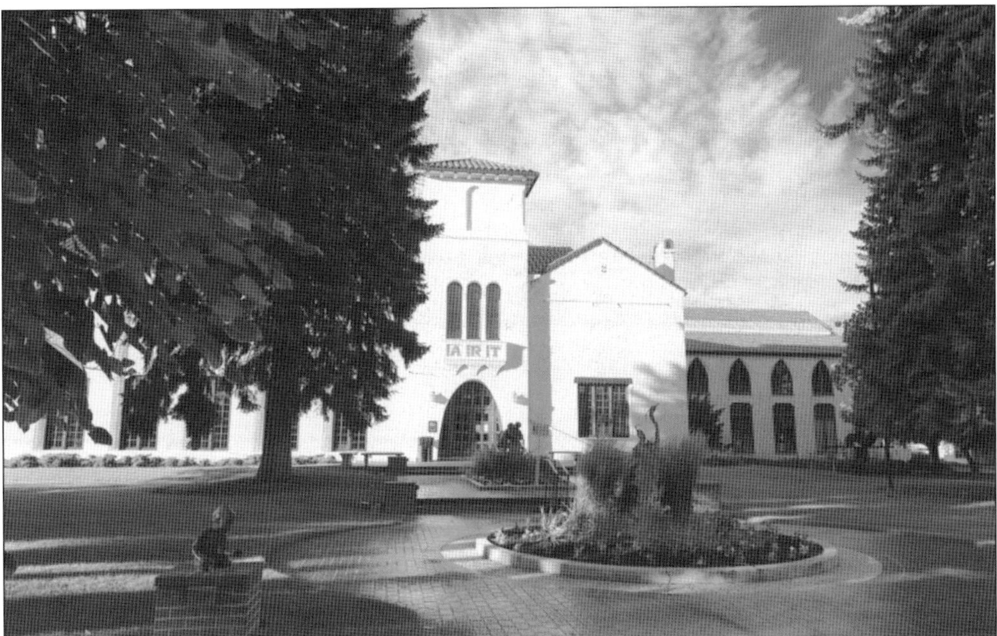

MUSEUM OF ART. The Springville Museum of Art is Utah's first art museum, dedicated in 1937 by David O. McKay. The permanent collection has 150 years of Utah art, along with Soviet realist and American art pieces. The art museum hosts many events throughout the year and is one of the reasons Springville is well known. (Courtesy of Dennis Robertson.)

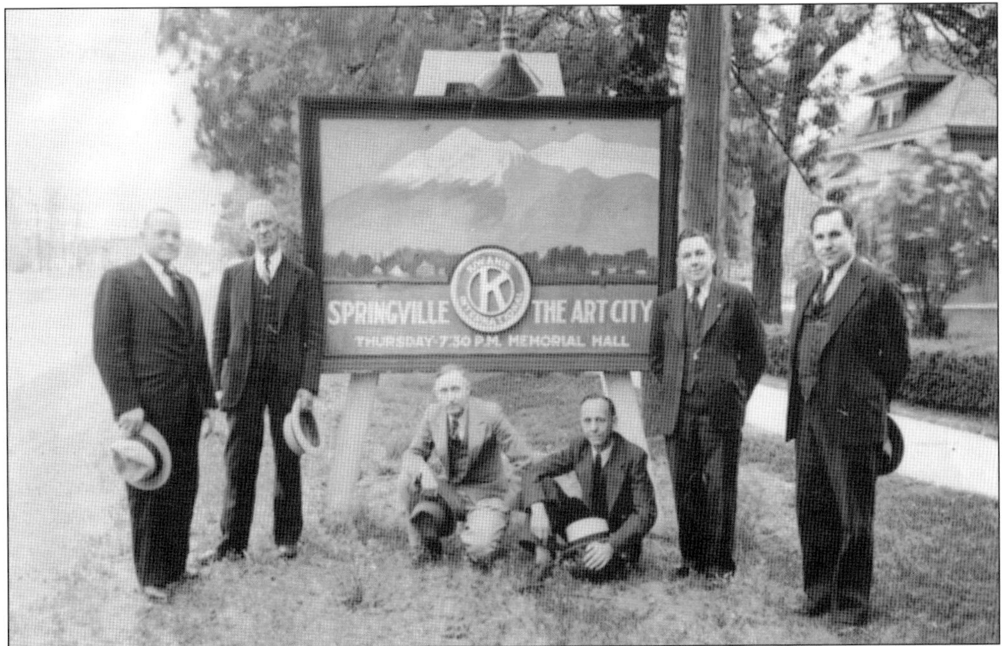

KIWANIS CLUB. The Springville Kiwanis Club started in 1922. From left to right are A.Y. Wheeler, Martin W. Bird, James F. Wingate, Harold Christensen, Milton Harrison, and Fay Packard. The club sponsors wonderful programs within the city to benefit the youth of Springville. (Courtesy of Springville Kiwanis Club.)

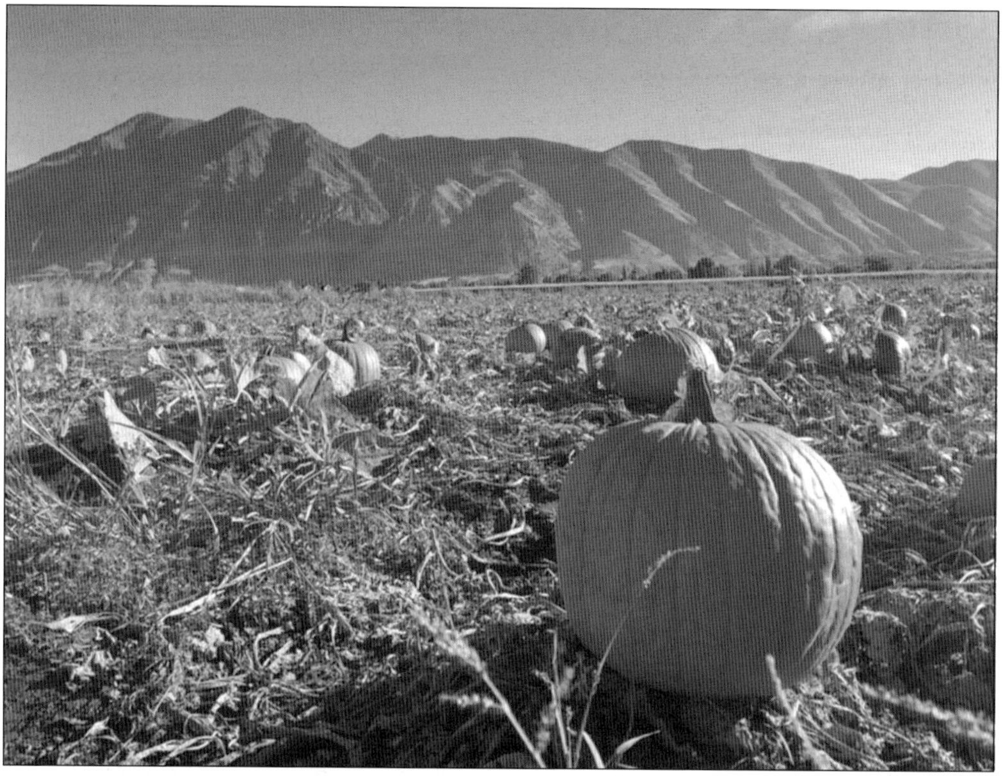

Pumpkin Field. Springville is a distinctive place that embraces many levels of society. This picturesque scene shows a pumpkin field ready for picking. The city is a splendid place to raise a family in an attractive area beneath majestic mountains. (Courtesy of www.servedaily.com.)

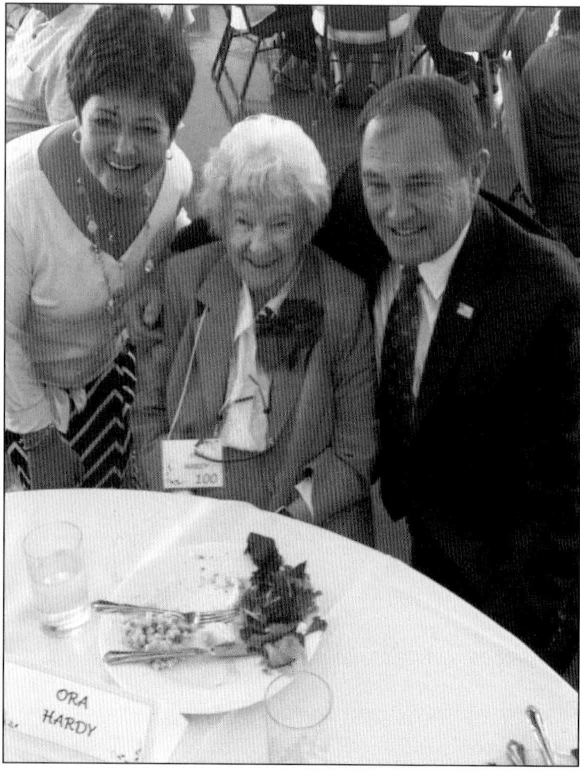

Centenarian Ora Hardy. Springville resident Ora Hardy (seated) is being greeted by Gov. Gary Herbert and his wife, Jeanette, at the centenarian celebration in Salt Lake City. Ora always said "be optimistic and be happy." She was born in Provo on May 10, 1916. Springville mayor Wilford Clyde declared May 10 Ora Hardy Day. Jeanette Snelson Herbert is a native of Springville. (Courtesy of Ora Hardy.)

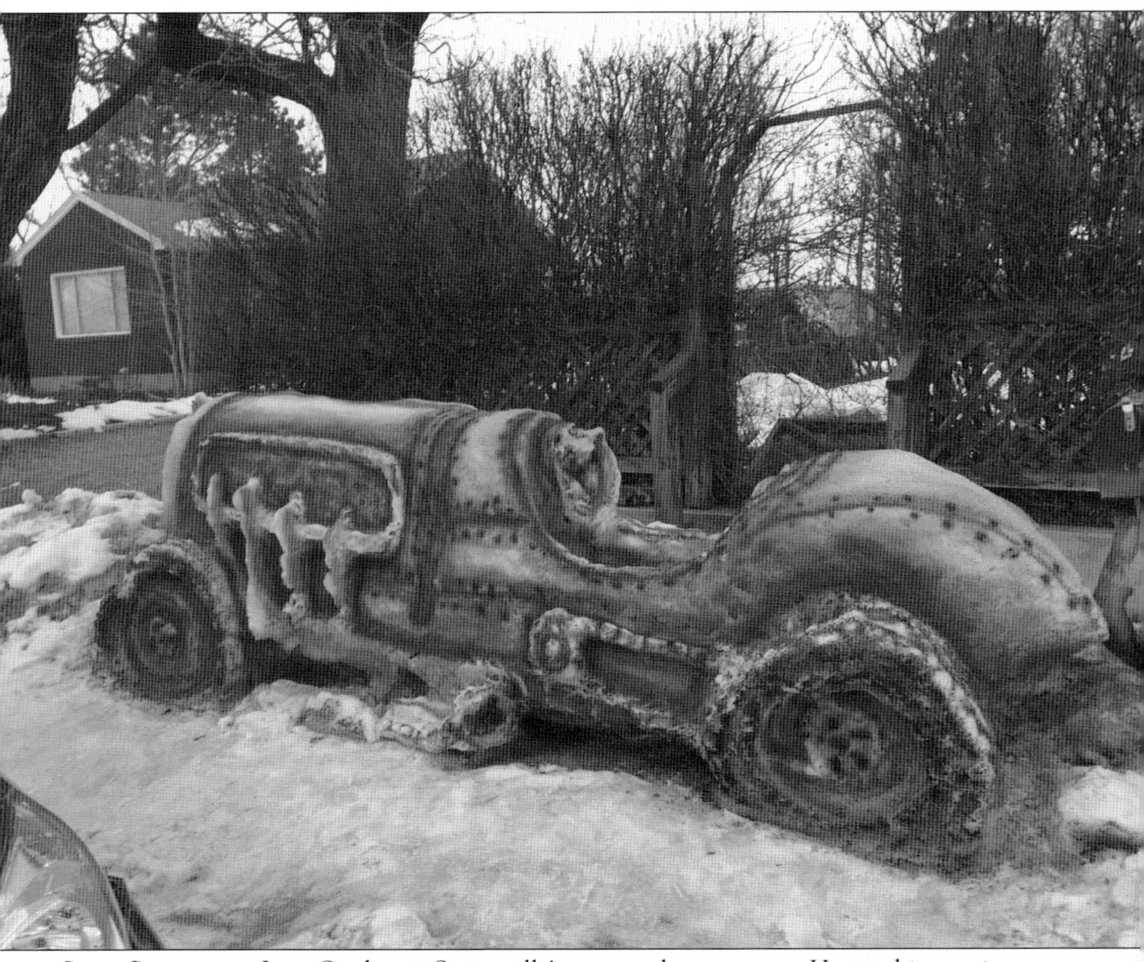

Snow Sculpture. Jerry Gardner is Springville's snow sculpture master. He uses his creations to wipe away the winter blues. His home off Canyon Road is a regular drive-by for many residents who want to see his latest creation each time it snows. (April Clawson photograph.)

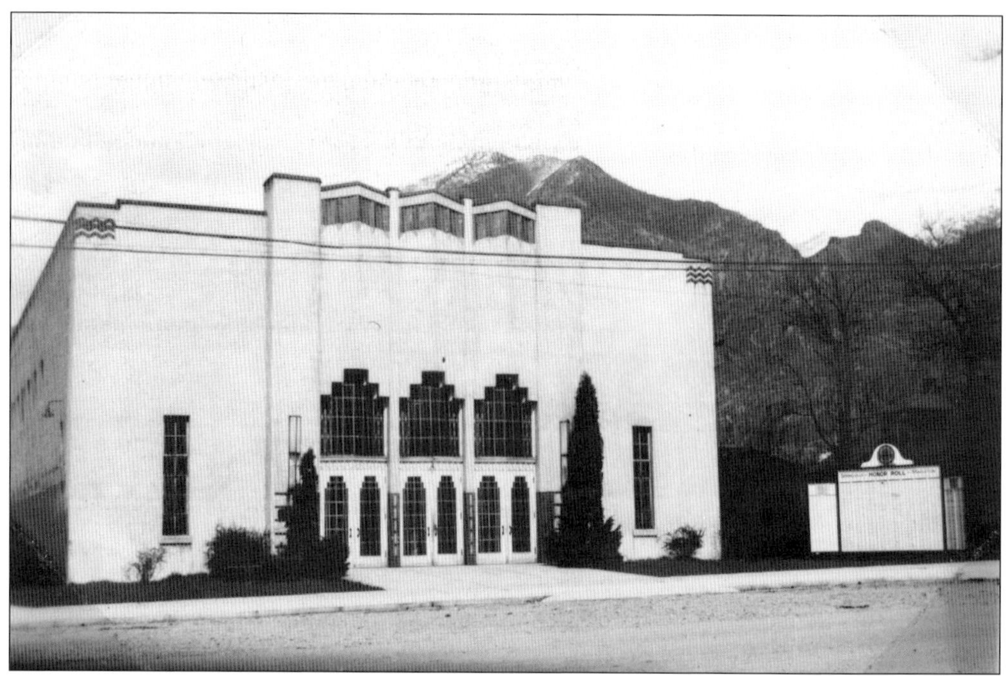

Memorial Hall. Memorial Hall was built by the American Legion in 1932 on the foundation of the original Springville Opera House, which burned down in 1929. This building is now the home of the Springville Senior Citizens Center. (Courtesy of M. Lee Taylor.)

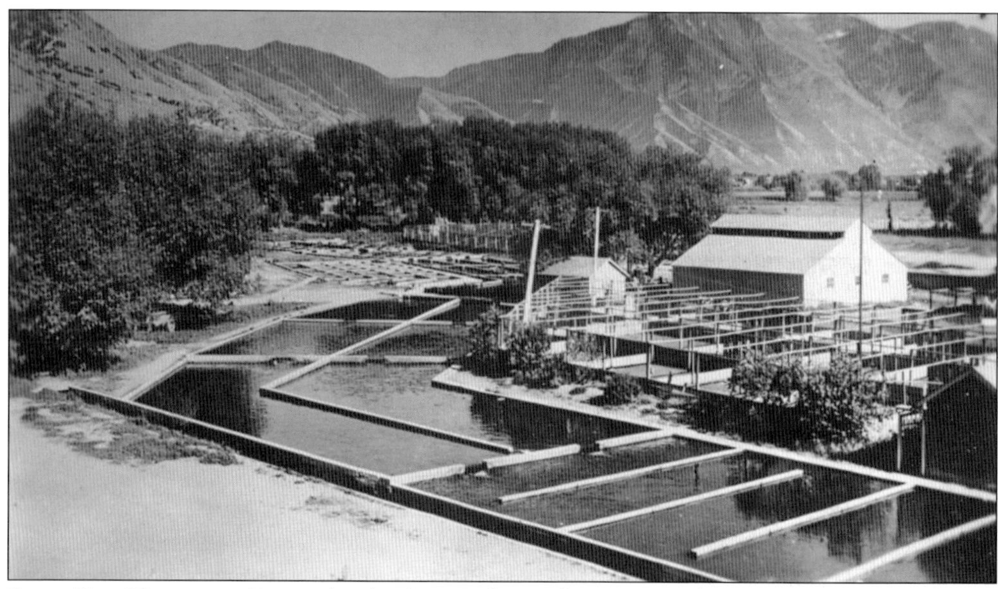

State Fish Hatchery. Pictured is the State Fish Hatchery on North Main Street. It is still being used, but is much changed. (Courtesy of M. Lee Taylor.)

Mark Twain. A Gary Price statue of Mark Twain was dedicated to the citizens of Springville on September 18, 2004, the town's 154th birthday. Many donors contributed to this artwork, and it sits in front of the Carnegie Library downtown. (April Clawson photograph.)

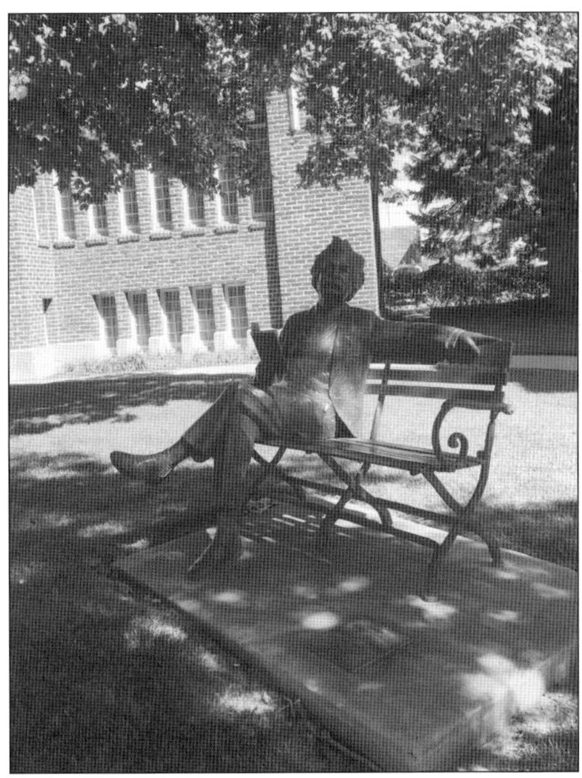

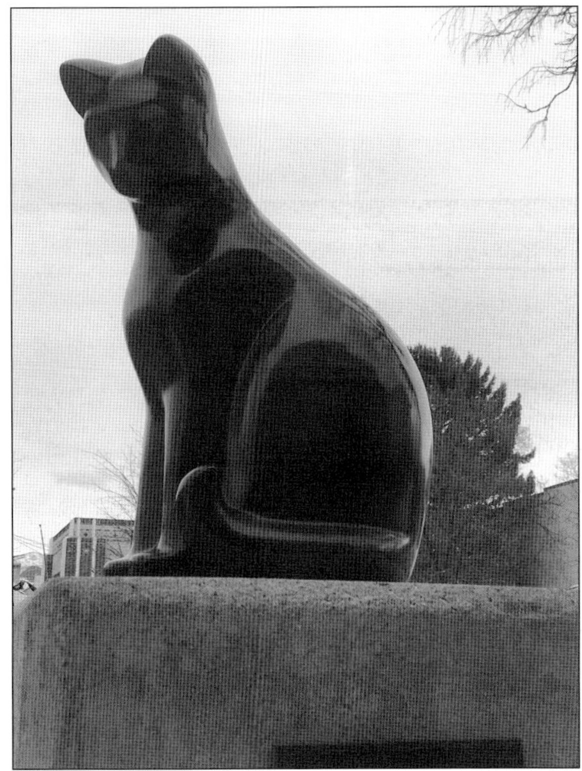

Cat Statue. The city is adorned with many statues, sculptures, and other art pieces. This one is called *Crystal* and was created by Jeannine Young. It is dedicated to the fathers of Springville past, present, and future. (Courtesy of Jacob Clawson.)

Consistent with our mission to preserve history on a local level, this book was printed in South Carolina on American-made paper and manufactured entirely in the United States. Products carrying the accredited Forest Stewardship Council (FSC) label are printed on 100 percent FSC-certified paper.

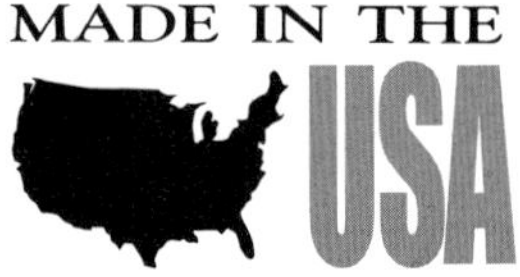